Listening as Spiritual Practice
in Early Modern Italy

The publisher gratefully acknowledges the generous support of the Ahmanson Foundation Humanities Endowment Fund of the University of California Press Foundation.

The publisher also gratefully acknowledges the generous contributions to this book provided by the Lila Acheson Wallace—Reader's Digest Special Grants Subsidy of Villa I Tatti: The Harvard University Center for Italian Renaissance Studies and by a University Co-operative Society Subvention Grant awarded by The University of Texas at Austin.

Listening as
Spiritual Practice
in Early Modern Italy

Andrew Dell'Antonio

⊞

UNIVERSITY OF CALIFORNIA PRESS
Berkeley · Los Angeles · London

University of California Press, one of the most
distinguished university presses in the United States,
enriches lives around the world by advancing
scholarship in the humanities, social sciences, and
natural sciences. Its activities are supported by the UC
Press Foundation and by philanthropic contributions
from individuals and institutions. For more information, visit www.ucpress.edu.

University of California Press
Berkeley and Los Angeles, California

University of California Press, Ltd.
London, England

Library of Congress Cataloging-in-Publication Data

Dell'Antonio, Andrew.
    Listening as spiritual practice in early modern Italy /
Andrew Dell'Antonio.
        p. cm.
    Includes bibliographical references and index.
    ISBN 978-0-520-26929-3 (cloth : alk. paper)
    1. Music—Italy—17th century—History and
criticism.   I. Title.
    ML290.2.D45 2011
    781.1'70945—dc22

                                    2011005496

Manufactured in the United States of America

20   19   18   17   16   15   14   13   12   11
10   9   8   7   6   5   4   3   2   1

UC Press, in keeping with its commitment to support
environmentally responsible and sustainable printing
practices, has printed this book on Cascades Enviro
100, a 100% post consumer waste, recycled, de-inked
fiber. FSC recycled certified and processed chlorine free.
It is acid free, Ecologo certified, and manufactured by
BioGas energy.

To my parents

Contents

Acknowledgments

With projects that unfold over more than a decade, the number of individuals whose assistance made the final result possible extends beyond the ability to count. I thus begin by apologizing to any of my friends, associates, and students whose support I do not name explicitly—I could plead insufficient space, but really it's just as likely to be waning mental capacity. I have been blessed many times over by my communities and feel inadequate to reflect that in words.

In the early stages of this venture, my doctoral advisor Anthony Newcomb wondered aloud to me about other early modern Italian writers on musical experience beyond the ones whose essays had already been excerpted and discussed repeatedly in scholarly literature; my quest to find and consider such writers was spurred by that query. Tim Carter and Susan McClary helped me frame the project, and without their encouragement and support it never would have gone forward.

My work truly moved into a higher plane during my Mellon fellowship year at Villa I Tatti, not only because I was helpfully compelled to expand my thinking into areas outside music, but because the marvelously collegial atmosphere created the ideal mental space for such an expansion. Among the wonderful 2001–2 community at I Tatti, I should single out Marilina Cirillo, Deanna Shemek, and especially Lawrence Jenkens (and his family Katherine and Emmie) for providing outstanding intellectual and emotional support. Nelda and Sandro Ferace truly took us in as family and have welcomed us back since; much joy was shared with them, and I hope that will continue. I have benefited greatly from the generosity of both then-outgoing director Walter Kaiser and then-incoming director Joseph Connors. A Lila Wallace—Reader's Digest Publications Grant, which made including illustrations possible, has been the most recent of the many essential contributions that Villa I Tatti has provided to this project. Kathryn Bosi, music librarian at I Tatti, has been a particularly invaluable resource, not only in her ideas on what materials in the library might be of most use (and her eagerness to obtain others for my specific purposes) but for her encouragement and intellectual acumen, both during the fellowship year and since.

While we had been in contact prior to that year, it was at I Tatti that Suzanne G. Cusick became an inspiring mentor and a treasured friend. Her work continues to be a model for my efforts, and her insights into early modern music and society a beacon for my thinking throughout the project. My intellectual debt to her is truly profound. It was thus with great delight that I had the opportunity to work alongside her with her advisee Amy Brosius as she put the finishing touches on a superb dissertation that further informed and reinforced the final stages of my own project—a *conversazione* that bore fruit for us both, I think, though I expect that her own insights will in time significantly surpass my own.

Many colleagues who work in early modern studies shared their invaluable expertise and insight as I attempted to refine my arguments. Describing their individual contributions would occupy much (though deserved) space, and presenting their names in anything but alphabetical order would give me the impossible task of comparing their equally incomparable assistance, so I will resort to the unvarnished list: Lorenzo Bianconi, Bonnie Blackburn, Todd Borgerding, Jeanice Brooks, John Butt, B. Harris Crist, Cory Gavito, Wendy Heller, Leofranc Holford-Strevens, David Hunter, Anne MacNeil, Melanie Marshall, Kimberlyn Montford, Giulio Ongaro, Massimo Ossi, John Potter, Deborah Roberts, Laurie Stras, Richard Wistreich . . . Thank you all. Robert Holzer does deserve special mention for helpfully sharing with me his very insightful paper "Beyond the (Musical) Pleasure Principle: Sanctifying the Sensuous in Early Seicento Rome," presented at the 1996 American Musicological Society national conference in Baltimore, which regrettably remains unpublished. While not early modernists, Robert Fink and Kimberly Fox were essential pillars of support to me through the final stages of writing.

Richard Spear was tremendously generous in sharing not only essential images and permissions but also his crucial insights as a foremost authority in early seventeenth-century Roman visual culture; the first chapter would have been much poorer without his help. Sir Denis Mahon was kind enough to provide permission for the reproduction of the Guido Reni painting in his collection that graces the cover of this book.

Faculty Research Assignment leaves from the University of Texas bookended my work on this project; I thank the university for the crucial time to focus that these allowed. My colleagues and students at the Butler School of Music make it a pleasure to come into the office each day; I especially thank Michael Tusa and the students in the Fall 2008 Foundations of Musicology class for the opportunity to present my work-in-progress to them. The Early Modern Study Group at the University of Texas provided me with a chance to "vet" some early chapter drafts with trusted colleagues: thanks to all, and especially to Douglas Biow for coordinating the group and Ann Johns for hosting. It may be rare to single out a student for thanks, and rarer still if that individual is a master's student; but Donald Patrick is yet a rarer individual, and working with him these last two years has sustained me in remarkable ways. I have learned much from him and am grateful for his friendship.

The anonymous readers from University of California Press provided trenchant suggestions and encouraged me to make this a much more streamlined book; I thank them enthusiastically for their essential contributions and take full responsibility for any good advice they proffered that I ungratefully overlooked. Thanks also to Eric Schmidt for careful guidance through the production stages, and to Elisabeth Magnus for her copyediting eagle-eye. Mary Francis is, I am fully convinced, the best editor an author can hope for: tremendously encouraging every step of the way, while unstinting in pushing for an ever-stronger result. I had already experienced her expert guidance during a previous project, and this time she was if anything even more helpful. I can only hope that in the future I will undertake more projects worthy of her support.

Susan Jackson accompanied me through the early stages of this project; while we have since moved apart, her partnership sustained me for many years, and I am grateful to her. Without her my daughter Miriam would not have come into my life and expanded it immeasurably—trying to be a good father to Miriam has fueled and sustained my emotional growth, and it will continue to be my most treasured identity.

Felicia Miyakawa became a presence in my life when this project was just about complete—but in just a year she has contributed more to it than she may realize.

My parents have been my rock for as long as I can remember. Their encouragement and genuine, heartfelt interest in my professional work over almost three decades are rare blessings for which I am grateful every moment. This project would have been absolutely unimaginable without the core inspiration for joy in knowledge and focused work— and the love of language—that I learned from them as a child and still learn from them every day. This book is dedicated to them, with my gratitude and admiration.

Introduction

Listening as Spiritual Practice

Music is the most "spiritual" of the arts of the spirit and
a love of music is a guarantee of "spirituality." . . . As the
countless variations on the soul of music and the music of
the soul bear witness, music is bound up with "interiority"
("inner music") of the "deepest" sort and *all* concerts
are sacred.

—Pierre Bourdieu, *Distinction:*
A Social Critique of the Judgment of Taste

Pierre Bourdieu's scare quotes around the term *spiritual* indicate that he
is arguing metaphorically and perhaps with a good dose of irony, drawing analogies between social understandings of religious transcendence
and musical fruition rather than postulating their direct equivalence.
While there would be much to say about Bourdieu's metaphorical characterization as it applies to the place of music in the post-Enlightenment
European tradition, for a group of influential thinkers in early modern
Italy (and Rome in particular) the link between sonic and spiritual transcendence was very direct. Leaders of the post-Tridentine Catholic Reformation understood the role of visual art as entirely bound to a deeper
understanding and appreciation of the sacred and placed the ultimate
onus of that understanding on the properly disposed recipient. Likewise, they set about positing musical experience, and most crucially the
listener's appropriate parsing of that experience, as a privileged path to
union with the divine. More specifically, a focused approach to musical
fruition—developed, primarily in elite Roman circles, in the first decades
of the seventeenth century—was a conscious response by the early modern
Catholic nobility and curia to the challenges posed by changing musical

styles. The Florentine-Roman "new music" was famously defined by the expressive power of its professional exponents, whose musical skill and effectiveness was often labeled as *virtù*—and the individual with such skill could become known as a *virtuoso* or a *virtuosa*. This use of the term was, however, potentially disruptive to early modern class and gender conventions, since *virtù* had long been understood as the defining quality of the noble male. Assigning the attribute of *virtù* to a member of the artisan class—or worse, a eunuch or a woman—ran the risk of bringing into question the nature of masculine noble identity itself.

The term *virtuoso/a* continued to be used in this context—though not without controversy—and indeed had become largely synonymous with "professional musician" by the late seventeenth century. However, an attempt was made by key members of the Roman religious elite to "reclaim" the earlier notion of *virtù* by redefining it as connected with listening rather than with musical performance, and further by characterizing it as a measure not only of earthly status but also of spiritual sensibility. In this way, a discourse of listening-based musical connoisseurship was deployed as a practice for establishing spiritual prestige and reaffirming noble masculine self-control.

One of the central contentions of this study is that the nonspecificity of musical description in seventeenth-century accounts (especially of sacred music) can be read as a purposeful strategy on the part of some writers to establish a nontechnical musical-descriptive frame, one designed to distance the writer from the specialized language of musicians—a language considered suspect because of its double association with lower-class (and often female) professionals and with scholastic pedantry. Indeed, art historians have seen parallels in the contemporaneous "growth of an articulate visual literacy" employing a language that is vague by modern technical standards.[1] To trace this move to a purposefully "nonspecific" descriptive frame, I will be exploring a number of examples of musical-descriptive strategies employed by early modern Italian elites. While these strategies will be the focus of subsequent chapters, some essential premises should be understood at the outset.

Scholars have long remarked on the formative musical patronage of the Barberini and other cardinal families of early modern Rome in the spread of the "new music" (Florentine and otherwise) in the first decades of the seventeenth century and have effectively traced the careers of the musicians who worked in the cardinals' *famiglie*.[2] In discussing the specific qualities of musical style and culture in early modern Rome, these scholars have turned their focus to the activities of musicians—composers and performers—who created soundscapes at the behest of the cardinal-ate courts. This approach is certainly essential, especially for the purpose of reconstructing specific sound events. However, it is less concerned about how the patrons (and their associates and *famiglie*) received or interpreted those sound events.

Indeed, it been a commonplace to characterize early seventeenth-century listeners as distracted or even uninterested in the "music itself." Those who have explored the tradition of comments on music by non-musicians in this time frame have evidently been frustrated by the non-specificity of such comments—a common conclusion is that audiences were making a show of appreciating music but didn't really care *what* the music was, and thus by implication didn't really pay attention. Frederick Hammond, in his magisterial study of musical patronage by the Barberini, repeatedly returns to this kind of assessment: "To judge from the chroniclers, it was necessary mainly to provide the right kind of music for each ritual; the quality of the music itself was immaterial. . . . Why and how music was employed in a given situation, and what kinds of music—vocal, instrumental, sacred, secular, loud, soft—were performed are questions whose answers are pertinent to a social and historical inquiry. The aesthetic nature of these artefacts, although a preoccupation today, would have been largely irrelevant and often incomprehensible to the audiences for whom they were created" (Hammond 1994, xix). Hammond later suggests that "accounts of seventeenth-century festivities essentially invert our own scale of values. Since the written or printed document constituted the permanent evidence of the magnificent but ephemeral occasion, the audience was at least as important as the performers. The singers were noticed only if they were famous virtuosi, the instrumentalists virtually never. The music was rarely examined in detail, and the librettist was more likely to be named than the composer. . . . Certain terms of description and approval recur constantly, suggesting that the mere presence of the thing described was more important than its quality" (128–29). Hammond further concludes that "the fact that Gerardi could find nothing more precise to describe the music at the Jesuit centenary two years later than to quote the same phrase verbatim points up the poverty of musical description in seventeenth-century Italy" (230). Hammond's characterization is reinforced by Claudio Annibaldi's distinction between "a sponsorship that reflects a patron's good taste and knowledge" (for which he coins the term *humanistic patronage*) and a "'conventional patronage' in which sponsorship involves musical repertories generically associated with the upper classes" (1998, 174). Annibaldi argues that conventional patronage was far more widespread and that cases of humanistic patronage were exceptional and deserve less attention in building a comprehensive understanding of early modern musical sponsorship. In other words, both scholars suggest that early modern patrons and chroniclers were generally not especially concerned with judging the quality of a musical work—or with articulating their "good taste and knowledge" through their assessment of that work. Rather, they were primarily concerned with expressing their class status through "generic" statements about music that would be expected of individuals of their social standing.

Scholarly attention to the political/social constructedness of the discourse of musical connoisseurship has been a salutary challenge to a prior tendency to perhaps take too much at face value the vaunted musical commitment of (for example) noble dedicatees of musical prints. It is also certainly true that the descriptive language concerning music in texts by nonmusicians tends to be vague, at least by modern scholarly standards of musical description. As an example, we might take the accounts of musical activities at the various churches in Rome in a mid-century guide to the city. Santa Maria dell'Orto, we are told, "is beautifully kept and officiated, with music, organs, and rich decorations. . . . On the eighth of June, the musicians of Rome come to honor this church, singing a solemn mass following a vow made to the Blessed Virgin in 1584" (60). At Santa Caterina de'Funari, "there is good music devoutly sung by the nuns themselves" (174). At San Lorenzo in Damaso, the Compagnia del Soccorso, instituted in 1602, "display the Holy Sacrament on the main altar of the church with a great apparatus, continuous prayer, sermons, and excellent pious music, beginning on *sexagesima* Thursday and continuing through the following Sunday" (221). At Santa Maria in Vallicella, the "Chiesa Nuova," under the sponsorship of the Congregatione dell'Oratorio, "there is devout, and excellent music. On every weekday, except for Saturday, there are four sermons lasting half an hour apiece, at the end of which some spiritual motets are sung; on holidays after vespers there is a single sermon. . . . From the beginning of November until Easter in the evening there are devout *oratori* with good sermons and music for an hour and a half" (227–28). Services at Sant'Apollinare "are officiated by the students [of the Jesuit Collegio Germanico] themselves, who collaborate with the choir on every feast day with excellent music" (262). The Chiesa and Compagnia del Crocefisso is "a beautiful church, decorated with lovely images, where on Fridays in

Lent the brothers ensure that one of the most worthy preachers in the pulpits of Rome delivers a sermon, accompanied by exquisite sounds and most beautiful music" (291). At San Lorenzo in Lucina, "they have spent many hundreds of *scudi* on silver vases, on altar decorations, and on the church, the organ, and other beautiful things, and every Saturday evening they sing in that church the Litanies and other praises of the Virgin with very good music, preceded by a sermon in praise of the Blessed Virgin by one of the aforesaid fathers" (332).[3] Modern scholars seeking musical specificity—names of performers or composers, let alone reference to specific musical works—could well be exasperated by the vagueness of these accounts. Nonetheless, through these descriptions the reader of the guidebook is clearly meant to become aware of the sonic "highlights" of sacred experience in the capital of Christendom and to understand that they deserve specific attention as part of the training of elite spiritual and protoaesthetic taste toward which the guidebook is designed. Ultimately, seventeenth-century elite nonmusicians would just as likely have rejected language that modern scholars might consider to be "accurately" musico-descriptive, considering it either inappropriate to their nonprofessional status or ineffective in conveying what was truly important about their engagement with music.

The nature of that engagement itself bears revisiting. A number of contemporaneous writers document the growing preference among Central Italian elites for listening to professional performers rather than participating in amateur music making. The predominant and most culturally appropriate way for elites to participate in musical activity—"musicking," to use the pithy term coined by Christopher Small (1998)—shifted in definition from creation of sounds to listening to sounds, or, more precisely, to *discourse about sounds*.[4] The case studies in the chapters that follow will explore how this shift was consciously designed and theorized to allow the elites to reassert the expertise and superiority on the field of musical meaning that had been challenged by the expressive power of professional musicians.

A central premise of Stefano Guazzo's *La civil conversazione,* one of the foundational "behavior manuals" of early modern Italy, is that "knowledge begins in conversation and ends in conversation" (1993, 1:30). This increased interest in the "conversational" display of knowledge in early modern Italy provides a framework for the idea that *discourse about music* can be a—perhaps even *the*—defining aspect of musical meaning.[5] Jonathan Brown finds a parallel concern with *discourse-about* in the visual arts, and his description of its dramatic effect on the changing cultural significance of painting bears an extended quote:

> Once painting had acquired intellectual trappings, it could be talked about in an intelligent way. Indeed, the ability to do so was taken as a mark of a person's quality. A fabulous gemstone might be admired for its size, rarity, brilliance and cut, but it provided no information or insight into human history and conduct or the mysteries and meanings of the faith. . . . The possession of fine pictures became [in the second third of the seventeenth century] a badge of identity for the social elite. This is not to say that the traditional trappings of wealth and power disappeared from view; the conspicuous consumption of luxury goods is an enduring characteristic of every hierarchical society. However, the prestige acquired by painting during the seventeenth century was unusual in this respect: by infusing display with a literary culture, it transformed notions about magnificence and the valuation, both social and material, of painting itself. (1995, 244)

Effective *discourse-about* (a marker of the civilized conversationalist) enables a change in the status of the object—indeed, in the case of music, encourages the idea that music (through careful assessment of the listener's experience) can somehow be "objectified" as an item for discussion. More importantly, *discourse-about* also brings attention to discourse as crucial to the creation of status and meaning (though the discourse itself may ostensibly be a transparent account of the item under discussion). Thus the sophisticated or elevated nature of the discourse can be seen as more important than its "objectivity" or "accuracy" (in technical terms) concerning the item around which discourse is taking place.

Given that this discourse—the *civil conversazione* codified by Guazzo and embraced by early modern elites—implicitly excludes individuals who do not have sufficient cultural training or leisure time to engage in such exchange, this framework can be very helpful in claiming/reclaiming the musical-signifying act for the leisure-class individual, shifting agency away from the professional musician. Indeed, this claiming/reclaiming plays itself out specifically with respect to music in Guazzo's book, as Roger Freitas observes: "In Guazzo's model *conversazione,* for example, the sole musical episode is provided by a professional who, during the course of dinner, enters the gathering, sings the praises of one of the guests, and then departs. The diners then focus on his presentation as a topic of conversation: although in this case the singer is not a member of the company, his contribution is treated just as if he had been" (2001, 518). To differ slightly from Freitas's reading, the company does not so much treat the singer as a member of its own group as appropriate the singer's rhetorical voice: after all, the singer does not *join* the company in conversation about his performance—Guazzo's noble interlocutors engage in *discourse about* the musician's activity. The company shows itself to be both conversant with the singer's art (though without any reference to specific sonic issues: the entire discussion concerns the words and sentiments expressed by the *musico,* with no description of what we today might call "the music itself") and entirely able to contextualize that art in a more sophisticated web than the professional-class singer would have been considered able to spin. Thus, as musical activity shifts from participatory to receptive, the conversation into which the music is inserted continues to "behave" as if the music were part of the activity of the noble conversers—*discourse-about* becomes a way of "musicking."

Through *discourse-about* (which parses and informs the listening experience), the noble conversers continue to claim ownership of the meaning of that music even if they are not creating the sounds. Their ownership becomes all the more secure because their tools to establish control and prestige (all of which are inherent in their sophisticated, elite cultural understanding and linguistic ability) are out of the reach of professional class musicians. On the other hand, the ability to produce sound through song or musical performance is something that elites share with their inferiors. It thus does not distinctively mark their superior sensibility and can safely be understood as less prestigious and less meaningful. Hence the ability to listen actively and parse the effects of that listening through *discourse-about* becomes a mark of social distinction and cultural control.

While some useful studies have attempted to trace amateur discourse about stylistic novelty to specific musical repertories (most notably Holzer 1992), there may or may not have been a distinctive new musical style that inherently *required* new modes of listening and related *discourses-about.* In any case, this study does not attempt to identify a set of musical repertories that may have been the locus of the new early modern rhetoric of *discourse about music,* or to describe the musical detail or "music-itself uniqueness" of such repertories—hence the reader will not find discussions or examples of individual musical works. In keeping with the concerns articulated by the elite writers who found it necessary to establish the new discourse, the study will instead focus on the rhetoric of the discourse itself, exploring how it posits expressive intensity and transcendence as inherently unnamable, without explicitly giving that rationale. Further, it will trace how *discourse about music* moves away from the precision of technical language (associated with the professional musician and/or the pedant, two different but equally undesirable images) and very purposefully toward the vagueness that marks its opposition or refusal.[6] Ultimately, this discourse is predicated on a new understanding of listening as an active process that implicitly highlights the sensibility of the listener as the generating source of the impetus toward discourse.

Superior understanding and vagueness are not only compatible stances but arguably perfectly complementary ones in this cultural frame: rational dissection belongs to the craftsman's trade, while the elite individual's understanding goes well beyond workaday matters. Indeed, it comes to him without any effort, by definition, and such effortless comprehension must be idealized so that he can reclaim agency over the affective power of music.[7] Further, the creation of an institutional place (and thus a need) for a *discourse about music* shaped by a subject position outside that of the musician reinforces the cultural prestige and employment opportunities for a group of individuals (let us now for now refer to them as noble connoisseurs) who wish to distance themselves from the artisan-musician in reinforcing their cultural and status-linked superiority. Thus the cultural value of an item in discussion is defined by the noble connoisseur's sensibility, but it also defines the connoisseur's job as a guardsman of the cultural patrimony. If that patrimony is not only cultural but religious, guardianship guided by elite understanding can be understood as all the more essential for the spiritual health of the church and its leadership.

The phenomenon of elite masculine musical connoisseurship is in keeping with what scholars focusing on the visual arts and the spiritual theory of the Catholic Reformation have found in their respective investigations into early modern Roman culture. Not only are the individuals concerned with the discourse surrounding music in many cases the same ones who establish a critical discourse on the visual arts at the same time, but the discourse itself is in many ways analogous to that on visual art. Indeed, the similarities are precisely what fosters a coherent approach that crosses several cultural concerns, unified by an overarching preoccupation with identity and subjectivity (and masculinity) that is fully in keeping with the social complexity of the early modern Italian "cultivated nobleman." As Stefano Lorenzetti (2003, 16) suggests, "The cultivated [early modern Italian] nobleman is nothing but a new-style orator who has replaced the forum with the court—an entity that is simultaneously real and ideal, both a physical and a mental place. His actions are designed for continuous and pervasive *persuasion*. Every aspect of his education fits into a rhetorical context that underlies its implicit finality, within a 'general rhetorics' in which all arts participate with a substantially analogous function." What distinguishes the connoisseur of the 1630s from his Castiglionian "grandfather" is the idea that while the arts are interdependent, they become unique in that each demands a varied set of "critical competencies." These competencies in turn require (create?) the notion of discrete art forms and discrete artworks, though of course the elite connoisseur is capable of negotiating both the specific competencies and the "general rhetoric" of the arts. While he alludes to some of these differences, Lorenzetti does not, however, address *spiritual* "knowledge/competency"—and I will argue that this last element is also crucial for a particular group of elite connoisseurs connected with the Roman curia more generally and with the Barberini papacy more specifically. These connoisseurs would be likely to have subscribed to the sentiment articulated in *The Roman Nobleman: Two Books of Nobility*. published in the late seventeenth century: "If the virtues make Man noble, whence comes the honor of families, religion must make him most noble of all, since it is a compendium of virtues. . . . If the warriors of the world claim nobility, those of God have an even better claim . . . It is very noble to be a courtier to the king; thus we should consider even more noble to be a courtier to God" (De'Crescenzi 1693, 155). It is this group of thinkers and writers on whom the present study will focus.

Against the idea that early modern listeners were either disengaged or indifferent to the nature and quality of the sounds they experienced, I argue that the new *discourse about music* establishes listening as an active rather than a passive practice, a very purposeful move in the wake of long-standing concerns about the dangers of musical "abandon" (especially in the presence of women) for the stable subjectivity and identity of the noble male. This rhetorical gesture also responds to the acknowledged shift in cultural prestige from collective amateur music making to the employment of highly trained professionals briefly discussed above. This perspective on "active listening" was strongly fostered—both explicitly and more subtly within a broader interpretative methodology—by Jesuit pedagogy, which became prevalent among the Italian ruling classes (arguably, indeed, European Catholic ruling classes *tout court*) in the early decades of the seventeenth century.[8]

I characterize this elite discourse on listening as a "spiritual practice" because the individuals whose writings we will be examining describe the phenomenon of listening as an active, carefully applied process (thus a *practice*) that is designed to establish a privileged connection with the transcendent experience of the divine (hence a *spiritual practice*). In this respect, such an approach to *discourse about music* is fully in keeping with the Jesuit self-training that was so influential in the identity formation of early modern European elites. Unlike some other Jesuit "practices," however, this was not one designed for widespread or proselytizing use: one of its main characteristics (and arguably, its aim) was exclusivity—or, in Bourdieu's term, *distinction*. Thus this sort of listening was intended to be, not a *normative* practice, but rather one that would mark the superior sensibility of those who could fully understand and deploy it. Certainly, however, those who theorized this exclusive approach to listening wished to portray it as a spiritually refined practice—one proper to the leaders of the Reformed Catholic Church. In that sense, perhaps, the approach to listening and *discourse about music* that we will be exploring can be seen as normative for a particular elite: for those institutionally influential individuals, it shaped possibilities of experience and created institutional assumptions about such experience crafted by individuals who were both "self-charged" and confirmed by hierarchical structures as the most legitimate producers of discourse around those acts.

One other essential aspect of this project concerns my suggestion that "aural collecting" formed an important aspect of elite listening practices in early modern Italy. As Margaret Murata rightly observes, the shift in vocal performance toward the stage and toward singers whose primary careers were operatic rather than directed at the chambers of the cardinal-ate courts led to a significant change in models of patronage and musical reception/consumption by the last quarter of the 1600s. Murata concludes that in the last decades of the century the collecting of scores had taken the place of direct sponsorship of musicians: "Collecting scores was a relatively inexpensive and passive form of having music, or showing interest in a fashionable but expensive occupation of current culture. . . . As both singers and the image of singers were de-cameralized, proprietary interest in music materialized in the library" (1990, 277–78). In this study, I argue that this emphasis on the score was not the first instance of collecting on the part of patrons and the professional tastemakers in their employ. Rather, I suggest that a different approach toward collecting, focused on listening experiences rather than on physical artifacts, was under way within the early decades of the century and was systematized during the years of Barberini rule.[9]

While collecting scores did indeed (as Murata characterizes it) constitute a less active sponsorship of individual musicians, it may have functioned in ways similar to the "aural collecting" that I will explore in the ensuing chapters in that it permitted the noble collector's engagement with musical meaning—with the *discourse about music*—without any direct agency on the part of a performer.[10] The increasing distance in the listener-performer relationship—both financial and discursive—may have encouraged the idea of placing agency in the direct communication between composer and listener, an idea that certainly begins to take hold by the closing decades of the century and may find some resonances in the time frame of this study as well.

The chapters that follow will expand on the general principles set out above with a series of four "case studies" that move from broader to narrower frameworks (in both philosophical and geographic terms) but are also designed to show intersecting concerns and thought processes among the "listening elites" that are the focus of this study. It should be understood that these case studies are meant to be, not the final word on the topic, but rather an opening excursus on a phenomenon of musical engagement by listening that remains to be explored much further (see, for example, the excellent discussions of the role musical *conversazioni* played in mid-seventeenth-century Roman elite circles in Brosius 2009). Thus the reader will not find any extended discussion of the broader scope of influence (beyond Italian, and more specifically Florentine-Roman, spheres) of the phenomena explored in the case studies, except in the closing Envoy, which brings to bear some recent scholarship on the emergence of systematic aesthetic theories of music in later seventeenth-century France, and what I see as the useful resonances between those theories and the earlier examples on the Italian peninsula that make up the case studies in this book.

The crucial nexus between gender, class status, and spiritual understanding that was forged by the framing of an ideal of "active listening" in early modern Italy allowed the act of listening to be theorized as a forceful interpretative ("musicking") stance rather than a passive reception of emotion-shifting sound. While the case studies presented in the following chapters are historically circumscribed, the nature of inquiry into listening practices (rather than musical works or music-making individuals) opens up the opportunity to consider broader methodological issues, and here I offer some links between my approach and other recent studies of listening practice.

This is by no means the first study to concern itself with historical approaches to listening, and I have found a number of other authors' case studies of great use to my thinking.[11] But I would go further: the *discourse about music* with which I am engaging in the following pages indicates a systematic approach to the understanding of sound as experienced that arguably provides an alternative model to the drastic/gnostic split recently posited by Carolyn Abbate (2004) as inherent in contemporary discourse about music. The common "gnostic" approach to musical meaning in modern/modernist aesthetics, Abbate suggests, implies both critical detachment on the part of the interpreter and a focus on music as text. Lost in that approach is the individual's immediacy of engagement with music (whether as performer or as listener), in a particular "musical performance's strangeness, its unearthly as well as its earthly qualities, and its resemblance to magic shows and circuses" (508). I find it intriguing that the "unearthliness" of what Abbate describes as the "drastic" potential of music is here described in secular terms—magic shows, circuses—rather than sacred ones. Were we to think of the "drastic" as a potential component of spiritual transcendence, the notion of "strangeness" described by Abbate would be, as we shall see, analogous to that described (in positive terms, as an essential aspect of "proper" musical understanding) by several of the authors we will encounter in this study. Thus we may tease out of the approaches to listening and its related discourses cultivated in early modern Rome a potential path to criticism (*discourse about music?*) that attempted to account for the drastic signification of sound.

In setting up his groundbreaking account of the "acoustic world" of early modern England, Bruce R. Smith suggests that "from the listener's standpoint, there are two quite distinct ways of attending to sound: one that focuses on the *there*ness of the sound, on the sound-producer; and one that focuses on the *here*ness of the sound, on the physiological and psychological effects of sound on the listener" (1999, 7). Smith then tells his reader, "What I am inviting you to negotiate in these pages is the difference between *ontology,* which assumes a detached, objective spectator who can see the whole, and *phenomenology,* which assumes a subject who is immersed in the experience she is trying to describe" (10). Smith's distinction is similar to Abbate's drastic/gnostic alternative. However, he takes the idea further, drawing on authors such as Barry Truax and Steven Feld in positing the importance of cultural identity formation through listeners' engagement with the sounds of their environment— what Feld (1996, 91) has characterized as *acoustemology,* which "recognizes that cultures establish their identities not only through things seen but through things heard and said." The approach that follows will not provide the thick accounting of soundscape that both Feld and Smith accomplish in their respective frames of reference. However, the pervasively oral/aural nature of the early modern Roman elite's *discourse about music*—its manifestation, even in written documents, as something either meant to be "performed aloud" or drawing its rhetorical structure from the essentially oral/aural metaphor of the *discorso*—will encourage me to posit the "active listening" practices discussed in the ensuing chapters as "performances" and to argue for the *discourse about music* as a model of "musicking" designed to engage or even compete with the "musicking" of the professional musicians and to establish authority over it.

Perhaps one more theoretical angle can be useful. Peter Szendy, in his discussion of the goals and nature of listening, has argued for the special value that musical arrangements provide in allowing the musician creating the arrangement to be "listened to while listening." In other words, the arrangement is "musicking about music," as it were, and Szendy considers this an especially valuable insight into the way music can be understood. Szendy repeatedly returns to the value of arrangements, in that "an arranger is a listener who signs and writes his listening," and he places his interpretative faith in such "*actual* attitudes of listening," since ultimately he maintains that "'verbalizations of their own musical experiences' . . . [tell] us nothing about listening *itself*" (2008, 102). Szendy's hierarchy relies on the notion that "musicking about music" is somehow a privileged interpretative gesture that can convey more about "the music itself" than narrative or verbal expression. Furthermore, Szendy's notion of arrangement implies a certain specificity of "musical text," with sound complexes retaining the locus of musical meaning. As we will see, this hierarchy is purposefully reversed in the writings of seventeenth-century Italian nonmusicians, a claiming of primacy for the drastic, phenomenological understanding of the response of the listening subject (Smith's *hereness* rather than *thereness* of listener engagement) made all the more possible by the careful skirting of the "work status" of the musical "object" (or nonobject?). Paradoxically, for the authors we will be exploring in this study, *discourse about music* is more truly expressive of the essence of musical meaning than "music itself." This is a key reason why in this study I purposefully refrain from attempts to identify or describe specific elements in musical repertories from the time that might have occasioned the discourse of "spiritual listening"—in doing so, I would be going pointedly against the premises of that discourse.

Szendy does observe that "*distraction, lacunary* listening, might also be a means, an attitude, to make *sense of the work;* that a certain inattention, a certain *wavering* of listening, might also be a valid and fertile connection in *auditory interpretation at work*" (2008, 104). Perhaps in our case we could posit, in the absence of an established concept of *work,* the possibility for another goal for "wavering" of engagement with music, which would not imply carelessness, lack of attention, or indifference. Rather, the ability for the individual to detach from the sonic experience—whether to reach moments of spiritual transcendence or to draw on memories of past experience or to draw connections with other relevant cultural artifacts, all aspects that we will explore in the ensuing chapters—again puts focus on the agency of the protoaesthetic actor and his ability to exercise control over his elite act of engagement with (and interpretation of) specifically/carefully chosen sonic moments.

In the closing stages of his argument, Szendy crucially suggests that contemporary individuals have an "irrepressible desire to listen to listening" (2008, 142)—that engaging in a dialogue with others about music is a defining tendency of the modern listener and that some "ways of hearing listening" (here again Szendy touts musical arrangements) are inherently more powerful because of the listened-to listener's successful engagement with the essence of the listening experience, which then makes for deeper communication of that essence to the listening listener. I would propose that the examples discussed in the ensuing chapters are relevant to Szendy's proposition in two distinct ways. First, they contextualize a historical moment in which Szendy's "desire to listen to listening" arguably first takes modern form—when the notion of a *discourse about music* is systematically broached in ways that eventually shape eighteenth- and nineteenth-century European theories of aesthetics. Second, they provide an alternative to Szendy's assumption that "musicking about music" is most effective when put in practice by musicians—that the essence of musical meaning is to be found in the making of additional music. The authors whom we will explore are purposefully drawing us away from the specificity of sound organization—they are "musicking about music without music." They attempt to locate the essential power of music in refined recollection of the ineffable drastic experience of sound and to understand that process of recollection as a link to experiencing the wondrous "strangeness" of the divine.

CHAPTER I

Rapt Attention

I turn to you, most blessed winged spirit, as you prepare to restore and comfort the languid and lovesick Francis with your song; ah, hold back the *accenti,* no longer play that harmonious instrument, which in being too lively brings him death and in lifting him too high oppresses him. Have mercy by stopping the course of so much mercy. If one more note comes out, it will relieve him of all life breath. If you wound that thin string one more time, you will cut the string of his life; nor can you handle that sweet bow again, for he will remain slain by its arrows. Thus Francis states when the music ends: the sensation of one more sound would render him senseless.

—Lelio Guidiccioni, *Discorso sopra la musica*

Since song and sound come from an intimate thought of the mind, and from the impetus of fantasy, and from an *affettuoso* delight of the heart, and striking with the air the already broken, distempered listener's spirit, the connection between soul and body, easily it can move the fantasy, delight the heart, penetrate to the deepest parts of the mind; and having penetrated, it works its effects, according to the disposition, and complexion of those who savor and delight in musical harmony.

—Lodovico Casali, *Generale invito alle grandezze, e maraviglie della musica*

The goal of expressing or evoking *affetto*—a term loosely but imprecisely translatable as "affect" that suggests the ineffable nature of human emotional/spiritual response—was introduced by advocates of early modern Catholic reform to justify the increasing focus on the recipient of a spiritual message rather than its creator. In this chapter, I will briefly discuss connections between the various uses of the concept of *affetto* in post-Tridentine discourse on preaching, the visual arts, and musical practice, particularly in the evocation and contemplation of mystical delight and transcendent union with the divine. I will then focus on musical manifestations associated with the presentation of the Eucharist, the moment in the Mass considered most crucial to early modern Reformed Catholic spirituality, drawing a connection from eucharistic devotional practice to a specific image of mystical transport through instrumental music: the iconography of the ecstasy of Saint Francis, who is often depicted in early modern Italy as responding to the sound of a violin-playing angel. The implications of this musical iconography will lead us through an examination of the role played by Jesuit ideas and institutions in reinforcing particular models of mystical contemplation and to some initial observations about spiritually informed listening and its role in the construction of ideal elite listening practices in early seventeenth-century Italy.

Some version of the claim that the goal of music is to "move the *affetto* of the spirit" (muovere l'affetto dell'animo) was invoked by many early modern composers of vocal and instrumental, sacred and secular music alike: for example, Adriano Banchieri suggests that modern composers "must work to imitate with harmony the *affetti* of the discourse/rhetoric/speech [gli affetti dell'oratione], so that the song may delight not only its composer but likewise the singers and the listeners."[1] The term was frequently used as a descriptive indication in the introductions to musical scores as well as within the scores themselves. Performers were encouraged to sing, or were described as singing, "with the greatest possible *affetto*"; and instances of the term *affetto* to denote passages of instrumental works are as widespread as they are idiosyncratic.[2] Given the variety and potentially contradictory nature of these usages, perhaps rather than attempting to determine a contemporary consensus on the precise meaning of the term it might be more useful to observe that claiming the existence of *affetto* in one's musical practice seems to have been an overriding concern in early seventeenth-century discourse on music.

This is understandable, for the term *affetto* permeated the discourse of post-Tridentine Catholic reform as an element of neo-Ciceronian theories of rhetoric and oratory. A straightforward instance is provided by Cardinal Gabriele Paleotti's 1582 commentary on visual images, in which

the cleric (an active participant in the Council of Trent and strong pro-
ponent of Tridentine reform) affirms that the artist must create a work
apt "to give delight, to teach, and to move the *affetto* of the beholder" (a
dare diletto, ad insegnare e movere l'affetto di chi la guarderà), echoing
the tripartite purpose of rhetoric *(docere, delectare, movere)* as defined
by Cicero and claimed for Christian oratory by Augustine.[3] Paleotti does
not, however, place sole onus on the creator of the work for the effectiveness of its meaning. In the passage immediately preceding his statement
about the artist's rhetorical task, he asserts that "the goal [to persuade]
is not within the power of the creator; his role [ufficio] is the endeavor
and the use of means proportionate to that goal. . . . Thus concerning the
painter, just as is appropriate for the writer, it can be said that his role is
to shape the painting in such a way that it be suited to engender/give birth
to [partorire] the goal that is expected from sacred images" (1961, 214–
15). Thus the recipient and creator had equal responsibility in the proper
cultivation of *affetti.*

In the generations following Paleotti's treatise, *affetti* became understood as "gestures and expressions that communicate the soulful feeling
of the senses," and for the commentators of the Catholic Reformation
affetti were closely linked with "the depiction of themes of moral significance that elevate the soul" (Spear 1982, 1:29, 36). An early seventeenth-
century definition of the term, from the Florentine *Vocabolario degli
Accademici della Crusca,* specifically highlights the spiritual nature of
affetto: "a passion of the soul, born of the desire for good, and the hatred
of evil."[4]

Creating works that would excite the recipient's *affetto* was the artist's task—but not only, indeed not primarily, the artist's. Preaching,
also a crucial aspect of the Catholic program of reform, was perhaps
the most explicitly theorized of the vehicles by which spiritual *affetto*
could be evoked. As a consequence, the ability to deploy eloquence and
rhetoric in the service of the divine was considered essential to the task
of moving the emotions to rectitude. Franciscans embraced the role of
"professional" preachers in the post-Tridentine reform, and by the 1570s
Rome was described as "a city flooded with preaching," in which clergy
"mounted the many stages there to practice and perfect their art."[5] Many
preachers were highly sought after (both in and beyond Rome), and contemporaneous commentaries speak to their effectiveness and popularity.[6]
Scholars have identified particular preaching schools associated with different orders or individual preachers and their followers.[7] Indeed, the

professionalization of the preacher proceeds in an interestingly parallel way to that of the visual artist and musical performer in late sixteenth- and early seventeenth-century Italy.

The preacher was increasingly characterized as a mediator between divine grace and human understanding, and that mediation was in keeping with one of the crucial principles of Catholic faith reaffirmed by the Council of Trent in opposition to the central-European Christian reformers, the concept of *justification,* or the process of acquisition of divine grace through righteous living. As McGinness (1995, 32) observes, "Like justification, preaching assumed that the grace to reform one's life is offered to every individual (indeed, the preacher is mediator of this grace), but there was the delicate matter of human co-operation with divine grace. The role of the preacher, then, was to move listeners, to persuade them, to cooperate with that grace." Thus the preacher was charged, not with *forcing* the faithful to worship, but with "persuad[ing] them to cooperate with [divine] grace," to choose freely the path to salvation, since this was an essential aspect of Catholic theology. The need for active cooperation on the part of the listener implied a need for oratory to serve not just as a tool for providing information but also as a resource for *learning to listen,* to assist the listener-recipient in becoming properly disposed toward God's message of grace.

A widely circulated "guide to delivering a sermon" by one of the most renowned and highly esteemed Franciscan preachers of the day (Girolamo Mautini da Narni, to whom we will return in chapter 4) specifies that "[the preacher's] oratory is not meant to astonish but to predispose the listeners to the word of God, to meditation on the truths suggested by sacred scripture."[8] Unlike Reformed-Evangelical or Calvinist preachers, Catholic preachers did not have as a goal of their practice their listeners' direct acquisition of the scriptural Word. Rather, they were charged with *interpretation* of scriptural text, and the ultimate goal was for the listener to perceive a glimpse of the transcendent Truth that words could only imperfectly adumbrate. Thus the preacher's message had to be not only doctrinally accurate and verbally persuasive but also "listener-friendly" beyond verbal content, containing within its structure and flow the incentives and instructions for the fruitful acquisition of the transcendent grace that surpassed the specific content of the preacher's earthly speech. Accounts of successful preachers (and many were popular and highly sought-after, especially recruited for events such as the *Quarantore,* on which more below) dwell at least as much on the sonic expressive power of the preacher's voice—and its effect on the listeners—as they do on the specific content of the sermon. One example of such an account will suffice here:

> The sonorousness of his voice has never been heard in others, it is not fully bronze nor fully silver, it shatters the air from afar and disperses opposing opinion, but in such a way that it soothes with thunder and sweetens with lightning. . . . He speaks with pauses as much as with words. Every one of his motions and his glances works effectively. . . . In excited actions he is fearsome, graceful in calm and composed ones. . . . A turn of his eye, a lift of his hood, his gathering or extending his body, with all of which (gravely) he accompanies the *affetti* of his discourse, configure others' spirits as he wishes. If he becomes heated in admonishing, out of the small pulpit comes a tempest as from a military machine. If he sweetens and comforts, there is no song more dear to the ears than his speech. All in all, in his presence, words, and actions, he is venerable, sublime, and penetrating, and altogether sweet, graceful, and lovely.[9]

The descriptive imagery is analogous to that used to praise contemporary singers by such contemporary chroniclers as Pietro Della Valle and Vincenzo Giustiniani, whose writings on music and the arts will be explored in subsequent chapters. For example, Della Valle writes that Modern Roman singers display "the art of soft and loud, of increasing the voice bit by bit, of softening it with *grazia*, of expressing *affetti*, of following with good judgment the words and their meanings; making the voice happy or sad, pitiful or bold as needed" (1903, 162). And according to Giustiniani, the female singers of Mantua and Ferrara distinguished themselves by "diminishing or enlarging their voice, now loud, now soft, narrowing or widening it phrase by phrase, alternatively drawing it out and speeding it up. . . . [Roman/Florentine singers] sang bass and tenor with a very wide range, with exquisite ways and *passaggi* and with extraordinary *affetto* and a special talent in letting the words be heard clearly" (1628/1878, 17–19). Indeed, Giustiniani links the sonic expressiveness of sermonizing and singing very directly. "A close acquaintance of mine chose to frequent a confraternity, prioritizing it over many others that were perhaps better, because the leader and rector had a beautiful voice in making his sermons, and sang the litanies well, with *grazia* and a delightful sonorous voice" (27). The term *grazia* recurs in these and other contemporary authors' texts as a central tenet underpinning *gusto*, and its appearance in a sacred context underlines the continuity between taste for beauty and divine understanding.

A widely influential manual on preaching by one of the most esteemed practitioners of early modern Italy—Francesco Panigarola's *On the Way to Compose a Sermon (Del modo di comporre una predica)*, first printed in Italian in 1581 and quickly translated into Latin and French—draws on a specifically musical image to describe the opening section of a sermon: he compares it to a performer's opening *ricercata,* from which "those who are present can immediately derive what they can hope from the [musical] performer's skill."[10] To be sure, metaphors connecting verbal and rhetorical expression to music permeate the controversies over the "second practice" and "new style" in early modern Italy, but in this case the metaphor is reversed, and the rhetorical power is seen as sonic and as building on nonverbal immediacy rather than as dependent on text and critical reason.

If moving *affetto* was an essential goal of the preacher, Paleotti also specified a further purpose: as Anton Boschloo (1998, 47) frames it, "As far as *affetto* is concerned . . . artworks must be created in order to achieve two objectives: 'move the senses' and 'excite the spirit to devotion.'" Indeed, for those who wished to build devotional rhetoric (preachers, visual artists, musicians), clarity of meaning was evidently less important than evocation and inspiration. "Preachers no longer look to impart a clear and distinct apprehension of doctrine (though in other circumstances this was important)," observes McGinness (1995, 106), "but instead to proclaim it, to draw out the affections, and address the heart." And it is to the importance of spiritual understanding based in the heart (which housed *affetto*—rather than the brain, home of *intelletto*) that we now turn. With the increasing concern for the recipient's predisposition and response to rhetorical stimuli, in the decades following the Council of Trent Catholic Church leaders began to make a distinction between different levels of affective response. In the process, they privileged specific models of response that became associated with the cultivated, upper-class individual. Perhaps as a reaction to the Evangelical Reformation's highlighting of textual study as a path to spiritual connection, we can see in late sixteenth-century Italy an encouragement to seek another path: in the words of one turn-of-the-century commentator, "the way of *affetto* and of love, which is found more through inspiration than through reflection."[11] This path was recommended not only for illiterate individuals (who would naturally not have access to texts for reflection) but also, and perhaps more directly, to the increasingly literate upper classes, who might otherwise have been tempted by the Protestant championing of humanism and individual textual interpretation. The scholarly, text-based path to divine understanding was increasingly characterized as long, difficult, and even pedantic—qualities entirely opposed to the ideal of effortless *grazia* that the Italian ruling classes had been cultivating as a defining trait in the decades following Castiglione's *Cortigiano* and Dalla Casa's *Galateo*. Better to gain inspiration to transcendent understanding through images—again quoting Paleotti (1961, 228; I have retained the construction of the original, despite its awkwardness in English, to highlight the image of the devout viewer/listener's body being penetrated by the breath of the depiction), "If words that are heard or read have such power to move our senses, with much greater force will penetrate us those images, from which we can see the breath of piety, modesty, saintliness, and devotion." This is not a circumstance governed by rational response but certainly one that has the power to move the emotions—though the agency in this case is interestingly obscured, since the paintings do not, of course, "breathe." Implicit in Paleotti's description is the "active reception" of the spiritual message on the part of the viewer of the image: we will return below to the implications of this notion of "active receptivity."

A new conception of the self was fostered in this period by the resurgence of Augustinian theories of spirituality: in William Bouwsma's words, "a view of the self as a mysterious and undifferentiated unity, its quality a reflection of another faculty previously little recognized, 'the heart'" (2000, 22).[12] Preachers encouraged their listeners to draw on the power of the heart rather than to rely on the intellect in reaching a deeper understanding of grace. New theories of art and artistic response were directed at this privileging of the heart as the locus of an individual's spiritual essence.[13] For Archbishop Federico Borromeo of Milan, visual images had the power to destabilize the heart, causing rapture or ecstasy and thus opening a direct path to divine insight.[14] Borromeo's valuing of visual art was paralleled by his estimation of music as a conduit to spiritual understanding, and in his sermons he praised those individuals (primarily nuns) whose musical activity became a path to ecstasy.[15]

Those who theorized the power of the heart in the reception of spiritual or artistic messages also emphasized the importance of a pure or well disposed heart, associating such purity with the refined individual, since Catholic dogma maintained that faith was a learned trait rather than an innate one.[16] A link was thus established between "correct" spirituality, artistic understanding, and refinement of training, with a further connection to class status—issues that will concern us in subsequent chapters.

Certainly strong arguments were made—and not just by musicians—concerning the power of music to enhance devotion, if only by drawing parishioners in and exposing them to the multisensory persuasive power of the church. Here is a concise summary from the end of the sixteenth century by Lodovico Zacconi: "People leave the public square and their homes to go to the holy Temple, invited by the sacred musical *concerti;* thus beyond those universal effects, which are by now known by all the world (which are to cheer our afflicted and saddened spirits, to console our soul, to please us, to make us well-disposed, and to entertain us with delight), [music] incites and pushes us also to devotion and to divine tribute. Because while God is praised in the churches with sweet and lovely sound, people run there, and running there they obtain mercy, since they never run there in vain, nor do they ever depart without having gained something."[17] Arnaldo Morelli has discussed the systematic increase in sacred musical activity in post-Tridentine Rome in the context of a renewed focus on drawing the faithful to rituals and spaces of worship.[18] Others (especially Culley 1970) have traced the growing dedication to music in key Jesuit institutions, particularly the Collegio Germanico, as an energizing component of the young pupils' attention to worship as well as a source of attraction to outsiders.[19]

Church functionaries were quick to respond to the usefulness of music to please the crowd not only on customary high feasts but also on other occasions. In an account of activities at Saint Peter's Basilica in Rome, we read that "after we had received [the pope after vespers on Friday of Passiontide, March 17, 1617], we went to the choir and sang compline in polyphony, and the organ was played almost continuously, [and] even though it is Passiontide and [scripture commands that] 'the sound of the organs should cease,' nonetheless it is tolerated because it draws a great number of people."[20] There were certainly dissenting voices within the church hierarchy who were suspicious of the potential for abuse in the deployment of "sensual" resources for divine purposes. However, other strong voices echoed the sentiment that "it is delight, after all, that prompts the soul to ascend to higher realms of the spirit" (McGinness 1995, 106) and that pleasure could be "an access" to spiritual transport (Holzer 1996; 2000).

Richard Goldthwaite (1994, 147) has remarked on the early modern Catholic tendency to intensify "the use of luxury to enhance the entire liturgical apparatus and . . . the further development of the pictorial arts to appeal to religious sensibilities." As we have discussed, one can easily extend Goldthwaite's nod to the pictorial arts into the entire multisensory sphere of Catholic devotion. And according to Louis of Grenada, one of the most widely read and esteemed Catholic mystics in the late sixteenth century, the interior experience of the divine and the experience of beauty are linked—in particular, they are not reflexive but active and are "ways of gaining perfection in love."[21] Active engagement in divine grace, as briefly discussed above, was an essential aspect of perceiving and contemplating the union between beauty and the divine: this was especially evident in rituals surrounding the Eucharist.

One of the elements of post-Tridentine reform was to respond to Evangelical challenges by explicitly championing crucial elements of faith and practice that the Evangelicals had rejected.[22] Among the most important of these practices was a renewed emphasis on the cult of the Eucharist.[23] The council encouraged the public worship of "this sublime and venerable sacrament"; indeed, during its closing statements on December 4, 1563, the Council of Trent "declared the Eucharist the holiest and most divine work that Christian faithful could do" (Wandel 2006, 230).[24] The Tridentine Catechism reinforced the importance of celebratory excitement, stating that it was the principal duty for the religious leader "to procure with all due diligence that the faithful be excited to love the immense goodness of God toward us, so that, fired up with divine ardor, they be enraptured to that highest and most perfect Good, in which they will find true and ultimate happiness."[25] Specifically, the catechism stated that faith was conceived from hearing,[26] and while the meanings of the words of faith must certainly have been the primary focus of that dogma, nonetheless we have seen above that the intense concern with other sonic effects—ranging from rhetorical gestures to noise to musical sound—provided the potential for a broader understanding of the resources available to move spiritual *affetti* in a well-prepared listener.

Examples of music accompanying eucharistic display, whether at the elevation of the Host at Mass or in the course of special eucharistic devotions such as the *Quarantore* or Forty Hours' Service, became frequent at major Catholic churches in the last quarter of the sixteenth century and expanded widely into minor churches, especially in Rome, in the first part of the seventeenth. The musical expression that became associated with the elevation is a particularly interesting case in point. Clement VIII's ceremonial guidelines of 1600 indicated the elevation as a place for "music of particularly solemn character" (Hammond 1994, 155). The most substantial collection of concerted music for the Mass Proper—the *Sacrae modulationes* published by Lorenzo Ratti, chapel master at the Jesuit Collegio Germanico, in 1628, probably under Barberini sponsorship—contains a full cycle of graduals and offertories for the liturgical year, each grouping also containing a paraliturgical motet specifically designated for the elevation (Chauvin 1970, 30 and passim; see also Culley 1970, 168–69). This would appear to indicate an institutional understanding that the elevation required specific attention as an occasion for sonic triggers to transcendence.[27]

While motets continued to accompany the elevation through the seventeenth century, instrumental music also played an increasingly important part in the sonic framing of this most crucial ritual. Girolamo Diruta, in his organ manual *Il Transilvano,* calls for the organist to imitate "with his playing the hard and bitter torments of the Passion" during the elevation (see Tagliavini 1998, 87); and Frescobaldi's elevation toccatas provide a remarkable example of sonic intensity in their use of dissonance and chromaticism.[28] Stephen Bonta has also convincingly shown the increasing association of ensemble instrumental music—and specifically instrumental genres or styles that become associated with the term *affetto* or *affettuoso*—with the elevation in Italian liturgical practice of the first half of the seventeenth century.[29]

The use of music to assist in focusing the *affetti* of the faithful on the Eucharist was a key aspect of the *Quarantore,* a practice that was instituted in Rome in the last decade of the sixteenth century and that initially came under the leadership of the Congregazione Mariana, a confraternity of Roman noblemen.[30] At the core of the *Quarantore* was the display of the consecrated host for forty hours on a specially prepared altar, accompanied by regular alternation of preaching and music; the goal was to create an intense and unbroken rhetorical space to encourage the faithful to connect with the sacrifice of Christ. The visual display of the host was designed to bewilder the viewer with its magnificence, and other artworks were frequently added to those regularly on display in the church to saturate the visual expression of *affetti.* Similar intensity was provided by the musical resources, which often framed the "headline" event—preaching by a featured preacher, recruited especially for the occasion by the leadership of the parish.[31]

The configuration of this devotional practice allowed for an unbroken forty-hour aural stimulation of *affetti* through speech and sound, which combined with other multisensory triggers (incense for the nose, visual decoration for the eyes, etc.).[32] Accounts of the *Quarantore* describe the role of the musical component of the devotion as a directly transcendent force in conjunction with the sermon: for example, the advertisement for an upcoming *Quarantore* at San Lorenzo in Damaso in Rome in 1604 specified that "once all are kneeling and the doors are closed, music will begin in order to raise spirits to God; then Father Fedele will deliver the sermon, and will act as mediator between the soul and God, in order to reconcile all with His Divine Majesty, and all will dispose themselves as our Lord God will inspire."[33] The significant spread of these devotions throughout Catholic Italy in the seventeenth century reveals the church's perception of the spiritual effectiveness of this intensified assault upon the *affetti*. Furthermore, the local nobility (whether in Rome or in other cities from which we have descriptions of *Quarantore* celebrations, such as Siena and Bergamo) tended to play a significant role in the sponsorship of, and attendance/participation in, the *Quarantore*—indicating their wish to appear especially engaged in (and appreciative of) this manifestation of transcendence through sound.[34]

In the early decades of the seventeenth century, Franciscans gained a reputation as expert *Quarantore* preachers.[35] Consequently, many of the most sought-after preachers were Franciscans, and an individual from the Franciscan Capuchin order was often symbolically chosen as the official preacher to the pope (the *predicatore apostolico*).[36] Indeed, Franciscan models of piety were resurgent during the post-Tridentine reforms and were deeply influential on the development of the Jesuit order, as we will discuss below. These models encouraged *imitatio Christi,* the direct emulation of Jesus's actions and emotional travails advocated by Francis; the goal of such emulation was a transcendent, mystical union with Christ. Franciscan models of devotion also drew extensively on the new emphasis on the Eucharist: as the religious scholar Steven Ostrow (1996, 109) observes, "In his *Testament,* [Saint Francis] extolled the Eucharist as the only means through which mortals could see God on Earth." More generally (and also following the saint's teachings), Franciscan preachers pointed to the presence of the Eucharist as a potential trigger for ecstatic transport.

An interesting association of Saint Francis with music, and particularly music that fuels transcendence, provides the basis for an iconographic tradition that flourished in the decades around the turn of the seventeenth century—a tradition that has intriguing implications for an assessment of listening as a spiritual practice. There are several accounts of Saint Francis's encounters with music in the stories of his life that developed and became standardized in the generations following his death. Some of these stories involve Francis seeking out music as comfort from his travails, others tell of his direct involvement with performance (one story relates that Francis was prone to singing the praises of Christ while "accompanying" himself on a stick held and "played" like a bowed string instrument).[37] The episode that caught the fancy of early modern Italian artists and their patrons derives from a devotional text that dates from long after the saint's death and that seems to have reached the height of its popularity in the sixteenth century: the so-called "Considerations on the Stigmata" appended to the *Little Flowers of Saint Francis*.[38] These five "considerations" (one for each of the five wounds of Christ, "stigmata," that Francis received on his body as proof of his devotion and saintliness) consist of short episodes from the life of Francis around the time he received the stigmata on Mount Verna, with simple commentary on the spiritual message of those episodes. The following episode closes the "second consideration":

> When Saint Francis was very weak in body, from abstinence, and his battles with demons, and since he wished to comfort [his] body with the spiritual nourishment of the soul, he began to think of the unmeasurable glory and bliss of those blessed with eternal life, and thus prayed to God that he give him the grace to taste a small portion of that bliss. And while he was thinking thus, suddenly there appeared to him an angel with great splendor, which had a *violetta* in its right hand *[sic]* and the bow in the left. And while Saint Francis was astonished at the presence of that angel, it drew the bow only once over the *violetta,* and immediately such sweetness and melody sweetened his soul, and relieved all bodily sensation, that as he later told his comrades [the saint] believed, that if the angel had drawn the bow [again], his soul would have left his body from the unbearable sweetness.[39]

The theme of Saint Francis and the "violetta"-playing angel was taken up by several artists in this period, in some cases repeatedly, and we shall consider two prominent examples below.[40] Unsurprisingly, given its attribution of transcendent spiritual power to music, it is also mentioned by a number of musician-commentators, such as Lodovico Casali:

> In the chronicles of Saint Francis, my protector, the tale is told that because [the saint] delighted in music, he desired to savor the sound of a *viola,* which was in the property of his dear companion, a holy man named Friar Pacifico . . . but since that friar refused, out of respect, God the Highest Provider of all things, who is pleased to console his servants, sent to him from heaven an angel, who, playing a *viola* as Saint Francis had desired, with the sweetness that can come only from a heavenly hand, consoled the soul and the afflicted body of the holy father.[41]

Casali here conflates the Celano and Bonaventure stories (both of which involve Francis being soothed by angelic music after requesting and being denied earthly music), cross-pollinating them with the "viola" of the *Little Flowers* (the other two stories involve a plucked-string instrument). Furthermore, while the wording in Casali's reference to "sweetness" is somewhat ambiguous, the story plays up the agency of the angel and his (its?) role in creating heavenly sounds. Likewise, André Maugars—a virtuoso bowed-string instrumentalist who visited Rome in the late 1630s and provided an account of musical activity in cardinal family circles—clearly focuses on the significance of the instrument chosen by God to bring comfort to Francis: "Saint Francis, when he asked God—in the fervor of his meditation—to let him hear one of the joys of the blessed, heard a consort of angels who played the *viole,* since it is the sweetest and most charming of all the instruments" (1993, 18–19). The single angel with the single bow stroke from the *Little Flowers* has here become several angels playing "en concert." While the idea of an angelic ensemble may be Maugars's own elaboration, it has striking parallels with an image that Maugars might well have encountered during his stay in Rome and that we will discuss below. In any case, as in Casali's account, the emphasis is on the performers and the power of the instrument to charm.[42]

While these musicians' perspectives on the scene of Saint Francis and the musical angel are interesting, the popularity of the iconographic tradition is probably more closely connected to its potential for a focus on the listener, since Franciscan spirituality—which generalized the saint's own practice of *imitatio Christi* to the goal of following Francis's own practice and spiritual focus—would probably have led the viewer to identify with the listening saint rather than with the performing angel. The opening epigraph for this chapter provides a particularly striking verbal description of the scene from the listener's perspective, and we will return to that description in chapter 4. Here we will dwell on two images of the musical consolation of Saint Francis by two individuals who were among the most celebrated painters in early modern Rome: Domenichino and Guido Reni.

Guido Reni's version of the scene is the earlier of the two, dating from about 1606–7 (fig. 1). It was possibly commissioned or sponsored by Cardinal Scipione Borghese, since Reni was "on retainer" in the cardinal's household (*famiglia*) by 1608 (Spear 1996, 554–56). The saint is pictured in a landscape, in a state of quiet repose. In his hand is a skull, and nearby is a crucifix, both common iconographic attributes of Francis's contemplative life. The saint's head is tilted to the side, almost as if Francis were turning his ear to the miraculous sound. The angel's performing pose is somewhat fanciful but reasonably close to a realistic gesture. In describing another Franciscan image by Reni, with the saint deep in contemplation of the crucifix, Marc Fumaroli (1998, 337) provides a description that I think resonates with this painting as well: "Reni invites the spectator of his paintings to view them inwardly *just as* Saint Francis views his sculpted crucifix, as a point of departure for the soul's ascent toward the

FIGURE 1. Guido Reni, Saint Francis Comforted by the Musician Angel, ca. 1606–7. Oil on copperplate. Collection of Sir Denis Mahon, currently in the Pinacoteca Municipale, Bologna.

inward vision and savoring (*gusto*) of the divine presence that is really experienced or, at least, 'considered.' "[43] In this case the point of departure is not a visual image but a sonic event—one, I would argue, meant to evoke concrete events experienced by the early modern viewer. Reni

FIGURE 2. Domenichino, Saint Francis and the Musician Angel(s), ca. 1626. Fresco. Cappella Merenda, Santa Maria della Vittoria, Rome.

invites his spectator to join Saint Francis's transcendent enjoyment of angelic music by depicting a very real sound, one that the Roman elite would have been able to recall from personal experience and might have associated with the expression of intense emotion, given the increasing presence of instrumental music at moments of spiritual intensity such as the elevation.

The second image is by Domenico Zampieri, known as "Domenichino," considered a chief contemporary rival of Reni among the students of the Bolognese Carracci school (fig. 2). As the art historian Stephen Pepper (1984, 24) observes, while Reni was described by his contemporaries as embodying the sophistication of image and color associated with the term *grazia*, Domenichino was often called the master of *affetti*, credited with being most concerned with the didactic depiction of spiritual messages. The image is a fresco from a cycle depicting episodes from the life of Saint Francis in the chapel of Ippolito Merenda in the church of Santa Maria della Vittoria in Rome. The church was rededicated in 1622 to incorporate an icon of the Virgin that had inspired the victorious Catholic armies in the Thirty Years' War. Merenda was a wealthy lawyer in the Barberini circle who had chosen Francis as his saintly protector and another Francis (Cardinal Francesco Barberini) as his earthly patron. Decoration of the chapel was probably begun in 1626, to commemorate the four-hundredth anniversary of the saint's death.[44]

Just as in the Reni depiction, here the saint is shown with his attributes—the crucifix and the skull—but now instead of one angel we have an entire angelic consort, fully in keeping with a performing ensemble for Roman concert music of the early seventeenth century.[45] Entirely unlike Reni's quiet and still Francis, Domenichino's saint is reeling under the unbearable power of the heavenly sound, "falling" toward the altar of the chapel. The experience of transcendent connection with the divine through listening is shown here not as a refined enjoyment but as an irresistible transport, one that involves the entirety of the body in connecting with divine power. Through the power of the listening experience, Francis is brought into a position much like that of the crucifix at his side, fulfilling his task of imitating the experience of Christ. The viewer is thereby encouraged to think of the listening experience as a vehicle for the imitation of Christ's passion, at least through an understanding—perhaps physical as well as spiritual—of divine intensity. Domenichino, like his patron Merenda, was associated with the Barberini protectorate, and his more spectacular approach fits well with the Barberini program of spiritual theatricality. However, Reni was arguably more favored by the Barberini, and as the art historian Anthony Colantuono observes, "It appears that the Barberini were promoting a form of diplomatic oratory rooted in Tassesque ethical and stylistic principles. . . . In Tasso's formulation, the quest for perfect beauty was inextricably linked to the end of perfect moral instruction. As the Barberini must certainly have recognized, Guido [Reni] was capable not only of portraying a sweetly lyrical kind of beauty but also of *using* that beauty as a rhetorical device, a device with which to persuade the beholder to accept virtually any moral argument" (1997, 174–75). In any case, notwithstanding the very different characterizations of the listening experience in the two paintings, both artists draw on contemporary musical images in depicting the musical angel(s), and both draw the viewer's attention to the personal experience of a saint whose example was repeatedly presented as a model for emulation in early seventeenth-century spiritual manuals.

The idea that the violin could represent (embody?) angelic intervention as an aid to transcendence finds interesting resonance in a passage from an Easter dialogue motet by the Milanese composer Girolamo Baglione (discussed in Kendrick 2002, 237ff.), in which the violin anticipates the voice of the angel calling to Mary Magdalen at the tomb of the risen Christ. Kendrick suggests that this is intended to be "the expression of joy at the Resurrection highlighted by the 'popular' use of the instrumental genre [canzona] and scoring. While Kendrick's point is well taken—the musical language of the violin in the Baglione motet is, after all, more akin to the diatonic and lively canzona than to the more chromatic and *affetto*-inflected instrumental styles generally associated with elevation-specific works—the violin may be doing double valence here for those listeners who could perceive its connection with Franciscan iconography. And indeed, there is at least one noteworthy depiction of musical-angelic consolation of the Magdalen, in a painting by Marcantonio Franceschini that shows the saint lying down with her ear turned to a *concerto* of two singing putti and two angels playing lute and violin (Gentili 2000, 65–67, 207).[46]

The characterization of earthly music as an analogue to heavenly sounds is not unique to these cases, of course; indeed, it could be considered a commonplace in Catholic commentary from the church fathers to the present day.[47] Yet as Burke (1987, 21) has observed, "The commonplaces and stereotypes so frequent in autobiographies and memorials are not so much hindrances to the historian as aids in the reconstruction of the rules or norms of the culture." The commonplace of musical transcendence does appear to be more intensely described and frequently evoked in early modern commentary and, even more significantly, becomes increasingly linked to subjective spiritual transcendence in an age in which the valorization of the self became a crucial concern of the ruling classes.[48]

Individual connection with the divine, a hallmark of Franciscan spirituality, was also at the core of the teachings of Saint Ignatius and the Jesuit order that arose from his leadership. While Jesuits also took part in the late sixteenth-century resurgence of preaching that has been briefly discussed above, their primary mission was pedagogical and was directed at the ruling classes.[49] Underpinning Jesuit spiritual and pedagogical practice was Loyola's *Spiritual Exercises*. One of the crucial texts of early modern Catholic spirituality and the core text of Jesuit religious pedagogy, *Spiritual Exercises* is based on the principle of "the spirituality of the heart" explored above, drawing on an individual's ability to harness the power of his or her own *affetti* in feeling the love and suffering of Christ. This approach was deeply indebted to the Franciscan tradition of the *imitatio Christi*.[50]

As Philip Endean (2008, 53) observes, "*Spiritual Exercises* is not a book to be read; Ignatius is quite explicit that the person making the Exercises should not have the full text to hand, and not know what is coming." The individual undertaking the *Exercises* (in Jesuit parlance, the "exercitant") must do so aurally, guided by a more experienced master (the "spiritual leader"), whose deployment of rhetorical imagery should aim to surprise (unbalance?) the ear and the imagination. The analogy with preaching is clear, though the frame is now changed from public to private. But the focus is still on the exercitant and his ability to look inwardly to achieve the identification with Christ that is the ultimate aim of the *Exercises*—perhaps all the more so since, unlike the preacher, the spiritual leader can and should tailor each phase of the exercises to the exercitant's specific path and "taste."[51] The individual response, however—as Loyola himself was careful to specify—had to be consonant with the hierarchical message of the Church Militant. Thus the choice of images and rhetorical strategies had to be very carefully managed by the spiritual leader, and the exercitant's journey had to be carefully monitored to avoid any appearance of heresy. This explains the remarkable efflorescence at the turn of the seventeenth century of Jesuit texts on rhetoric, which carefully analyzed and codified the means by which the discourse of transcendence and identification with the divine was to be framed.[52] Scholars have remarked on the emphasis placed, within this systematic concern with rhetoric, specifically on *elocutio*—the oral delivery (both structural and sonic) of the spiritual message, whether in public preaching or in private exercise leading, and its reception by the listener.[53] This emphasis on active listening as the path to the acquisition of faith is certainly in keeping with the variety of cases we have examined to this point.

While the Jesuits continued to advocate that the initial practice of the *Exercises* be aurally driven and led by a well-trained spiritual leader who could both deploy rhetoric effectively and ensure adherence to established dogma, the popularity of the *Exercises* led to their broader use in regular devotional practice.[54] This expansion necessarily transferred the responsibility for rhetorical deployment of devotional ideas from the (now absent) spiritual leader to the exercitant himself and—even more importantly—made the exercitant further responsible for monitoring his own response to the transcendent moment.

Many texts designed to feed the hunger for daily-use Ignatian practice were published in the early decades of the seventeenth century, several featuring the key word *exercises*. For example, a book entitled *Spiritual Exercises within Which Is Demonstrated an Easy Way to Make Fruitful Prayer to God* (*Esercitij spirituali nei quali si mostra un modo facile di far fruttuosamente oratione a Dio* [Rome: Fetti, 1613]) contains many short meditations and images, with vivid contrasts of intense emotion, and the author/editor suggests that they be spoken out loud or internally as a series of "exclamations" (rather than careful intellectual reflections) designed to jar the devout exercitant into an ecstatic state.[55] Here the reader (or perhaps "user," since silent dispassionate reading is clearly not sufficient to gain proper benefit from the text) is asked to take on simultaneously the roles of preacher (or spiritual leader) and listener/exercitant in a process of "self-oratory." The oral/aural component is explicit, though paradoxically it can occur internally, without the actual sounding out of the rhetorical message. The essential component for the success of this set of exercises is the "active-receptive" state of the exercitant, who is called upon to "listen" internally as well as externally and to respond with the kind of immediacy that characterizes the sense of hearing rather than the distance and cogitation inherent in processing text through the sense of sight.

Fumaroli (1998, 235) rightly observes that early modern Catholics considered meditation a discipline in which "the task is to concentrate attention and to transform it into a spiritual habit," understanding it as sharing with rhetoric "the same goal, which is to persuade, to modify the judgment, the will, the behavior of its 'recipients.'" I would further observe that "meditation" in the case of the recipient of aural rhetoric (whether preaching or music) does not require reflection or rational cogitation, but rather a disposition to the immediacy of transcendent connection with the divine. Jesuit training would have aimed at guiding the individual to reach a "proper understanding" of that transcendent connection within the hierarchical framework of the Church of Rome.

Early modern Catholic rhetoric emphasized the importance of "active receptivity" to stimuli that could trigger transcendent connection to the divine. While the sense of sight was an essential resource for the "active recipient," it was not the most uniformly privileged conduit, and the sense of hearing (in some cases, as we have seen, evoked by the sense of sight) was at least as crucial—perhaps in many cases even more so. The message of the Church of Rome—through preaching and the arts—was designed to "mak[e] clear that membership in the Church depends above all on a 'correct understanding' of Catholic doctrine, and that one's moral progress depends on this as well" (McGinness 1995, 37). Where artistic experience and doctrine are linked—for example, in the depictions or descriptions of musical transcendence/transport—it becomes equally clear that this "correct understanding" (the Latin term is *recte sentire*) is also related to what we might characterize as protoaesthetic experience and thus that "moral progress" also depends on proper disposition to the reception of *affetti* through art.[56] Thus the new characterization of the listening experience was designed to highlight the possibility of individual transcendence, to connect that transcendence to the spiritual and social message of early modern Reformed Catholicism, and to further associate that transcendence to a notion of refinement that was becoming the defining trait of the ruling classes.

Post-Tridentine theories of the heart as seat of affective spirituality were directed at fostering a renewal of participatory spirit in the devotional practice of the Church of Rome.[57] However, a key difference between Roman and Evangelical practice lay in the *nature* of such participation. For if Evangelicals defined participation as personal involvement in the creation of ritual and interpretation of spiritual messages, the Church of Rome had to redefine participation as a *receptive* activity: in other words, to theorize the notion that the viewer or listener has equal status in the creation of meaning to the person performing the ritual—and by extension, creating the artwork or playing the music. This perspective resonates well with the ideas of "self-oratory" that are reflected in many texts that draw on Loyola's *Spiritual Exercises* but make the devotional process self-contained, allowing the exercitant/recipient to both initiate spiritual ecstasy and control its interpretation. In fact, when combined with the importance of individual connection to the sacred that was highlighted in the neo-Augustinian heart-based spirituality discussed above, the importance of the recipient/viewer/listener becomes greater still, and the ritual (or artwork, or music) can be understood as a "mere trigger" for the individual's spiritual understanding, which becomes the true measure of social distinction. The process by which this shift is achieved, and its rationales, will be our concern in the next two chapters.

CHAPTER 2

Aural Collecting

And if your Excellency felt as if transported out of your mind
once long ago, as you have told me, when you heard Correggio play in Parma, I have also heard (perhaps you can recall)
that another time, a few years ago in Rome at the house of
Monsignor Raimondo, you were seen, as it were, melting
with sweetness when you heard sung some of those Virgilian
verses that are elegantly set to music by the elder of the
Mazzocchi brothers.

—Pietro Della Valle, "Della musica dell'età nostra"

By collecting artistic and natural artifacts and wonders, the early modern
cultivated individual sought to achieve connoisseurship through the careful balance of receptivity to the marvelous and repeated, careful parsing
and categorizations of items. Through the display of the collection, such
connoisseurship could then be deployed as evidence of the individual's
sophistication, and thus as a marker of elevated class status. Collections
are described in contemporary literature as contributions made by con
noisseurs to the shaping of artistic taste by providing models from which
artists could draw, underlining the increasing role of the educated connoisseur in the determination of artistic meaning and worth.

Musical scores and instruments were collected alongside other artifacts,
and musicologists have addressed this aspect of early modern collecting.[1] However, scholars have not reflected on the fact that connoisseurs
of this era also "collected" sonic experiences, in the form of musical performances. The collecting of musical scores (especially in manuscript) appears to have been more common in the later seventeenth century, while
the sponsorship of musical performances was crucial in the spread of the
"new music" through the Italian courts a half century earlier. Description

of the sonic experience of those performances—and their evocation and categorization—becomes a central concern in nonmusicians' accounts.

Drawing on contemporaneous commentary on connoisseurship of both visual artifacts and musical performances, this chapter will examine a transition in the early seventeenth century from a conceptualization of music as one aspect of celebratory ephemera to a separation and "objectification," as it were, of music—an attempt by connoisseurs of the early *Seicento* to collect and evaluate sonic experiences. A result of this process is the connoisseurs' attempt to characterize a sonic experience as analogous to a visual artwork and thus as equally dependent on the perspective of the elite recipient—and the sharing of that perspective among sophisticated peers—for its significance and signification.

Axiomatic among the ruling classes of early modern Italy was the understanding that elevated social status had to be accompanied by material ornaments that would reflect magnificence as an outward expression of the central virtue in Aristotle's *Ethics,* magnanimity.[2] Cultural display presented a possibility to embody or enact one's *gusto:* the well-honed taste that was open only to those of elevated status and that—in a circular process—the noble individual needed to embody on a regular basis in order to certify his place in the social order. The ability to exercise *gusto* could also be a pragmatic skill that could benefit one's chances for employment: with the increasing complexity of the art market, acquisition of works of art (or for that matter, recruitment of musicians) was increasingly by proxy, and seventeenth-century princes "increasingly [relied] on the advice of 'connoisseur' subordinates to make correct financial investments and behave according to depth of taste" (Southorn 1988, 44–45). The linking of taste and upper-class status fed an increase in demand for cultural goods, which resulted in a proliferation of skilled craftsmanship to cater to that demand; the concomitant pursuit of novelty and distinction helped drive the dissemination of several kinds of "new music" (as well as novelty in other arts). This process led to the gradual establishment of a self-perpetuating class of specialized artist/artisans in several cities of the Italian peninsula—Rome foremost among them, given the massive financial resources and political/cultural mutability of the theocratic state, which demanded ever more elaborate ornaments for the support and celebration of the Church Militant.[3]

But a further and specifically Roman agenda for the display and proper understanding of cultural artifacts through *gusto* partly explains the broadening of the ideal of connoisseurship to the lower nobility and upper bourgeoisie connected with the cardinalate courts: an understand-

ing that proper appreciation of beauty was a vehicle for the apprehension and promotion of the True Faith. This essential link between
beauty and morality—posited as a central aspect in the writings of Tor-
quato Tasso, one of the earliest critical essayists on poetry as well as
a renowned poet himself—was embraced in post-Tridentine Rome.[4] As
the art historian Janet Southorn (1988, 38) observes, the seventeenth-
century connoisseur Francesco Scannelli specifically suggested that the
highest quality in art was "a sentimental, emotional truth which [ap-
pealed] to the heart of the observer and [carried] him closer to the apprehension of divine beauty which, to Scannelli, was the true end of
connoisseurship."[5] Francesco Panigarola, a renowned early modern
preacher, directly compared the four stages of spiritual connection with
God *(cogitatio, studium, meditatio, contemplatio)* with the four stages of
viewing a painting: viewing attentively, studying, understanding, and
gustare—"savoring."[6] In Panigarola's four-stage description of increasing connoisseurship, the link between spiritual and sensory experience
goes both ways, not only making spiritual experience more concrete but
also elevating sensory experience by its analogy with spiritual bliss.

The outstanding cultural vibrancy in early modern Rome was driven
by the political structure of the theocratic state.[7] The pope was simultaneously the God-chosen pastor of the Roman faith and the elected temporal prince *(primus inter pares)* of the nominally equal-status rulers of
the church hierarchy, the cardinals. Given the tremendous financial and
political opportunities provided by the papal office and its complex network of ministers, powerful families (both in and beyond Rome) were
eager to gain and consolidate influence through their members and allies appointed by the pope to the cardinalate. This meant that Rome had
dozens of "princes," each conscious of his potential to influence (or even
be) the next pope, and each prepared to insert his own hierarchical structure (the *famiglia*, consisting not only of blood relatives but also of trusted
associates and prestige-building creative people) into the changing mech-
anisms of the state. Political mobility was more dynamic than elsewhere
in Europe, since it depended not on direct bloodline succession (as in all
the other principalities) but on the will of God as reflected by the consensus of the cardinals' conclave.

Cardinals thus invested heavily in creating and maintaining their level
of cultural prestige and in displaying that prestige to each other and to
their political opponents and allies. In doing so, they fostered cultural
workers (writers, architects, artists, artisans) who would not only most effectively contribute to their image but also help build a solid and dedicated

network through various kinds of affiliations.[8] There was regular interchange between the *famiglie*, whether through sharing of resources (both material and human) or through events hosted by various cardinals; some scholars have usefully characterized this latter phenomenon as a "circuit."[9]

As one example of such events, we might take an example of an extended *villeggiatura* at Tivoli hosted by Cardinal Alessandro d'Este in 1620: "The poet Fulvio Testi visited Tivoli in October 1620 and reported to [his patron] Cesare [d'Este, brother of Cardinal Alessandro]. The hospitality, he wrote, was 'grand' but not 'ambitious,' and guests included a different foreign prelate every day and always 'rare literary talents.' The day began with prayers, then discourse, study, reading, games and walks through ever-changing garden vistas. . . . Music was made at Tivoli (by Frescobaldi as well as Alessandro's regular musicians) and new epic poems were written, or at least begun" (Southorn 1988, 21). It is clear in this account that Cardinal Alessandro d'Este carefully shared *experiences* of his prized possessions (which included the creative services of renowned musicians such as Girolamo Frescobaldi) with his distinguished guests and that the guests' interactions with each other in the context of such refined cultural resources were at the center of the proceedings.

As one more example of the "cardinal circuit," we might consider the following account of Cardinal Del Monte entertaining on May 29, 1624: "Cardinal Del Monte held a banquet yesterday morning in his garden near Ripetta, for Cardinal de Medici and other Florentine noblemen, with great splendor, and copious delicate seasonal food, courses with ice [statues?], celebratory ornaments, and most exquisite statues; and besides entertaining them with music and song by the foremost *virtuosi* in Rome, provided them with great *gusto* by showing them his distilleries, geometric devices, and many other curiosities in which His Lordship delights greatly."[10] Again, the account highlights Del Monte's *gusto* and sociability in engaging his guests interactively ("showing them") through the display of visual art, curiosities, gastronomic delights, and, of course, musical entertainment.

Through their participation in this "circuit of entertainment," upperclass Romans would be honing their own connoisseurship by the experience of new wonders and the assimilation of these experiences into a system of cultural knowledge. While members of the curia could collect musical artifacts (and certainly several owned collections of musical instruments), they also could collect musical *experiences*—experiences that

they could remember and compare to subsequent experiences, establishing in their mind criteria of genre, style, and historical/artistic influence
that may well have been analogous to those that were reflected in the display and viewing of visual artworks. We will dwell more extensively below on the idea that early modern Roman elites were keenly aware of
the process of "collecting" experiences as well as finished artifacts and
of the crucial importance of shared discourse about those experiences
and artifacts.

The cardinals' musicians described above were specialized professionals, as were the gardeners who cared for the paths through the vistas, the
architects who had designed the villa and gardens, the visual artists whose
paintings decorated the palace, and the cooks who prepared the exquisite
refreshments. All these individuals would have been generally understood
as belonging to different social strata than the honored guests and would
likely not have mingled with them more than briefly. However, the individuals who wrote the epic poems, and who facilitated the flow of discourse, would also have been "professionals" of a sort: the Roman courts
created a tremendous demand for literate and articulate administrators,
who might serve as "secretary" or as "majordomo" or in similar capaci-
ties.[11] These individuals came to play an essential role within the cardinal
circuit: in their writings we find a new systematic approach to the collecting of art—and of musical experience. As Marc Fumaroli (1994, 54) observes, these authors bring about "a metamorphosis in literature on art,
which transitions in Rome in the 1620s–1630s from being a monopoly
held by artists to one held by erudite spectators, enlightened judges of the
Roman art scene." These individuals, who tended to come from the nobility or rising middling classes, become professional "tastemakers" for the
curia: in Fumaroli's (1994, 57) apt characterization, "*virtuosi* of taste,
worthy partners of the *virtuosi* of doing." These will be the individuals with whom we will be most directly concerned for the remainder
of this study, since as we will see they took on the task of theorizing
and defining their role and its importance both within the church hierarchy and for the intellectual and spiritual goals of post-Tridentine
Catholicism.

These professional "tastemakers" (whom, following Fumaroli, I will
henceforth term "*virtuosi* of taste") occupied a crucial social position
within the *famiglia* of a cardinal.[12] On the one hand, they were members of the leisure class, tendentially from families of the lower nobility:
their avocation was inherently detached from daily labor, and many of
them were also prelates or held other significant positions within the

hierarchy.[13] On the other hand, the *virtuosi* of taste also engaged directly with artists/artisans in the process of assembling collections of cultural artifacts either on behalf of their patron or for their own use—indeed, they tended to be much more involved in the logistics of the art trade(s) than the cardinals themselves. Some scholars have fruitfully explored the concept of "brokerage" in this context, observing—for example—that "an early modern patron was often a broker, a liaison between the client and a more powerful patron" (Cole 2007, 749).[14]

The *virtuosi* of taste were associated with a number of cardinal *famiglie,* but they gravitated strongly toward the most prominent and wealthy, who tended to be most closely associated with the reigning pope. For example, Cardinal Scipione Caffarelli-Borghese was a magnet of cultural prestige during the papacy of his uncle, Pope Paul V; and the nephews of Urban VIII Barberini, like their uncle, attracted *virtuosi* of many stripes to help shape (and publicize) their cultural projects. We will return to the *virtuosi* of taste associated with the *famiglie* of both the Borghese and the Barberini below.

An essential specialized activity undertaken by the *virtuosi* of taste was to collect and evaluate cultural artifacts. They did so largely on behalf of cardinals—their evaluative skill was ultimately in the service of the leader of their *famiglia*—but they also had to "perform" or enact their taste as a matter of daily behavior in order to demonstrate their suitability and worthiness to serve in their capacity, and thus they often developed their own collections. Furthermore, the role of *virtuoso* of taste had to be defined very explicitly as separate from that of the creator of the artwork or artifact. While artistic advisors to princes in preceding generations had been practicing artists, *virtuosi* of taste contended that artists were "the worst theorists and critics of art . . . too deeply involved in judging and evaluating their rivals' products."[15] Visual artworks were an important target of the *virtuoso*'s collecting process, and we will explore some of the criteria pertaining to this collecting approach below. However, the objects or works themselves were ultimately secondary to their reflection of the taste of the *virtuoso*—which spanned several cultural media—and his ability to engage that taste in the creation and fostering of high-level *discourse-about* within the events of the cardinal circuit.

The work of the *virtuosi* of taste depended on their ability to negotiate and indeed govern two categories of space, both essential to the identity of the cardinal circuit: the *galleria* and the *villa*. Both categories of space were intended to foster sociability and interaction and were sites for "performances" of prestige and sophistication of taste.

By the second decade of the seventeenth century, arguably following the model established by the Medici at the Uffizi under first Francesco I and then Ferdinando I in the last quarter of the 1500s, wealthy families throughout the Italian peninsula began reconfiguring rooms within their living quarters as spaces dedicated to display of cultural artifacts: "These days in Rome, Genoa, and other Italian cities there is the custom for the kind of constructions/rooms that are called 'gallerie,' perhaps because they were first introduced in *gallia,* or France, for the strolling purpose of persons at court. Their proportions are derived from loges, but they are somewhat less open than the latter."[16] This passage from a 1615 architecture manual highlights the association of the *galleria* with leisurely interaction and elite culture. The importance of owning such a space in order to project an image of belonging to that cultural sphere meant that even members of the Roman curia who were not from the wealthiest families made an effort to assemble and advertise their own *gallerie.* For example, Girolamo Frescobaldi's son Domenico—who was a minor though active member of the Roman curia in the middle third of the seventeenth century—was described as having a "studio of rare drawings by excellent painters, paintings, and compositions in tablature for harpsichord handwritten but not published by his famous father, Girolamo."[17] The guide to Roman galleries and palaces in which the younger Frescobaldi's collection is described, Giovanni Bellori's *Nota delli musei, librerie, galerie et ornamenti di statue e pitture ne' palazzi, nelle case e ne' giardini di Roma,* was published in 1664—by which time the presence and public display of galleries had saturated Rome, and the phenomenon of collection and connoisseurship of artworks had become firmly established. Still, there are other descriptions and guides, both manuscript and printed, that reflect the *galleria* as an essential space for cultural display starting from the first quarter of the century.[18] It is noteworthy that these early descriptions tend to characterize the *galleria* as a place for gathering and interaction, for sociable interchange in the presence of the collected artifacts—that is to say, *discourse-about.* Implicit in the characterization of the *galleria* is also the presence of a company of social equals, who build a collective understanding through interaction and dialogue, facilitated by the collectors or their advisors—the *virtuosi* of taste—who serve as interpreters and facilitators of the elite community's interaction.

Parallel to the *galleria,* but on a larger scale, was the *villa* (sometimes referred to as the *vigna*): wealthy Roman families established buildings and gardens either on the outskirts of Rome or in the surrounding foothills, designing their architecture and contents specifically for display and convivial enjoyment of cultural refinement. Cardinal Scipione Borghese was a prominent exponent of this practice, establishing his first *villa* just outside the city walls around 1613:

> Unlike the Quirinal garden palace [residence of the Borghese family], the Pincian villa was a site of reception, where the cardinal arranged lavish festivities for foreign emissaries and princes as well as intimates of the family. Unlike the Quirinal garden palace, it offered no accommodations for overnight visitors, not even the cardinal. Instead, the casino was a permanent home, a veritable museum, for the cardinal's collections. Despite the enormous extent of the grounds, the villa was used primarily for evening entertainments. In the formal gardens Scipione held alfresco banquets in a sunken grotto, where upon his command fragrant petals were released from the ceiling. Meals were accompanied by music and followed by hunts staged in the park, which visitors viewed from a safe distance. Lelio Guidiccioni conducted tours of Scipione's fine works of art. (Ehrlich 2002, 41–42)

Guidiccioni, whose work we will examine at length in chapter 4, was at the time the leading *virtuoso* of taste in Scipione Borghese's *famiglia*. Ehrlich's description conveys the continuity of space and purpose between the works of art within the *casino* (a building designed for the purpose of housing such artifacts, a sort of self-contained *galleria*) and the open-air delights (hunting, banqueting, etc.) of the grounds. The constant thread within Scipione's entertainment was provided by the assembled guests, who could be expected to interact among themselves (perhaps facilitated by such expert tastemakers as Guidiccioni) in building a discourse of shared refined interpretation that would cement their shared cultural heritage and social standing. This provided an updated opportunity to engage in the courtly behavior made normative by the pervasive circulation of Castiglione's *Libro del cortegiano* and Guazzo's *La civil conversazione* among early modern Italian elites.

The above description of evening entertainments at Villa Borghese mentions music as an "accompaniment" to meals, and while this was certainly one way that music was integrated into the cardinal circuit, in many instances music was designed to be the center of attention, as we can see in the following account by Emilio De'Cavalieri, reporting to Ferdinando Medici on February 1, 1602:

> The day before yesterday, Cardinal Paravicino [*sic; recte* Palavicino?] and [Claudio] Acquaviva went to the *vigna* of Cardinal Dal Monte because of the beautiful weather, where Dal Monte showed him his entire building [casino] to their great enjoyment [gusto]; and fortunately Signora Vittoria [Archilei] came with Antonio also to see the *vigna,* not knowing that cardinals would be there; since Paravicino was most desirous of hearing her sing, as

was Acquaviva, they entreated her to favor them; and they called for the instruments; and since Signora Vittoria was in a fine mood [? imbarbarescata] and also because they were in a room with a vaulted ceiling, I certainly haven't heard her voice in better condition; and she gave such satisfaction that Acquaviva said, "I am embarrassed that I did not weep."[19]

In this account we can see the importance of the interaction between the refined protagonists, whose collective *gusto* is stoked by the visual surroundings and then further stimulated by Archilei's singing. Despite Cavalieri's praise for the singer's voice, the focus here is on the intensity of the listeners' experience and their assessment of that intensity—with Claudio Acquaviva (general of the Jesuits, and as such one of the most spiritually noteworthy individuals in the curia of the time) regretting his own inability to reach a sufficiently transcendent state.

Indeed, the interaction of elite individuals is central to the description of the nature and purpose of the *galleria* and *villa* in the architecture treatise by Vincenzo Scamozzi that we have encountered above: "[The *galleria* in a *villa* is designed] for the placement of paintings, sculptures, statues, columns, bas-relief stories, portraits of men illustrious because of arms and letters, and similar things, which may give the opportunity to discuss, and pass time honorably [virtuosamente]."[20] Again, the focus is on the process of passing time, through conversation and *discourse-about*, in a manner appropriate for the cultivated gentleman; and note that a cognate of the word *virtuoso* is used to describe the quality of this refined pastime.

The items listed by Scamozzi are relevant as a function of their ability to engender such discourse and interaction. The superiority of collective and interactive engagement extends, according to Guazzo, to moments of spiritual transcendence as well: "While God welcomes devout and emotionally intense [affettuose] prayers in every place, nonetheless we are especially obliged to seek him in that public, sacred place that has been ordained for this purpose, where we are compelled to pray with greater fervor by the most holy sacrament that is exposed there and by the devout prayers of others" (Guazzo 1993, 1:22–34). Guazzo's mention of the combined power of the Host and of others' prayers resonates usefully with the importance of the *Quarantore,* as discussed in chapter 1.

The *galleria* and *villa* provided the Roman elites with spaces and opportunities for shared fruition of refined cultural artifacts and for their parsing through discourse that differentiated those elites from the artist/artisan producers of those artifacts. Paradoxically, the individuals who facilitated and coordinated that discourse—the *virtuosi* of taste—were just as specialized in their craft as the artist-artisans, though their status as close companions to the leaders of the *famiglie* depended on their noble identity and their distance from the artisan class.

The role of academies in expanding the ideal of elite interaction developed in the *galleria* and the *villa* to the satellite cities of the papal states and to other cities and courts of Italy remains to be fully explored. Certainly the spread of academies was considerable in early modern Italy, and they were important hothouses for the cultivation and display of intellectual sophistication and connoisseurship.[21] Leaders of cardinal families were aware of the importance of sustaining a set of shared cultural values with the nobility of Catholic Europe, one that would include new ideals of connoisseurship and discursive exchange and would supersede established traditions of academic training.[22] Elite visitors to Rome were eager to learn the Roman fashion and to build the kind of knowledge necessary to participate in refined discourse within that society; for example, Marquis Enzo Bentivoglio, who from Ferrara was closely in touch with developments in Roman high society, was informed by an associate in Rome: "Yesterday, upon request, I brought the Flemish ambassador with three or four other distinguished men from Flanders to hear the *Napolitana* [Adriana Basile?] play; he liked it very much, and wanted to know her first and last name, and that of her husband, and he wrote it in his book; he also wanted to hear Ippolita [Recupito?]."[23] In this case the Flemish ambassador is making notes about his aural experience of the individuals involved in the performance, presumably to recall and discuss that experience with his Roman peers and perhaps also to know how to seek out or request a similar experience in the future.

It is worthwhile to dwell briefly here on the example of the Roman Accademia degli Umoristi, since it was the primary collective cultural meeting place of the Roman elite during the first half of the seventeenth century and (as we shall later see) was arguably the crucible for the cultural projects of the Barberini, as well as a likely inspiration for later French intellectual initiatives. John Evelyn provided this summary in 1645: "The Witts of the Towne meete on certaine daies, to recite poems, and prevaricate on severall Subjects &c."[24] Central to Evelyn's description (and analogous to what we saw above of *galleria/villa* culture) is "prevarication," the interactive quality of the event, in which the topics to be addressed are by implication ultimately less important than the discourse by which the "witts" perform their worthiness and identity.

The Accademia degli Umoristi reputedly began as a series of gatherings stemming from wedding celebrations for Paolo Mancini, scion of one of the oldest and wealthiest families in Rome, in 1600. In 1611 the group created a constitution, which specified that membership should include "people considered worthy because of nobility of birth, more than mediocre literary worth, or excellence of some respectable artifice" (Alemanno 1995, 99). This *accademia* was thus created—presumably in descending order of priority—for the ruling nobility of Rome, for the *virtuosi* of taste whose literary-rhetorical training in *discourse-about* could facilitate their sophisticated interactions, and for the artist/artisans whose creations might be honored by the members' discourse.[25]

Urban VIII had been a co-founder of the Umoristi decades before his election to the papacy, and significantly religion was the most common topic of discourse in the Accademia. Strongly present in accounts of topics were also the *affetti*—those refined and ineffable affects/emotions, often linked with spirituality, that we briefly explored in chapter 1. Another common topic for discussion was politics—but exclusively in the broader theoretical context of the relationship of the prince to his secretary in the court hierarchy, a topic that must have been very close to the heart of the *virtuosi* of taste and their cardinal patrons, who certainly embodied such relationships.[26]

The Accademia degli Umoristi welcomed some of the most renowned professional musicians of the day, most notably Adriana Basile and Francesca Caccini, and Adriana's daughter Leonora Baroni was reputedly given honorary membership (Hammond 1994, 86; we will return to the significance of this point in the next chapter). But even if Baroni was granted such an honor, professional musicians would not have been participating in the cultivated discourse as equals—rather, their performances would have provided material for such discourse, in ways analogous to the scene relayed above concerning Vittoria Archilei at the *vigna* of Cardinal Montalto or the episode from Guazzo's *Civil conversazione* discussed in the Introduction.[27] In a way, then, the musical performances by professional guests functioned as "artifacts" of a sort, their value and meaning contingent on the sonic experience and discursive interaction of the members of the Accademia present at the event.

In this light, Hammond's observation (1994, 103) that "almost any gathering" could be termed an *accademia* in early modern Rome might be qualified with the idea that an *accademia* may more precisely be understood as a site for sophisticated *discourse-about*, its focus the interaction between the *virtuosi* concerning the performance or presentation rather than the performance or presentation itself. Further on the connection between notions of *accademia* and the idea of the cultivated *virtuoso*, one might observe the presence of at least two gatherings named *accademia dei virtuosi*—one presided over by the cardinal-nephew Ludovisi in the early 1620s, before the accession of the Barberini pope (Mario Rosa [2002, 81] describes this *accademia* as "a sort of curial training ground where men at the start of their career might exercise themselves under the stimulus and guidance of others more expert than themselves"), the other founded by Francesco Barberini as cardinal-nephew in 1624, and even more closely connected to musical matters (Susan Shimp [2000, 24] observes that "the [Accademia de Virtuosi] met in Cardinal Francesco's apartments to hear madrigals and discuss Greek music theory"). Indeed, the noble-masculine quality of *virtù*—which will be the focus of chapter 4—can be seen as a defining quality of all academic enterprise: as Gino Benzoni (1978, 181–82) suggests, "Within the academy one is cultivated; those who are cultivated are *virtuosi*; the academy, which makes its members *virtuosissimi*, is the apex of *virtù*—a *virtù* inconceivable by commoners, which thus separates one from that class."[28] Of course, establishing one's separation from the commoners was especially crucial in a social framework—that of early modern Rome—that combined elements of upwardly mobile meritocracy with the need to maintain stable hierarchies. Academic endeavors were thus essential not only for the development of intellectual and rhetorical skills but also for shaping and reaffirming the boundaries of social exclusivity consonant with the agendas of the post-Tridentine curia.

An important aspect of the Accademia degli Umoristi was its role in supporting key political efforts, most notably what Alemanno (1995, 101) characterizes as "the Francophile orientation pursued by the papal curia during the first third of the seventeenth century." The cultural-political connection with France had roots in Florentine Medicean politics of the previous century, given the advocacy exerted by Ferdinando de'Medici on behalf of Henri of Navarre in the process of his conversion to Catholicism and assumption of the throne of France. While the Medici-Bourbon relationship was not always smooth in the last decades of the sixteenth century (especially given Florence's strong overtures toward the Hapsburg Empire), the marriage of Henri to Ferdinando's niece Maria in 1600 helped to solidify the alliance. The families of the "Florentine nation" associated with the Medici sphere of influence in Rome (which Fosi [2008, 31] characterizes as "a dominant elite in the sixteenth and seventeenth centuries") became even more strongly involved on behalf of the French monarchy. These families may well have been drawing on Medicean models when they recruited "artists, 'connoisseurs,' and amateurs with the purpose of reinforcing local art schools and creating a style and a 'visual language' closely connected with the principate and the dynasty." The formulation (from Solinas **2000**, 5) specifically describes the Medici, but it can readily be applied to Medicean allies in seventeenth-century Rome.[29]

Perhaps the first prominent Florentine-allied cardinal to foster diverse cultural projects (with a strong musical component) through his *famiglia* was Francesco Maria Del Monte (1549–1627). A member of the household of Ferdinando de'Medici while the latter was still a cardinal, Del Monte followed Ferdinando to Florence when he relinquished religious life to become Grand Duke of Tuscany in 1587. Returning to Rome in 1588 following his own election to the cardinalate, Del Monte continued to correspond with Ferdinando, especially in the planning of the latter's wedding festivities in 1589, and in the process he emulated and replicated Medicean practices of cultural sponsorship and display.[30] For example, having moved into Palazzo Madama (a gift from the Medici), he reported to Ferdinando on November 22, 1589, that "today [Cardinal] Montalto spent a while here in my house, where I have had a room set up with harpsichords, guitars, the *chitarrone,* and other instruments; and he was so delighted that he says he will often do me the honor of coming to dine with me."[31] Note that Del Monte here does not even mention any musicians, even though presumably Cardinal Montalto (who was renowned for his passion for and sponsorship of music, as John Walter Hill [1997] has thoroughly demonstrated) would probably have been delighted by performances he heard in Del Monte's "musical room" rather than just by viewing the instruments. In any case, the crucial point of the report is the sharing of sophisticated experience between the two prelates.[32] Closely connected to these powerful religious leaders of the Florentine nation in Rome at the turn of the seventeenth century was Vincenzo Giustiniani (1564–1637), also a *virtuoso* of taste and brother of a cardinal, whose perspectives on collecting (musical as well as otherwise) we will soon discuss at some length.[33]

In the generation that followed, the most important family of the Florentine nation in Rome was of course the Barberini. Maffeo Barberini (1568–1644) was papal *nuncius* in Paris in the early years of the century, where his contemporary and friend Vincenzo Giustiniani visited him during a sightseeing tour of Europe.[34] Created cardinal by Paul V Borghese (who was also from a Tuscan family allied with the Florentine nation), he made common cause with Cardinal Scipione Borghese during the short reign of Gregory XV Ludovisi and was elected pope as Urban VIII in the conclave of 1623. Maffeo/Urban's extraordinary patronage of artists and musicians, as well as that of his nephews Francesco (1597–1679) and

Antonio (1607–71), has been extensively documented and does not need to be rehearsed here.[35] One aspect of the Barberini approach to patronage is, however, especially important for the purposes of this study: their reliance on *virtuosi* of taste as advisors to and facilitators of their cultural projects, continuing the tradition established in the turn-of-the-century cardinal circuit and systematized by Scipione Borghese.[36]

This reliance is most evident in the increased concern with collecting artifacts in post-Tridentine Italy. Once again Rome is an exemplary case study, as Renata Ago has explored in her masterly study *Il gusto delle cose: Una storia degli oggetti nella Roma del Seicento (The Taste for/of Things: A Story/History of Objects in Seventeenth-Century Rome)*. Ago (2006, 125) observes that already in the mid–sixteenth century "collections represent a way to gain prestige, to transform money into social superiority," an essential resource in the fluid political and social context of post-Tridentine Rome, where nobility was essential for leadership status but was frequently in tension with successful social mobility through ecclesiastical careers. "A great part of objects' value," continues Ago, "comes from the fact that they belonged to a particular individual. At the same time, a great part of that person's reputation comes from the fact that he collected and owned those objects; the sacrifice of utility that he made for this purpose has demonstrated his ability to use his riches not for lowly, utilitarian purposes but in order to pursue higher objectives" (223). It was thus especially important that the collection not be dispersed and that it be preserved as an inalienable whole. After all, Ago (xix) observes, "Controlling inalienable goods is the instrument of the perpetuation or the overthrowing of hierarchies. It is thus vitally important to be able to preserve." While the leaders of noble Roman *famiglie* tended to follow Ago's characterization, gathering collections that they designated as inalienable in their wills, *virtuosi* of taste often built collections of a more transitory nature—after all, they would customarily acquire artifacts on behalf of the head of their *famiglia* or would provide artifacts as gifts to those individuals or their friends as an integral part of their display of professional taste.[37] Though there may well have been commercial criteria for the collections' ephemeral nature, a fluid collection also allowed the *virtuoso* to continuously display his taste as a proactive activity. This fluid collecting practice would have provided him with new opportunities to choose items or give them away as practices of teaching/advising, both making his role necessary to the leader of the *famiglia* and attempting to focus attention on the active connoisseur rather than the "passive" artistic object. For example, in his will Lelio Guidiccioni singles out a painting of the Virgin (to whom he was especially devoted) as requiring special treatment/attention. While he does not mention the artist's name, he asks his ultimate patron the pope "to enjoy it, and to make it so that when God calls you to your reward of your great efforts it may be placed in Saint Peter's under the Tribune facing your tomb, where it may be readily seen and judged by men of valor for its worth."[38] Thus deployed, the painting (as a reflection of Guidiccioni's taste) could serve several functions: decoration of holy space and inspiration for public onlookers, but also continuation of *discourse about art* by "men of valor" (those in the elite community shared by Guidiccioni and the pope) beyond the death of both individuals. Ultimately, to compensate for the transitory status of their collections, Roman *virtuosi* began to define their own taste and discriminating ability, as well as their taste-making legacy, as their "inalienable collection"—hence the importance of memory to these individuals, as we will explore below.

As a number of scholars have observed, *virtuosi* of taste increasingly replaced painters as authors of early seventeenth-century commentary on the visual arts.[39] Giulio Mancini (1558–1630), physician to the Barberini, was one of the leading *virtuosi* of taste in early seventeenth-century Rome. Mancini was the author of an essay on painting (*Considerazioni sulla pittura*), probably drafted in the second decade of the century, which was widely circulated in manuscript—though never printed—and very influential to the nascent "profession" of visual-art collecting and connoisseurship.[40] At the start of his *Considerazioni*, Mancini advises his readers that paintings can be judged expertly by those who have no practical experience in their creation: "One needs merely a good judgment, trained by having seen many paintings both by oneself and relying on the judgment of several connoisseurs. . . . A man of good natural judgment, with a thorough experience of things, with knowledge of *disegno*, can judge the perfection, the value, and the proper placement of paintings."[41] With experience and guidance, Mancini suggests, the person of good breeding ("good natural judgment") can gain a more perfect knowledge than the artist, who has a single-minded focus on his own approach and financial situation and does not have "prudence as a habit" (l'habito della prudenza; 8). Mancini indicates that such knowledge is to be reached through the experience of communal enjoyment and *discourse about* the works, relying on both one's self-training and the judgment of (and interaction with) several *virtuosi* of taste.[42]

Mancini's stated goal is to facilitate the judgment of "perfection and value," thus categorization, and the appropriate display of the results of the connoisseur's judgment. In the *Considerazioni,* he provides descriptions of four schools of living painters, including names and specific traits within the schools, and extensive lists of subjects and genres with the parameters by which they are to be judged.[43] Similarly, Vincenzo Giustiniani, in his *discorso* on painting, lists twelve types of painting style in increasing order of artistic excellence, providing names and examples for each.[44] Many *virtuosi* of taste did not leave explicit discussions of their criteria, but on the basis of extant descriptions and catalogs of collections (whether of artworks or other marvels), a concern with categorizing artifacts or experiences by their stylistic tendencies and approaches to different genres seems to have been a common characteristic of the early seventeenth-century *virtuosi* of taste.

Most importantly, once categorized, artifacts had to be displayed in such a way as to publicize the connoisseur's discernment, not only to reflect on the *virtuoso*-collector's supreme *gusto,* but also to instruct and guide others—patrons, aspiring *virtuosi,* or even artists—in the ways of art and of Christian morality. Mancini's criteria for interpretation—and hence display—were connected with genre (portraits, religious stories, landscapes, etc.), historical period, regional school, artistic influence, and other parameters that reflected the connoisseur's understanding of the nature of the work, most notably the potential effect of the painting on particular types of audiences (Mancini 1956, 141–43). More specifically, Mancini suggests, connoisseurs should place their artwork

> according to the subject, the type of color scheme, the time in which they were created and the school according to which they were made. . . . One should first place the oldest . . . and of these first the *oltramontane,* then the Lombard, then the Tuscan and the Roman, for in this way the spectator will be able to see and enjoy them more easily and, after having seen and enjoyed, keep in his memory the pictures he has seen. But I would not suggest that all the same school and manner be placed together. . . . Rather, I would suggest that they be alternated with those of other manners and schools of the same century, because in this way, because of their variety, they will delight more, and through the comparison of the variety of ways of painting, they will be felt more strongly without offending the [viewer's] taste, as would happen if one alternated among these some paintings from another century.[45]

Note the importance Mancini places on the ease of interpretation on the part of the viewer, and further on the viewer's ability to retain the images in memory, presumably to assist with the development of taste/judgment (*gusto/giudizio*) through experience and comparison that Mancini has established as crucial for the proper formation of the artistic connoisseur. We will return to the crucial role of memory in collecting (especially with respect to the collecting of ephemeral experiences such as musical performances) below. Note also the ideal of a balance of variety (which brings delight and presumably stimulates both the *virtuoso*'s own comparative thinking and the potential for discussion of similarities and contrasts and thus refined social interaction) and the ideal of moderate decorum of good taste (potentially offended by the introduction of a vastly different style), which reflects on the "proper judgment" of the connoisseur.

While many of these criteria for placement of artworks may seem perfectly natural to a twenty-first-century reader, since they correspond to the way most art museums now display their collections, they are in fact an invention of the early seventeenth century. Previous displays of visual artworks were almost invariably tied to specific political or dynastic purposes by the commissioning prince, or to spiritual purposes chosen by the commissioning order or pontiff. The truly new aspect of these collections is the idea of comparative, simultaneous display of various artists' works for reasons connected to *gusto*—the display as embodiment of the superior discernment of the *virtuoso* of taste, his contribution to a shared "discourse" of display.[46] These displays were often organized not only (or even primarily) by subject matter but by the common artistic "language"—as defined by the expert collector.[47] Thus the real subject matter of these collections was not the artifacts themselves but the *virtuoso* who had skillfully assembled them and could interpret them in the company of his peers.

The collecting, display, and evaluation of visual artifacts was evidently Mancini's central concern and was certainly a primary preoccupation for many Roman *virtuosi* of taste. However, we have touched on the presence of music in the refined activity of the cardinal circuit, and many of the same *virtuosi* who assembled collections of visual art also turned their "tastemaking" to the understanding of sound. Before addressing these individuals' pronouncements on the subject of sound and music, we should briefly reflect on the changing context of the Italian nobility's personal engagement with music at the turn of the seventeenth century, and primarily with the contemporaneous perception that noble "musicking" was increasingly—and appropriately—becoming associated with listening rather than performance.

While the tradition of solo singing to instrumental accompaniment is documented at least as far back as the fifteenth century in Italian courts and continues to be mentioned in sixteenth-century sources (including Castiglione's *Cortigiano*), professional singers (such as Virginia Vagnoli, employed at the court of Urbino in the mid-1500s) were described as exceptional presences in an ideal of courtly participation in music making.[48] Musical trends in North Italian courts of the last decades of the century lead to a transformation of the status of musical performance from a noble-amateur activity to a professional craft. Reflecting on this phenomenon, the *virtuoso* of taste Vincenzo Giustiniani provides a specific reference to convivial music making as passé:

> During the present course of our age, music is not much in use, in Rome gentlemen no longer practice it, nor is it the custom to sing in several parts *al libro,* as in years past, despite the fact that there are many occasions to get together and hold conversations. Music has been reduced to an unusual and almost new perfection, as it is performed by a great number of good musicians, who . . . bring great delight to those who hear them with the artifice of their sweet song. . . .

> In times past it was customary [for noblemen] to entertain [themselves] with a consort of *viole* or recorders . . . [but] experience has taught that such entertainment, given the uniformity of sound and consonances, quickly became boring and was more conducive to sleep than to passing the time in the afternoon heat.[49]

Giustiniani is careful to distinguish here between "gentil huomini" and "musici"; the former gather for noble interaction following the model of Castiglione and Guazzo, but instead of making music of their own (which would be by implication "imperfect" and sleep inducing) they enjoy the "great delight" provided by the "artifice" of the professional singers. Furthermore, the importance of noble interaction is foregrounded by Giustiniani not only explicitly in the first passage but implicitly in the second, since his reader would understand that "passing the time" would imply useful and artful conversation (*discourse-about*), which is counterposed to the laziness of sleep.

Giustiniani's observation is reinforced by several of his fellow Roman *virtuosi* of taste.[50] For example, Pietro Della Valle observes that "these days not many [madrigals] are composed, because it is unusual to sing madrigals, nor are there occasions in which they are sung, since people prefer to hear memorized music sung with instruments in hand and with conviction, rather than seeing four or five friends singing at the table with book in hand, which is too much like school and study."[51] Not only does Della Valle explicitly invoke the pedantry (and perhaps the "schoolboy" immaturity) of convivial singing, he also carefully contrasts "hearing" the (presumably professional) self-accompanying solo singer with "seeing" the group of comrades singing with book in hand—implying that the listener will not gain much from the latter scenario, or perhaps even that the circumstance of collective song does not really require *listening* in the same way that engaging with the solo professional does. This perspective is perhaps echoed by Giovan Battista Doni, who moved in the same Barberini circles as Della Valle, here describing madrigal part-singing in 1635: "It is an able man who, hearing a [madrigal] he has not heard before, can understand half of it. Perhaps composers do not realize this, for because they know what is being sung, they can more easily understand the words, but this does not happen to the listeners, who because of this tend to depart dissatisfied with this kind of music."[52] Again, the listeners' dissatisfaction is key to the lack of success of the part-singing madrigal style in the judgment of the early modern *virtuosi* of taste.

These comments are in keeping with other evidence that the *virtuosi* of taste and their patrons increasingly relied on professional musicians.[53] Solo singing was not new (though some, like Giustiniani, argued that it was "newly perfected"), but consort singing was perceived as losing ground, leaving solo song as the primary expressive resource. And the "newly perfected" style of solo song was largely characterized as difficult, requiring professional specialization: of course, this characterization frequently came from the professional musicians themselves, who understood that their success derived from their perceived sonic power. One example among many can serve as representative: the composer and organist Lodovico Casali, writing in 1629, suggests that "this is the fruit of modern concerted music: it is created not for all, but for a few. I will add that if concerted music is not performed by singers who have adequate training, it will never please. . . . If one will taste sweetness and delight from the perfect singer, from an imperfect one one will feel distaste, and the worth of the music will decrease, which will damage the reputation of good musicians."[54]

The importance of professional singers for the success of new musical styles was also reflected in sacred establishments. This was perhaps most evident in the practices of the Jesuit Collegio Germanico in Rome, where the founding tradition of involving the student body in the singing of the offices was gradually eclipsed in the first decades of the seventeenth century by a reliance on specialized *putti soprani* (who were recruited for their vocal ability and provided with basic education in exchange for their musical service) and even of professional musicians from the cardinal *famiglie,* who were sent to train with the musical establishment of the Collegio (and with the often-distinguished *maestro di cappella*) in exchange for their service at special celebrations.[55] The curia's fostering of this system of musical professionalization—the children of the elites who trained at the Collegio would have been learning to listen, rather than sing, during ritual—indicates its normative status.

If only "a few," in Casali's formulation, could convey the power and delight of the "new music" through performance, it is reasonable that those who were excluded from that agency—but who were accustomed to controlling cultural discourse—would have been eager to reclaim a role in "musicking." Given the changed parameters of fashion, they would have understood that they would have to do so from the listener's perspective. Accordingly, some *virtuosi* of taste during the early decades of the seventeenth century attempt to articulate the parameters of "collecting" and categorization with respect to music. They do so largely by conceptualizing the musical *experience* as something to be collected. As Margaret Murata (1990, 276) has convincingly argued, later seventeenth-century patrons and connoisseurs gathered collections of musical scores, especially as the tradition of chamber singing began to give way to a greater emphasis on stage performance, and the repertory of the chamber cantata became, in Murata's terms, "library music." In the earlier part of the century, the score was not an artifact closely associated with the essence of the music; rather, the performer, and the memory of the performance, were the "objects" that *virtuosi* of taste chose to collect, categorize, and discuss.

In some cases the performer and sonic experience may have been evoked by visual depictions; such is perhaps the case with the two "lute singer" paintings by Caravaggio, which have been discussed in several contexts by Francesca Trinchieri Camiz and Agostino Ziino.[56] To summarize Camiz's nuanced arguments, Caravaggio created two versions of a portrait of a singer (Camiz suggests this is Pietro Montoya, a castrato in the *famiglia* of Cardinal Del Monte) for Vincenzo Giustiniani and Cardinal Del Monte. In each version, the singer is accompanying himself on the lute and appears to be performing from open partbooks of madrigals by mid-sixteenth-century composers (Arcadelt, Berchem, Layolle). As Camiz suggests, these depictions may draw not only on the professional singer's practice of self-accompanying and solo adaptation of part-song but also on the repertories that Giustiniani and Del Monte would have associated with formative times of their youth. In other words, the image may have facilitated the "sonic recollection" (and parsing/categorization/comparison) of different musical events—the part-singing of the patrons' youth and the solo song of their professional employee. In this case, I would argue, it is likely that the "madrigals themselves" were less important than the web of associations occasioned by the recollections of their sounding, which could well have occasioned fruitful discussion of a shared cultural heritage when the painting was viewed in a group of peers. This discussion, in turn, could have brought back the idealized Castiglionian "space" of collective participation in song, while still affording recollection (and probably anticipation) of the savoring of professional voices.[57]

Another—perhaps the primary—means of "collecting" and thus "recollecting" sonic experiences was to place them in memory and find appropriate strategies to revisit the memorized events and the feelings they might have evoked, and in the process to establish categories whereby those musical experiences might be parsed and then "displayed" through discussion with fellow *virtuosi*. A well-cultivated set of interpretative categories could then be useful to the *virtuoso* in evaluating and savoring a new musical performance/experience, and likewise in engaging with his peers in the discourse surrounding that sonic event.

This sort of creative deployment of memory as a display of cultural sensibility was an increasing concern in early modern Italy as earlier models of mnemonic constructs were giving way to a valuing of memory itself as a "treasure chamber" and as inextricably linked with connoisseurship.[58] Memory of cultural artifacts was understood not just as recollection of objects but as the cultivated individual's embodied understanding of the objects—once again establishing an active role for the *virtuoso* "rememberer" in the creation of meaning and correspondence between phenomena.[59] Indeed, a post-Tridentine resurgence in the influence of the writings of Saint Augustine reinforced this reconfiguration and revaluing of memory, since Augustine himself had placed significant emphasis on the importance of memory to spiritual imagination.[60] A number of treatises on memory circulated in early modern Rome, both in manuscript and in print. Some that focused on human physiology (for example, that of Ambroise Paré, physician to the last Valois kings of France in the last quarter of the sixteenth century, whose works circulated widely and are still present in the Barberini holdings in the Vatican Library), "invited people to think of their memory as something physical and graphic: a trace in the brain tissue that could practically be seen and touched" (Smith 1999, 108).[61] Others specifically referred to the use of memory as a tool for listening. For example, Giambattista Della Porta states in his influential *Art of Memory* that "whenever I hear the *aria* of a madrigal that is similar to another, I remember that other one and the one who sang it."[62] Note that the memory of the earlier musical experience includes the performer and that drawing connections between the current and previous musical experience (presumably both the sound and the performer) is essential to Della Porta's account.

Memory was considered a valuable tool in the cultivated discussion that was considered integral to the collective construction of standards of connoisseurship. Vincenzo Giustiniani, writing in his "instructions for traveling" (which Giustiniani claimed were based on his own extensive traveling experience), tells the would-be *virtuoso* traveler:

> As soon as one arrives in a place, it will be good to query the keepers and servants of the place of lodging about the notable things of that place that are worthy of being seen: especially public and private buildings that are outside the norm, and likewise gardens, machinery and fortresses and waterworks, paintings, statues, and other appropriate things. And while such worthy things are seen, it will be good for the entire company to be present and observe, and for each member to say what occurs to him about it, because this way, not only are the events better impressed into memory, but there is also more opportunity to converse and gain pleasure in remembering through subsequent conversation.[63]

Memory alone might not suffice, however, so Giustiniani advises that his connoisseur travelers should take notes whenever possible, to further stimulate recollection and *virtuoso* discourse: "If in the company there is someone who will write in detail the progress of the voyage with its circumstances, making specific note as if creating a report of the notable things that are seen and that happen, it will be something that will bring great enjoyment [gusto] to all members of the company, through the rereading and conversation that they will be able to engage in when they have returned home, and on occasion this might be of use in important situations."[64] Likewise, Cardinal Giulio Sacchetti admonished his nephews, who were about to embark on a "learning tour" of Europe,

> Your goal should be not only curiosity to see new things, but to document, as you encounter a diversity of other customs and behavior, your learning of a more perfect set of rules for your own behavior and customs. For this purpose, it will be good for you to use your pen to make note [fare memoria] of what you hear and see, comparing modern events and ancient ones, reflecting on those accounts/histories about which you learn and creating an abstract of them, all of which will be useful to you at all times not only for customs but also to understand political interests and natural things.[65]

Sacchetti specifically links memory and writing-down, indicating that information gathered by this process will provide the core for sophisticated interaction by the young elite male. Indeed, Giustiniani tells us, collecting and memorizing are essential to the modern individual: "In short I con-clude that if one does not observe well those worthy things that one sees and if one does not ensure that they are solidly retained in one's memory, one can save the expense and avoid the travails of traveling, which would ultimately be superfluous, and instead enjoy the quiet of one's paternal home."[66] The collection of experiences, their "impression" on one's mem-ory, and the ability to recollect and compare perspectives among an elite group are all essential elements of the formation of the elite individual, who leaves "the quiet of the paternal home" to create his own identity. Identity here is seen as a socially formed characteristic, since the observing and remembering are happening as a collective, discursive effort.[67] Thus collecting, recollecting, parsing/categorizing, and sharing experiences were seen as essential activities of the sophisticated individual. Again drawing from contemporaneous physiological theories about creativity and mem-ory, Smith (1999, 109) observes that "in most situations the brain's three faculties were imagined to function in this order: first fantasy or imagina-tion gathers sense impressions; then reason processes those impressions; finally memory stores the result. . . . In certain situations, fantasy might not only supply sense impressions for cogitations but take cogitations and turn them into sense impressions." This final observation is essential: the culti-vated, experienced sensibility could re-create the emotional intensity of a remembered item or event, or even a synthesis of two or more item/events, giving the *virtuoso* the opportunity to exercise creativity of a greater sort than that of the individual artisans responsible for singular cultural artifacts.

How did *virtuosi* of taste apply their approach to memory to their experiences with music? Bizoni reports several examples of musical expe-riences in his account of travels by Giustiniani and his *famiglia*— which included visual artists and musicians—throughout Europe in 1606.[68] These events are described in a "sketchy" fashion, presumably to assist in their recollection (and their use as resources for sophisticated discourse) rather than to convey their every detail (which could have been seen as a pedan-tic endeavor).[69] While Bizoni was not as prominent a *virtuoso* cultural broker as Giustiniani, he engaged in productive negotiations with artists and musicians in his own right, especially working with the Bentivoglio family, close friends of the Giustiniani: for example, writing to Enzo Ben-tivoglio from Rome on July 28, 1607, Bizoni reports that "Giuseppino gave me the enclosed madrigal as a new work, and here it is considered very beautiful, and that is why I send it to your grace; [though] it is true that our Roman *arie* are more successful when they are heard then when they are written down."[70] Bizoni is here clearly drawing on his own connoisseurship of musical quality and evoking the memory—presumably shared with Bentivoglio—of the sonic power of the Roman style, which must be enjoyed in person (and by definition by *virtuosi,* in an exclusive collective space).[71]

While earlier noble patrons had been more concerned with the overall effect of a multimedia event than with information about the individuals who took part in the performance, *virtuosi* of taste in early seventeenth-century Rome made a systematic point of listing singers' names, just as they proudly listed the names of the painters and sculptors whose works graced their art collections, using the reputation of those professional artisans to reinforce their own reputation as professional connoisseurs.[72] Indeed, several discussions of music by early seventeenth-century *virtuosi* of taste can be characterized as catalogs or even "galleries" of musical experiences, in which the reader is guided through a succession of musicians, styles, genres, and schools as if strolling through a seventeenth-century collection of paintings. Two such discussions—by Vincenzo Giustiniani and Pietro Della Valle—are most relevant to this issue.[73]

In his unpublished *Discorso* on music, Giustiniani provides a numbered list of developments in musical style, almost as if each item were in a different room of a gallery, divided by historical/stylistic approach or by genre, and with separate description of subgenres within each item entry. What follows is a summary translation and description for each numbered "room" of Giustiniani's "sonic gallery"; the labels for each "school" are mine.

1. [Oltramontani school, ca. 1540–80] In his youth Vincenzo's father sent him to study music, and Giustiniani noticed that the best compositions were by Arcadelt, Lasso, Striggio, Rore, and Monte; or for singing with one voice with an instrument, the Villanelle Napoletane; he mentions Pitio/Pizio as one composer of these.

2. [Roman(?) school, ca. 1580–1600] "In a little while the *gusto* for music changed," Giustiniani tells us, and Marenzio and Giovannelli's works appeared, "with a newly delightful invention," both for ensemble and solo/accompanied singing; their excellence consists of a "new melodic style that delights the ears" (nuova aria e grata alle orecchie). Palestrina, Soriano, and Nanino began to write church works around this time.

3. [Ferrarese/Mantuan school, ca. 1575–90] "A new way of singing very different from that which came before" started around 1575

and for a few years following, "especially in the custom of singing with one voice alone *sopra un instrumento*." Giustiniani lists Gio. Andrea Napoletano, Brancacci, and Alessandro Merlo, who all sang bass with a range of twenty-two pitches, with a variety of *passaggi* that were new and pleasing to the ears of all (grati all'orecchie di tuti).[74] (Note the repeated reference to pleasing the ears and to the collective enjoyment of the elite listeners.) Giustiniani mentions competition between composers, specifically citing Wert and Luzzaschi, and between the different *dame* (not citing them by name) of Mantova and Ferrara; here he provides an often-cited list of different vocal effects used by these singers (excerpted above in chapter 1), with specific reference to a Roman falsettist (Gio. Luca) who took a contrasting approach.

4. [Roman/Neapolitan school, ca. 1575–1610] Following the example of the Mantova/Ferrara courts and of the Neapolitan bass singers, a new way of composing began in Rome; Giustiniani lists Gesualdo, Stella, Nenna, and Scipione de Ritici as examples of this "school," though it should be noted that they were all at least initially Neapolitan rather than Roman.

5. [Florentine/Roman schools ca. 1575–1620] At this same time, Cardinal Ferdinando de'Medici, "stimulated both by his own *gusto* and by the example of the abovementioned princes," sponsored many musicians, whom Giustiniani lists first by precedence, then by voice type, then by regional "school": Vittoria [Archilei] and Antonio di Santa Fiore as the originators; Giulio Caccini, Giuseppino, Gio. Domenico, and Rasi (the latter learning from Caccini) as tenor/basses; falsettists Gio. Luca, Ottavio Durante, Simoncino, and Ludovico (all Roman), and falsettists or *castrati* Onofrio from Pistoia, Mathias from Spain, Gio. Gironimo from Perugia, and others left out for the sake of brevity. Cardinal Montalto (who also sings and plays "with a sweet and *affettuosa* manner") keeps instrumentalists "Cavaliere del Leuto, Scipione Dentici del Cimbalo, [and] Orazio sonatore raro d'Arpa Doppia" and singers "Onofrio Gualfreducci eunuco, Ippolita napoletana, Melchior basso," and many others. Note that in this case Giustiniani mentions one of each type of instrumentalist and vocalist, as if he were providing a representative sample; and it is with this new Florentine/Roman school that Giustiniani's focus shifts almost entirely to individuals known primarily as performers rather than composers. Giustiniani

states that these and many others, along with other above-mentioned performers, have "revived the performance of music, to the point that many nephews of popes and other cardinals and princes have delighted in it" and that many Roman musicians have trained successful students in this style. The account here makes it clear that the ultimate measure of the quality and perfection of the new music is the approval and delight of the individuals with whom Giustiniani, as *virtuoso* of taste, would have wanted to be most closely associated.

6. [Sacred genres, ca. 1575–1610] "Up to this time there have been many composers," such as Monteverdi, Nanino, Anerio, and others, who have taken Gesualdo's lead but have "taken care to sweeten and facilitate the style and way of composing, and specifically have written many works to be sung in church."

7. Giustiniani suggests that musical styles, like fashions of clothing, "[vary] with the various *gusti* of the gentlemen and princes that delight in [them]." Giustiniani clearly wishes to establish that it is the agency of those who delight in music that matters; styles change, not because performers (or even composers) initiate the change, but because listeners understand and can identify ("catalog"?) the change.

8. [Landscape room] In addition to the ways described above, each nation, province, and city has its own different way of singing; a short list of cities and towns follows, without specific description of the different regional *arie* that Giustiniani mentions.

Along with Giustiniani's *Discorso*, Pietro Della Valle's unpublished essay "On Music of Our Time, Which Is Not in Any Way Inferior, but Rather Is Better Than That of Past Times" (dated January 16, 1640, in an eighteenth-century print, and dedicated to his friend and fellow *virtuoso* of taste Lelio Guidiccioni) has been extensively excerpted and mined as one of the most explicit discussions of the qualities of "modern music" in midcentury Rome.[75] Della Valle's "gallery" is less systematically divided into "schools" than that of Giustiniani, though like the latter he is quite explicit about evoking/invoking individual musicians. He first lists, by instrument, the most marvelous instrumentalists he has heard perform—Frescobaldi on the keyboard, Kapsberger on the *chitarrone*, Orazio on the harp, Michel'Angelo on the violin—and then comments on the necessary traits for ensemble playing, which requires "not so much the artifices of counterpoint, rather the *grazie dell'arte*" (Della Valle 1903, 159) in being able to coordinate with other musicians. After making a similar comment about ensemble singing, he begins listing singers he has heard. First, in the older school, "Melchior basso, Gio. Luca falsetto, Orazietto, Ottaviuccio, Verovio"; he says they did not have the "art of soft and loud ... and of other *galanterie* that are excellently executed by singers nowadays" (162). He remarks that Rome did not witness this latter new style until "Sig. Emilio de'Cavalieri brought it to us from the good Florentine school, in his last years; he was the first to give a good example of it in Rome through his little *rappresentazione* in the Oratorio of the Chiesa Nuova, at which I was present as a very young man" (163). Singers of this new style are the "Nicolini, the Bianchi, the Giovannini, the Lorenzini, the Marii, and many others." (Note that despite Della Valle's use of specific names he uses the plural form, as if the singers were generic types rather than individuals with specific artistic agency.) Della Valle continues his "exhibition" of modern singers by voice type: Guidobaldo, Cavalier Loreto, Gregorio, Angeluccio, Marc'Antonio, and so on (all castrati, "whom we now have in great abundance," and who are the paragons of good taste).[76] He goes on to list women singers, first those in secular contexts (Giulia, Ippolita, Leonora and her sister Caterina and their mother, Adriana, Maddalena, Sofonisba, Lucrezia Moretti, Campane, Valeri, Francesca Caccini), then those who have taken orders (Verovia in Santo Spirito and several unnamed nuns in several convents, including "those of Santa Chiara, whom one goes to hear in order to marvel" (164).

At the close of his "gallery" of illustrious musicians, Della Valle takes a more abstract perspective and addresses the issue of genre and good judgment, *giudizio:* "I praise the *giudizio* and wisdom of those composers who can keep the correct decorum in every place and time and in every work." Different types of music are appropriate for church, theaters, scenes, streets; and within street music, different for processions and for *mascherate/serenate;* wedding music should not be the same as funeral music; and in churches different music should be played for Christmas, Easter, Lent, and Holy Week. Della Valle concludes, "There is no doubt that *giudizio* should play into all these aspects" (175). Note again that the discussion of genre-appropriate "placement" of cultural artifacts is parallel to that provided by Mancini in referring to the placement of visual artwork; and *giudizio,* balanced good judgment, is a term solidly associated with the upper circles of the Roman curia at this time.

In the opening section of his *discorso,* Della Valle explicitly refers to the ability of new-style musicians to trigger transcendence: "The [singing] masters of our time . . . express the *affetti,* the graces, and the lively sense of what is being sung; and this is what truly enraptures and brings one to ecstasy."[77] Of course, the individual who is "truly enraptured" and feels the ecstasy is the refined *virtuoso* of taste who is recollecting and commenting upon the musical event—someone such as Della Valle himself. One additional contemporaneous essay deserves mention in this context: Gratioso Uberti's *Contrasto musico,* published in Rome in 1630.[78] While Uberti does not list specific performers or musical "schools," his booklet is a musical guidebook of sorts: the two interlocutors in his dialogical account ("Severo," who is suspicious of music, and "Giocondo," who defends its benefits) are *virtuosi* whose path takes them through the various spaces of music making (and listening) in early modern Rome. First they go to a music school, then to a (noble or upper-class) home, then to the prince's court; from there they progress to the church, then the oratorio; after a brief discussion about music out of doors, they briefly stand outside the homes of musicians and composers, though they do not enter. Each location occasions a number of topics for discussion appropriate to the use of music in that space, each of which is provided with appropriate citations in Latin from biblical, patristic, and humanistic sources. The *Contrasto musico* reads like a guide to *discourse about music* for the aspiring *virtuoso* of taste, providing good "descriptive licks" and learned *exempla* so that the reader may learn how to elegantly hold either side of a sophisticated discussion on music. We will return to specific passages of this book, particularly those that suggest normative perspectives on listening in a sacred space, in the next chapter.

These descriptions are demonstrations of connoisseurship, in which the discerning *gusto* of the *virtuoso* of taste is displayed through the evocation and then parsing and categorization—by schools of singing, compositional style, genre, instrumental specialization, location—of musical experiences.[79] These experiences are crystallized as artifacts in the connoisseur's ear and memory and like visual artifacts can then be put in a gallery of sonic recollection, down which the contemporary reader can figuratively "stroll," revisiting particular sonic artifacts through recollection and discussion with equally experienced peers.

It is noteworthy that in these accounts the *gusto* of the narrator is grounded in personal familiarity and in the ability to compare and evaluate—through remembered experience—disparate sonic events based on the same kind of firsthand knowledge that Mancini postulated as crucial for the proper assessment of visual works. According to Mancini, to gain a correct understanding of the value of visual artifacts "there is nothing but observation made over long periods of time, and nothing can be said other than one must practice, watch, and ask."[80] Compare this to Giustiniani's reference to his "lunga pratica" on which his discussion of musical traditions is based: the two paradigms of acquisition, description, and comparison are absolutely analogous. In the foregoing discussion, the *virtuosi* of taste clearly posit the collection, assessment, and display/recollection/discussion of musical artifacts as an active process. It is precisely in this context that authors begin to stress the importance of the recipient in the creation of artistic meaning.[81] The ideal of moving the affections could be achieved only through active participation on the part of the recipient: persuasion, according to contemporary rhetorical and spiritual theory, involved the cooperation of the subject being persuaded.[82] In the critical language developed by the *virtuosi* of taste, receptivity to the beautiful—like receptivity to the divine—was considered an active rather than passive endeavor.[83] Emanuele Tesauro, a literary critic of the time, suggested (1995, 462) that "ingenuity understands more than the tongue speaks, and the concept of the listener supplies what is absent in the voice of the speaker. Indeed, wit loses its insight when a saying is too clear." And in the visual arts, in Colantuono's formulation, "the beholder was not seeking passive entertainment, but would actively and eloquently translate the pictorial images into appropriate rhetorical or poetical forms, thus bringing its *concetti* to life by uniting them into a coherent discourse."[84] Crucial here is the idea that the creation of a coherent intellectual message is the task of the informed recipient rather than the artist. And as the more educated and sophisticated of the two parties by virtue of their higher class status, *virtuosi* of taste claimed the knowledge and the discernment to dominate the negotiation of meaning surrounding the artwork. For example, Lelio Guidiccioni, in his *Eneide toscana* (1642) dedicated to Francesco Barberini, describes Aeneas as "turning with ease to contemplate a spacious painting; an object, as we know, that must be carefully viewed, and not—as those who do not apply themselves do—without thought. And we thus gather that the taste [gusto] for painting is princely."[85] Furthermore, Gabriele Paleotti, whose commentary on sacred images we encountered in chapter 1, suggests that painters should be careful to "satisfy learned people" with their work; otherwise they will make errors that will "discredit that work, leaving the painter with the appearance of not being able to create well-considered things."[86] This new deployment of *gusto* with the aid of memory to concretize musical experience begins to change an important feature of sixteenth-century musical sponsorship, ably argued by Claudio Annibaldi in several essays, and most recently eloquently outlined by Franco Piperno in his discussion of patronage at the court of Urbino: the notion that figurative arts, architecture, and urban planning produce fixed results, which can be discussed and praised systematically, while music's transience renders it evanescent, nontransferable as part of courtly "treasure," and especially subject to changing fashion.[87] The solution for the Roman *virtuosi* was to construct their own listening taste as a constant, defining both a notion of "tasteful" music to be evaluated by the connoisseur and, by extension, the notion of music as a quantifiable "artwork."[88] As Annibaldi (1998) has astutely observed, the last decades of the sixteenth century see a shift from a traditionally "metonymic" notion of artistic patronage—in which noble things gain value largely through their association with noble people—to a new "metaphorical" notion, in which noble people are distinguished by their noble *understanding* of things.[89] The phenomenon of "aural collecting" that develops in the first decades of the seventeenth century is a further refinement of this shift to "metaphorical" patronage.

The choice made by connoisseurs of the later seventeenth century to collect manuscript musical scores may thus reflect not only economic concern but also an increasing fashion for a concept of music as an artistic artifact to be collected rather than an event to be sponsored.[90] As Murata observes, mid-seventeenth-century musical manuscript collections of cantatas and other secular vocal works are often too sketchy to be functional performing scores, especially for nonprofessionals. I would add that in this they differ from the printed scores of the previous century, which could be used by their collectors to initiate collective musical events. On the other hand, such seventeenth-century manuscripts (especially in the latter years of the century) tend to reflect a variety of repertories and composers and may have functioned as visual aids to the recollection of musical experiences, allowing the connoisseur to retrace in his memory the events and/or emotions that formed part of his "aural collection."

Virtuoso discussion of musical collecting—whether aural or in manuscript—may well have touched on the problematic issue concerning the true locus of the musical work: Was it the score, one ideal performance, an aggregate of performances that the listener could recall? In any case, while the notion of a musical work may have fluctuated for musicians and composers in the later sixteenth and seventeenth centuries, in early modern Rome the idea of an identifiable musical work became relevant for elite listeners.[91] More importantly, this was also a circumstance in which *virtuosi* of taste began to theorize about the nature of "music" as an independent category of experience rather than as a component of multimedia (dynastic or courtly entertainment, or spiritual celebration). The connoisseurship of the *virtuoso* now determined the relevance of the notion of a musical work: the idea of an artistically autonomous musical artifact might be relevant from the composer's point of view, but it was obviously relevant when patronage began to define it and value it as such. As connoisseurship became understood as a crucial marker of class status, the concern with a "correct" understanding of music increased, coloring the reception, sponsorship, and production of musical culture: we turn to this topic in the next chapter.

CHAPTER 3

Proper Listening

Thus, in my judgment, while the voices and instruments are
tuned, the spiritual individual might consider within himself
how well his thoughts are tuned with the precepts of nature,
and his *affetti* with the laws of God; and while the musicians
use the sad style, and then change to the joyful, thus the
devout man could grieve for his sins, and at the end console
himself in God's forgiveness.

—Grazioso Uberti, *Contrasto musico: Opera dilettevole*

Spiritual leaders of the Catholic Reformation developed a devotional
model often characterized as *recte sentire*, a "true way of feeling/thinking"
that could guide the righteous Christian toward correct understanding
and embodiment of the One True Faith. Then as now, *sentire* also trans-
lates as "to hear": while the Roman church establishment was not primarily concerned with codifying that aspect of spiritual experience, much
evidence points to a significant awareness of the rhetorical potential of
music to work both for and against the purposes of religious edification. Certainly, an increasing interest in guiding the "proper" evaluation
of visual or verbal artifacts—particularly those that could be understood as sensual or erotic—was part of the project of the Roman curia
in the early *Seicento*. The burden of understanding potentially ambiguous messages as spiritual and transcendent rather than earthly or sensual was increasingly placed upon the discerning individual, whose
"correct" taste would be informed by spiritual, as well as protoaesthetic,
connoisseurship.

This chapter traces the connections between ways of discussing devotion through listening, on the one hand, and prayerful attention to
spiritual texts or transcendent interpretation of religious images, on the
other, to indicate an important shift in the characterization of listening—

posited as active and ideally transcendent rather than passive and dangerously sensual. We shall also examine how the new characterization of listening is fully in keeping with changing notions of identity in early modern Rome, especially the goal of shaping identity as simultaneously integrated within hierarchy (both religious and social) and enacting freely chosen thought and action.

Describing the *Viaggio per Roma,* an appendix to the widely circulated treatise on art by Giulio Mancini that we considered at some length in chapter 2, Marc Fumaroli (1994, 72) suggests that the *Viaggio*—a description of visual artworks in the churches of the city—was indispensable not only for the "edification of the pilgrim, but also, and this provides its novelty, for the formation of the Christian spectator of the arts and the maturity of his erudite *gusto.*" Indeed, the importance of the Catholic agenda for the display and proper understanding of cultural artifacts through *gusto* and connoisseurship came from the theory, again quoting Colantuono (1997, 174–75), that "the quest for perfect beauty was inextricably tied to the end of perfect moral instruction."

And "perfect moral instruction" was, after all, a crucial concern of the Tridentine reforms. As the Church of Rome set about its task of renewal in the later sixteenth century, the preaching orders were greatly strengthened and were assigned the task of emphasizing that the avoidance of vice or the pursuit of virtue would not suffice for the true Christian's moral progress and social identity. The faithful needed to acquire a "correct understanding" of Christian (read Catholic) doctrine—often referred to as *recte sentire,* "to feel/understand correctly" (McGinness 1995, 37). As we have seen in chapter 1, by the end of the 1500s the Church of Rome instructed preachers to focus on the emotional and spiritual power of the sacred mysteries. As McGinness points out, "Preachers frequently invite listeners to 'contemplate' a mystery, but it is not contemplation in the restricted sense of St. Thomas, but that of rhetorical theology that involves the entire personality and demands love in response. They invite their audience to embrace affectively *(sentire),* to enter with their whole personality into the mysteries of Christ's Redemption" (94). It must be clear that such individual contemplation was meant to be achieved through the acceptance and understanding of orthodox models: the preacher was to direct the listener "toward the authority of the Christian masters, faithful interpreters and protective shield against any interpretation that would be too personal" (Tiacci 1999, 112). The term *personal* here stands for heretical, unschooled, imprudent, a *sentire* that is not *recte.*

We will return again to the careful balance between individual under-standing and acceptance of orthodoxy that was inherent in the reformers' goals, since Jesuit leaders saw "personal" interpretation within parame-ters of orthodoxy as essential. Still, preachers were encouraged to enlist the delight sparked by rhetorical *concetti* in their invitation to *recte sen-tire*, since delight was thought to facilitate the soul's ascent to elevated spiritual realms.[1]

But the preacher's rhetorical skill was not considered sufficient for the creation of transcendent spiritual delight; as we also noted above, Tridentine reforms emphasized the importance of justification, the need for human "cooperation" with divine grace. Grace required an active participant, an individual whose mastery of *recte sentire* allowed him access to the mysteries of spiritual beauty—in other words, a *virtuoso* of taste, and more precisely one whose taste would specifically exemplify high-level spiritual understanding. Such an individual required proper training, both through formal instruction and through self-discipline, since post-Tridentine spiritual teachings held that faith did not come from grace alone but demanded schooling and sacramental study. For example, to return briefly to the topic of the Eucharist, that most central concern of early modern Catholicism, "The Eucharist had come to require in-struction. . . . Understanding the full meaning of the Eucharist could only come with time and with knowledge. . . . The ritual of the Eucha-rist was no transparent representation of a universally understood mean-ing, nor 'natural,' something grasped by native intelligence. . . . The Eucharist was a complex communication between God and humanity, multivalent, historically embedded, highly susceptible to misunderstand-ing through ignorance and human frailty. Abuses, therefore, were all the more important to curb" (Wandel 2006, 228). The attempt to avoid such abuses was perhaps most evident in the Jesuit pedagogical practice known as the *praelectio*, a daily practice in the *collegia* in which the teacher read the text to the student, explicating it with the goal of giving the latter the tools to read it (and analogous texts) properly on his own.[2] Given the predominant place of the Jesuit *collegia* in the education of the Catholic nobility and upper classes at the turn of the seventeenth century, this systematic process of "initiation" and modeling was likely to be at the core of the early formation of a *virtuoso* in an early modern cardinal's *famiglia*.[3]

Loyola's *Exercises*, traditionally undertaken at the start of the Jesuit novitiate, took this training a step further, combining the authority of the *praelectio* process with the obligation for introspection. Saint Ignatius

himself, during his sickbed conversion, "had recognized a difference, perhaps a subtle one, in the *quality* of his reactions" as he moved from a delight in worldly things to one in the "heroic exploits of the saints" (Endean
2008, 55). Thus, while a more experienced spiritual leader is still present (as we saw in chapter 1, the prompts to the Exercises are meant to
be *heard*, rather than read) and can provide a useful guide, nonetheless
"Ignatius wants the process to be driven by the exercitant's responses to
the text, and he rather expects that these will be conflicting. . . . The hope
is that cumulative reflection on responses will gradually lead to clarity
regarding the overall shape of God's invitation to the exercitant. . . . The
phrase 'asking according to what I feel in me' is another indication that
it is the person's responses and desires which determine the process. . . .
The whole process is aimed at the clarification of desire" (56). Loyola's
Exercises thus transfer the ultimate onus from the guide to the exercitant, who is simultaneously self-training and being trained. Furthermore,
Loyola specified at the end of the second day of the *Exercises*—when
discussing the action, or *election*, to be undertaken as a consequence of
the insight gained from the process of the *Exercises* themselves, that "it
is necessary that everything about which we want to make an election
should be indifferent, or good, in itself, and should be allowed within our
Holy Mother the hierarchical Church, and not bad nor opposed to her"
(Loyola 1914, 48). The *Exercises* thus normalizes the idea of building an
individual free identity that is entirely contingent on hierarchical obedience. From a modern, post-Enlightenment standpoint these two concepts
may seem antithetical; for Jesuit exercitants they became the two necessary faces of the same coin.

Specifically regarding the role of the senses in understanding and
parsing experience, as well as the individual's role in controlling sensory
understanding, early seventeenth-century Jesuit pedagogues (such as
Emmanuel de Goes, Francisco de Toledo, and Francisco Suárez, authors
of textbooks on Aristotle's *De anima* for a university curriculum) argued
that while the senses are inherently passive (following Aristotle's characterization) "in so far as they receive the sensible species from material
objects . . . the senses must themselves do something in order for sensation to occur."[4] This modification of Aristotelian thought was thus connected with the central importance of agency and self-control—within
the hierarchical bounds of nature as God's creation—that underlies the
Exercises and hence all aspects of advanced Jesuit thought.[5]

In the previous chapter we encountered the preacher Francesco Panigarola's four-stage description of increasing connoisseurship, in which

spiritual and protoaesthetic experience are seen as direct analogues—or better, protoaesthetic experience is understood in the framework of spiritual transcendence, in a transition to higher understanding that resonates strongly with Loyola's *Exercises*. Cardinal Gabriele Paleotti, a Tridentine reformer whose ideas on the use of images in devotional practice we first encountered in chapter 1, similarly posits a threefold distinction in types of understanding (cognizione) and hence enjoyment (dilettazione). The three types of understanding are "animal" (animale), which comes solely from the senses; "rational" (rationale), which combines reason with the senses; and "supernatural" (sopranaturale), which "is born from a divine light infused into us by faith, through which we can believe and know things that not only exceed the capabilities of the senses but surpass all human discourse and rational intelligence; and this we also call *spiritual* understanding, which is given to pure and innocent souls by the singular grace of God" (Paleotti 1961, 216). Paleotti postulates that each type of understanding generates specific emotional states ("certi affetti"), giving rise to three categories of pleasure. Here he gives the example of a person delighting in the beauty of the starry sky, seeing "such a numerous army of stars, as if many lights placed from afar, some larger, others sparkling, some moving, some standing still; and from their variety and beauty the senses feel tremendous pleasure" (217). The individual then can intellectually understand the sizes of the stars, the order of the heavens, and so on; "thus the intellect is greatly pleased with this and rejoices." Finally, the most complete understanding comes from contemplating the glory of God, who has created the starry universe, and "with what providence and wisdom he has wished, through these creations, to give men the inspiration to contemplate eternity and excite them with desire of heavenly matters; from which the soul feels a pleasure within itself, so much greater than the ones mentioned above, since this last one comes from a much more lofty and perfect source" (218). This tripartite progression is clearly the result of an increasingly disciplined approach to perception and understanding.

Paleotti's exegesis is fully in keeping with the resurgent Augustinian notion of beauty as "a reflection of a higher, immutable divine 'reason.' . . . All perceptible beauty is an 'admonition' to mind to ascend to a spiritual plane where intelligible beauty is one with truth and wisdom" (Furley 1999, 403). Those who championed this Augustinian perspective understood delight in the beautiful—even intellectual delight, which was of course more elevated than sensual delight, as Paleotti himself makes clear—as an incomplete understanding, one that reflected a less-than-perfected inner self. As Tarquinio Galluzzi stated in a treatise on preaching, "'Pleasure is not the wages nor the cause of virtue, but an access' to greater virtue."[10] And Cardinal Federico Borromeo, in his own writing about sacred art and its connection to devotion, suggested that "beauty is never separated from virtue" (Quint 1986, 72). In sum, as we also saw in the previous chapter, the post-Tridentine reforms saw an effort by Catholic thinkers to theorize that receptivity to the divine was to be an active rather than passive endeavor. Following the same reasoning, receptivity to the beautiful, as a path to the true understanding of the transcendent perfection of the divine, must likewise be understood as an active process.

But active receptivity—if this formulation is not too much of an oxymoron—was only part of the principle of *recte sentire* as it applied to both spiritual and protoaesthetic experience: equally important was the self-discipline—generally gendered masculine with the term *virtù* (note the term in the quoted passages by Galluzzi and Borromeo immediately above)—that the active recipient needed to cultivate in order to embody the qualities of the spiritual and social elite. It was, after all, quite possible to *sentire*—to feel deeply and completely—in a way that was *not* proper. Those without good judgment might be inclined to interpret a work of art incorrectly or to ascribe to it improper meanings. Paleotti chooses an especially vivid metaphor to illustrate this concept, its reference to poison a clear allusion to the spiritual poisoning of minds through misinterpretation of scripture: "The same image will create several different [effects], depending on the various interpretations [concetti] that the viewers will make of it, as the schools say in a different context: all that is received has in it the nature of the recipient and not of the thing received. Thus we see that from the juice of the flowers in the fields bees make sweet honey, and spiders extract deadly poison. This happens similarly in many other cases, as everyone can understand" (1961, 172). A cautionary tale was cited at the time concerning a painting of the sacrifice of Isaac by the artist Cigoli, which an imprudent man implied was too erotically charged: "[When the painting was] seen by one who perhaps wanted to appear a better man than he was, he said, not knowing about painting, that the painting was beautiful, but it seemed to him that it was too moving; when the cardinal [Pompeo Arrigoni, owner of the painting] heard this, he answered with serious prudence that moving depended on the excellence of Cigoli, and being moved on the weakness of the viewer." (Brown 2001, 302 n. 57). The nature of "good judgment" (in this case "serious prudence") is implicitly linked with status—the image of the individual "who wanted to appear a better man than he was" evokes the culturally ignorant (and by extension morally suspect) poseur. Conversely, Cardinal Arrigoni's *seria prudenza* is a mark of his *recte sentire,* which defines and reconfirms the legitimacy of his spiritual and temporal status.

While the collection of artworks in Cardinal Scipione Borghese's villa on Pincian Hill was initially open to any individual who was "well educated" (*bene educato;* an alternative translation is "well behaved," which emphasizes the connection between outward behavior and inward discipline), after 1612 its access was restricted because of an unnamed *fiammingo* who had responded inappropriately to some works that he had considered lascivious (Spezzaferro 2001, 6). Similar concerns are expressed by Federico Borromeo, who—while commenting that "the Virgin Mother of God is so much more admirable in her singular charm, she inspires a sacred respect and sweeps out of every mind every unchaste thought," also observes that "whatever sin against decorum is committed in works of art remains perpetually and is insuppressable . . . how much more so when committed on sacred and divine subjects" (Quint 1986, 73).

It was thus important to establish a shared understanding of parameters of decorum, not only on the part of the artist or preacher who was to deliver the spiritual message, but more importantly by the individual recipient of that message. The *virtuosi* needed to define themselves as separate from those who lacked the intellectual and spiritual ability to engage fully with the repercussions of divine beauty on earthly matters, and to articulate/understand this separation as a natural manifestation of the hierarchical order that justified their social status. Various initiatives by the papacy and the prominent cardinals facilitated this definition. For example, early modern popes inaugurated a tradition of choosing a distinguished preacher as *predicatore apostolico,* who would present sermons to the assembled Roman hierarchy using both topics and rhetorical approaches that were understood as more "refined" and thus suited to the higher level of discernment of the upper curia (Tiacci 1999). By their appropriate response to this elite spiritual experience, the *virtuosi* who were members of the cardinals' *famiglie* could confirm their spiritual discernment. We shall return to a specific account of one such response, which dwells on various aspects of sound and listening, below.

Another curial initiative, and one that resonates with the focus on the Eucharist that we explored in chapter 1, was the foundation in 1629 by Pope Urban VIII Barberini of the Congregazione Urbana, designed for the "material protection and spiritual elevation" of gentlemen who worked in various offices of the Roman court. The members of this congregation were especially charged to be assiduous in visiting the Most Holy Sacrament in the churches, where the Prayers of the Forty Hours are held, in order to show themselves as true courtiers of the Supreme Prince and Lord of the Universe" (Fragnito 1998, 77). According to the goals of the institution, more expert members of the congregation would offer *letture* to assist the more inexperienced in becoming "knowledgeable about those most civilized disciplines, which are useful for the government of oneself, of the *famiglia,* and for service at the court, all of which greatly facilitate the acquisition of civil prudence" (77). Thus the goal of the Barberini papacy was to train the "godly courtier" to understand service of the divine hierarchy and its earthly manifestation in the curia as integral to his identity, both social and spiritual.

The focus on the devotion to the Eucharist as a central "training ground" for the members of the Congregazione Urbana was useful partly because of the hierarchical notion of receptivity of that sacrament pronounced by the Council of Trent. The council determined three types of reception of the Eucharist: "Some, being sinners, receive it only sacramentally; others receive only spiritually, namely those who have the desire to eat the heavenly food that is before them, and so experience its effect and benefit by a lively faith working through love; the third group, who receive both sacramentally and spiritually, are those who so test and train themselves beforehand, that they approach this divine table clothed in a wedding garment."[7] Through repeated and systematic devotional focus and training, the younger members of the Congregazione Urbana could gain access to the highest level of receptivity. Indeed, within the context of the priestly tradition that was reaffirmed through the Catholic reform, the high-status (and highly dedicated) member of the curia had a higher duty to connect with the transcendent power of the eucharistic mystery, on behalf of spiritual "inferiors" who could not reach that transcendence. For if only the celebrant at the altar could perform the act of eucharistic union with Christ's actions—and this was one of the most important reaffirmations of Catholic doctrine at the Council of Trent, countering challenges (both internal and external) concerning eucharistic agency by the congregation—it was incumbent on those present to "actively receive" the sacramental action, to fulfill the role of the apostles whose reception of grace completed the divine mandate.[8] Crucial here are the multiple hierarchical layers of "receptivity" and submission, idealized as paths to individual fulfillment as well as solidifications of social and spiritual belonging.

To accompany this definition of exclusive spiritual (but also social) sensibility, there were also efforts to characterize differences between the spiritual/social status and response of the *virtuosi* and those of lesser individuals, whose social inferiority would be partly manifest through their lack of spiritual understanding. After all, the cardinal *famiglie* included individuals of lowly extraction. While these individuals' duties were considered menial, in their exercise they would come into regular contact with the *virtuosi,* and in some cases their actions or products (food, visual art, music) could specifically constitute the topic of interaction between the *virtuosi.*[9] It was understood that different modes of speech or discourse were appropriate for different social classes and could mark the distinction between those strata.[10] The cardinal court projected its model of spiritual-courtly life as ideal and thus to some extent available to all whose spiritual dedication would be sufficient to reach the required mark. Cardinals were also increasingly encouraged in the post-Tridentine era to monitor and encourage spiritual focus and devotion by members of their *famiglia,* offering both the possibility and the evidence of spiritual and social "upward mobility." However, this was paradoxically contrasted with a reinforcement of notions of enduring hierarchy, making the model of spiritual sensibility the purview of a privileged few.[11]

A central principle underpinning the argument for an enduring hierarchy (with parallel resonances in spiritual understanding, framing of taste, and social roles) was that of a "new classicism," which gradually took form through the first quarter of the seventeenth century in discourse concerning not only the visual arts but all expressive media and arguably reached its peak in the cultural projects sponsored by the Barberini papacy and its allied cardinal courts.[12] As the art historian Elizabeth Cropper (1984, 157) observes, this notion of "individual perfection based on judicious imitation . . . [assuming] that these individual perfections referred to an ideal, rather than aspiring to licentious innovation," was actually grounded in the Jesuit *ratio studiorum,* which was established as a guideline both for preaching and for transmission/ interpretation of cultural rhetoric in 1599. Through the *ratio,* "the Jesuit orators sought to encourage the formation of a personal style based on good judgment through the imitation and mastery of selected ancient models. . . . Through this new urbane eloquence the ancient grandeur of Rome might again be united with the mission of the Roman Church; a Roman rhetoric could serve in the recovery of the Christian empire"

(157). While there is evidence of visual artists taking on the principles of this "new classicism" into their thinking about creative strategies, whether entirely of their own initiative or in order to curry favor with the *virtuosi* and patrons whose commissions they were seeking (for example, Cropper explores such a tendency in the writings of artist Pietro Testa), these principles were most thoroughly discussed by the *virtuosi* of the cardinal courts. One of the leaders of this viewpoint was Agostino Mascardi, a Jesuit appointed by Urban VIII to a special chair of rhetoric at the University of Rome, who argued that it is incumbent on the *virtuoso* to become an "educated critic" and to gain knowledge of the possibilities of a "creative ideal" on any subject (particularly those connected to spiritual matters), imagining the ideal ways a rhetorician or artist might create an *affetto* so as to be able to judge the quality of an individual creative effort with respect to that ideal.

This is fully in keeping with the notion of the *virtuoso* as "more artist than the artist himself": the importance of Mascardi's theorizing is its connection of the evaluative mission of the *virtuoso* to a higher purpose. Following the practice of the Jesuit exercitant, the *virtuoso* can carry the moral lessons he has gained through spiritually informed reception of the beautiful into everyday life, when he can reflect on them in his memory and apply the ideals he has derived to his actions.[13] In this way, the spiritually trained *virtuoso* of taste has the opportunity to claim a more important role (especially in the early modern Catholic hierarchy) than that exercised by powerful patrons or "event programmers" (the figures who had dominated the commissioning of cultural artifacts to that point). His role is to master a sufficiently vast experience in order to judge the circumstances in which the meeting of the artist and the "spiritual public" can be most favorable and fruitful for the painter, for his spectators, and for the church. As we will see below, this dynamic applies not only to the visual arts but to sonic artifacts (preaching, music) as well.

Before considering the traces of "proper listening" as a mark of superior discernment early modern Roman commentaries, it is worthwhile to dwell a while longer on the consequences of these formulations for the collection and assessment of visual artifacts. Visual media were more explicitly discussed at the time than music, and that discourse has been amply and usefully considered in modern scholarship: a reflection on both historical and contemporary discussion of visual works will provide fruitful parallels in our assessment of the more diffuse discourse on the reception of sound. The cultural historian Renata Ago (2006, 124) points out the significance of the early modern process of accumulating goods that are "destined not to be used or exchanged, but only to be 'viewed'; it is precisely this 'sacrifice of utility' that elevates them to the rank of *semiophores,* messengers of that which is invisible." In selecting items to collect (whether physical or sonic/intangible), the *virtuoso* of taste (whether enacting his professional role individually or on behalf of the leader of his *famiglia*) indicated his superior discernment precisely by a symbolic "refusal" of use value, thereby demonstrating his understanding of a transcendent purpose beyond use value. This resonates greatly with the notion of transcendent refusal of earthly matters in order to gain understanding of the divine, a central trope in early modern Catholic spirituality, especially in both Franciscan and Jesuit practice. Thus we might go one step beyond Ago, who justly observes (xxiii) that "only people who are not deprived—under any point of view—can allow themselves the lightness necessary to sacrificing the useful in the name of the purely delightful." The *virtuoso* of taste in the context of the Roman curia can display a "spiritual lightness" in recognizing the value of the "delightful" as a path to understanding the divine: an artifact that can be contemplated as beautiful has the inestimable value of offering insight into spiritual transcendence, and the individual who can discern that potential and articulate it to (and even model it for) his assembled peers is indeed a valuable member of the *famiglia.*[14]

The notion of a "well-disposed" recipient, able to exercise prudent judgment against the dangers of sensuality, was also a common trope in early modern commentary on the visual arts. For example, not only practicing artists but also the *virtuosi*-critics who eclipsed them in leading *discourse about art* in early modern Rome lavished the greatest praise on creative issues that addressed the intellect (foremost among them *disegno* and *proporzione,* the most controlled and masculine aspects of art) rather than the "surface" sensuality of color (often understood as the more "feminine" side of the craft).[15] Federico Borromeo, in his writing on collecting visual artifacts, maintained that "through its elegance form excludes lasciviousness" (elegantia forma lasciviam excludit; Quint 1986, 235) and suggested that careful attention to propriety in depiction of sacred images would yield not only personal piety but also greater understanding of and adherence to moral and doctrinal hierarchical truth.[16] The work of Caravaggio was famously controversial: some contemporaries defended it for its remarkable ability to express *affetti* by conveying immediacy and "reality," while others (and this is the perspective that eventually prevailed among the Roman *virtuosi*) "felt that the excessive naturalism compromised the spiritual content of his works" (Poseq 1992, 28), challenging the recipient's ability to engage the image with the appropriate decorum.[17]

Mancini himself was careful to dwell on the need for proper care in deploying the potential for sensuality, suggesting how a prudent collector could control the *affetti* just as much as the painter who created the works, demonstrating his command over the expressive power of a visual work, whether within the *famiglia* (which here Mancini seems to circumscribe to the immediate family, though the meaning is not entirely unambiguous) or for wider effect: "There must be great care in placing [pictures] in their [appropriate] places, both when one is the father of the *famiglia,* and when one is a public person or a prince, with respect to the behavior/customs and *affetti* that they can produce when they are viewed." There follow a series of suggestions for placement of particular kinds of images within the more public spaces of the collector's dwelling, finally including the advice that "lascivious pictures are appropriate to places where one entertains oneself with one's consort, because such a sight aids greatly to excitement and to making beautiful, healthy, and lively children."[18] Erotic art, in Mancini's formulation, is not inherently problematic. Given the importance of strong offspring to dynastic succession, especially in the complicated politics of early modern Rome, it can be of great use—as long as the collector controls its message and effect appropriately, limiting it to the most private places and purposes.[19]

Appropriate control of the effect of and response to sound (especially, but not only, musical sound) was also a primary concern of post-Tridentine Catholicism. Early modern writers expressed considerable ambivalence concerning the potential effects of music—an ambivalence that continued long-standing debates that had only intensified with humanist reconsideration of classical texts. While some celebrated the ability of music to enrapture the spirit, others decried the impossibility of evading the power of sound, since ears—unlike eyes—could not be closed to avoid temptation, and temptation that entered the soul through the ears was thought to be especially powerful and irresistible.[20] Some were especially concerned about the potential of music to sap the inherent qualities of noble manliness that underpinned the possibility of *recte sentire,* namely the trait of *virtù* (we will return in more detail to the nuances and implications of this attribute in the next chapter). Richard Wistreich adduces to this point the remarks of Francesco Bocchi, whose *Discorso sopra la musica* of 1587 asks, "Who doesn't know that he, who abandons himself entirely to the study of music, closes the path to the workings of *virtù,* and to the gravity of life, and dries the fount of valor, and of glory, as enveloped by delightful song he places strong and virile actions in oblivion?" (Wistreich 2007, 266). As Wistreich observes, Bocchi is probably drawing directly from a parallel passage in Plato's *Republic* that warns that a man's overindulgence in "abandoning himself to music" can "cut out as it were the very sinews of his soul." Too much "musicking" (the term *studio* is ambiguous and does not necessarily imply performance; indeed, the latter half of the quote makes it entirely feasible that the subject is listening to rather than creating music) can create a feminine space. As such, "musicking" can distract from the kind of "serious prudence" that the early modern *virtuoso* is expected to uphold.

Within this concern for loss of control, Suzanne Cusick (2000) has argued that Florentine proponents of the "new music" paradoxically yet purposefully put themselves in the position of being ravished and unbalanced by sound. In this formulation the listener assumed a position of (presumably) passive receptivity and, in the eyes of critics of the "new music," risked becoming (like the adolescent knight Rinaldo under the spell of the sorceress Armida in Tasso's *Gerusalemme liberata,* one of the literary touchstones in early modern Italy) "seduced by deceit, luxury, sensuality, and his own narcissism—an incomplete man in the control of the object of his desire" (Cusick 1993a, 13). Following this criticism, the new styles (in Cusick's elegant paraphrase of Artusi) aimed at the "pleasures of a nonperforming audience" of "dazzled but passive listeners" and "[turned] listeners into 'women.'"[21]

As Cusick (2000, 88–90) points out, the listener's lack of control was understood by critics in opposition to the self-discipline and control required of singers in the new style, and the fact that the singer was often female made the potential passivity of the male listener especially dangerous, particularly in the context of early modern Catholic concerns with female sinfulness as a threat to the order and sanctity of the church hierarchy.[22] After all, as Austern (1998, 623) remarks, "It was the powerful transitive magic of music, with its strong sympathetic connection to imagination and memory . . . that was most closely linked to the burning, inescapable passions of erotic desire." At stake in this situation were the "dangers of mere activation of the body's audio equipment" (644) without the establishment of control over the results of such activation.[23] The association of music making with courtesans in early modern Italy only contributed to both the seductive allure and the potential dangers (social, cultural, and even medical) of musical activity.[24] The prominent cultural presence of outstanding female professional musicians in elite Roman circles of the first half of the century fed the flames of controversy about female sonic agency.[25]

Furthermore, several early modern authors condemned the use of inappropriate music in church, expanding on the sole cryptic decree of the Council of Trent to avoid music in which "there is an intermingling of the lascivious or impure, whether by instrument or voice."[26] These condemnations seem to have taken two general paths: either to castigate music making by specific types of individuals (most prominently women) or to decry "lascivious" or inappropriate musical choices. The latter, interestingly enough, often refers to dancing and even to "dancing women," so that both lines of condemnation have clear resonance with the "feminizing" or "emasculating" potential of sound. The former, focusing on women (almost exclusively nuns) making music in sacred spaces, has been ably and extensively explored, with principal studies in English by Robert Kendrick (1996), Craig Monson (1993; 1995; 2002), Kimberlyn Montford (1999; 2000), and Colleen Reardon (2001). I will not rehearse their complex arguments here, referring the reader to their studies, but will perhaps let a statement from a Roman decree of 1604 provide a sample: "And while music can create good effects in some [female] servants of God, elevating them and ravishing them to the consideration of heavenly song, ordinarily it creates great harm, most especially in our unhappy times." The author/prelate goes on to quote Saint Augustine on the pitfalls of taking pleasure in musical sound, then concludes: "Thus, desiring that nuns serve God usefully and with purity of heart, we prohibit music—both vocal and instrumental—even in days of any solemnity or feast."[27] While accepting the potential for individuals—even outstanding women—to gain spiritual transcendence through music, the author of this decree concludes that such potential does not overcome the more likely scenario of distraction and spiritual harm. In this he is probably following the widely shared notion that women by their nature lacked the kind of self-control that, as we have seen, was considered essential for effective reception of expressive meaning, whether spiritual, sonic, or visual.[28]

The second line of attack, which is perhaps more directly relevant to our concern about "proper listening," can be seen in remarks by Agostino Agazzari, composer and director of music at the cathedral of Siena in the first half of the seventeenth century, who writes in his treatise on ecclesiastical music, "I myself have heard psalms and motets—and even the holy words of the Mass—set to the *ciaccona* and the *gagliarda* and other well-known profane melodies, all things that distract the mind from God, enticing it with sensual delight and curiosity."[29] Severo Bonini, writing in the same time frame from a Florentine perspective, spends several pages chastising musicians who "profane the house and temple of God against all propriety and contravening the council"—for example, playing "some little tune similar to the *spagnolettta* or the *romanesca*" as organ responses to psalms or mass versets.[30] Bonini observes that such inappropriate music making is readily perceived and condemned by "pure ears and devout persons" (gl'orrechi [sic] purgati, e le persone divote; 43). Thus one should not blame music but rather "those who make ill use of it" (chi male se ne serve; 45). Indeed, Bonini and others turn to Augustine for confirmation of the positive power of music in those who are properly disposed—here is Bonini's paraphrase of a well-known passage from Augustine's *Confessions:* "Oh how I wept, Lord, when I heard psalms and hymns in your praise sung sweetly in your church! Those sounds/voices [voci] penetrated from my ears to the depth of my heart and there illuminated to me your truth; my *affetto* burned, my eyes flowed with tears to my incredible delight. . . . I must say that this pious custom of singing is greatly useful, since as a most efficacious means of moving the spirit, and igniting it to the desire to praise God, it prepares us and makes us worthy of paradise."[31] Bonini does report Augustine's concern that he might take more delight in the sound of a voice than in the holy words that were being sung (and that if this occurred he would want to stop listening). However, he counters it with the contention (which he attributes to Thomas Aquinas) that "even if the words are not heard because of the singers' deficiency, nonetheless since the people know that one is playing, and singing with the goal of praising God, because of this alone they are moved to devotion" (Bonini 1979, 109). Note, however, that the reference to "playing" as well as singing is added by Bonini—and this opens up a large interpretative space, since of course instrumental music cannot convey words, so that an interpretation of its effect as devotional is entirely transferred to the listener. Gratioso Uberti, while refraining from adding a reference to instrumental music to Aquinas's original, comes up with a similar paraphrase that dwells more explicitly on the listener: "Even if the singer, who does not sing to give pleasure [but rather for devotional purposes], sometimes may become distracted from the sense of the words, and also the listener sometimes does not hear that which

is being sung, it is nonetheless sufficient that they both know the purpose for the singing. Thus says Saint Thomas" (Uberti 1630/1991, 116).
In other words, the well-disposed listener may reach transcendence
through sound alone, by understanding the delight experienced by that
sound as a means to spiritual understanding rather than an independent
sensual pleasure. In his formulation Uberti appears to play up the "distraction" of the musician, possibly implying a more focused dedication
on the listener's part. In following up on this observation, Uberti brings
together a counterargument to both forms of post-Tridentine condemnation of musical activity: "It is thus proper that the sweet, devoted
song of the sacred virgins [nuns] be heard by everyone; so that everyone
be moved to devotion, and be excited to praise God. But if anyone ap-
proached [the convent] for his shame with evil thoughts, let him be
certain that the angels charged to protect that place are faithful accusers
of sin. And God is a just avenger of every wickedness" (117). Uberti suggests that the onus for interpreting nuns' music as problematic lies in the
listener's inability to perceive it as transcendent, so that the agency—as
well as the potential for moral failing, sure to be punished by God—is
not in the singer but in the listener.

Bonini agrees, bringing the quality and prudence (and status) of the
recipient even more to the foreground: "It is very true that this honest
and holy singing, while it may in itself create wondrous effects, will
nonetheless work differently depending on the variety of the [listening]
subjects, because in the souls of sensuous individuals it is mostly cause
for filthy thoughts, [while it creates] heavenly thoughts in pious and
devoted souls" (Bonini 1979, 105–6). He speaks further specifically to
the inherent suitability of the *virtuoso* to achieve a proper understanding of sophisticated music:

> I have said that the recipient must be disposed and able to receive a given
> passion; and this can happen in a variety of ways, whether the listener or
> recipient is a person of quality, or a low person with a coarse mind, as are
> farmers, artisans, and the like. If he is of quality, that is to say noble or *vir-
> tuoso*, it cannot be that hearing pitiful or joyful situations, performed with
> beautiful poetry and excellent harmony accompanied by perfect and noble
> musical instruments by a skilled and *grazioso* singer, [the listener] will not be
> moved to happiness or tears, especially if the listener is inclined to a specific
> topic; because, if it is a warlike topic, the soldier will delight in it, if a peace-
> ful one, the religious and God-fearing man will [delight in it], if tragic, such
> as the story of Arianna and similar topics, all will be moved to compassion;
> if the topic is lascivious, then unbridled young people, accustomed to lascivi-
> ousness, will feel extreme pleasure. Thus one cannot say that song moves all

listeners absolutely, but only those who are inclined toward one specific subject or another.

And if [the listeners] are ignorant and low-class or coarse-minded people, such as lowly shopkeepers and farmers, they will not take so much pleasure as those mentioned above; they will take more [pleasure] in hearing blind men sing with a lyre, a guitar, or a panpipe. . . . When farmers hear a run-of-the-mill preacher, as long as he shouts loudly and has a booming voice, it matters little what topics he chooses, they esteem him greatly. . . . Shopkeepers will take greater pleasure in hearing some foolishness sung by a foolish and besotted brayer. . . . Heroic songs would be pearls placed before swine, as the proverb says; thus it should be no wonder that they are not disposed toward such topics, since they are disproportionate to their nature. 124–25)

The ability to fully appreciate sophisticated music is explicitly a mark of social class; note that the inability to assess "sonic quality" extends to preaching as well as music in Bonini's pantheon of listening ability.

It is likely that Bonini is reflecting a widely shared perspective on this matter. We have, for example, a record of the members of the confraternity of the Misericordia Maggiore in Bergamo expressing concern in 1606 that devotional music at their cathedral might be viewed as insufficiently sophisticated, using similar parameters: "At that time [when vespers are held early and musicians are not fully in attendance] very few listeners are present, and the ones who are there are shopkeepers and salad sellers, never are there any noblemen; and if a foreigner by chance comes by, hearing weak music and imagining that all musicians are present, he leaves dissatisfied."[32] While the primary objection appears to be the musician employees' lack of dedication to the service, the possible perception that the quality of music associated with their institution is "unsatisfactory" to the sensibility of their peers is also of evident concern to the noble members of the confraternity.

Concomitant with the desirability of a properly trained and well-disposed listener was an obligation for that individual to listen carefully in a variety of contexts. First of all, Guazzo had postulated careful, quiet listening as a crucial sign of "gravity and prudence": "Since listening quietly is one of the most difficult things there is in this world, it is necessary for our weak self to dispose itself to hold back this appetite [for speaking] and, resisting oneself, become slowly accustomed to keep one's mouth more closed and one's ears more open. . . . No less admiration follows being silent well than speaking well, because just as the latter uncovers eloquence and knowledge, the former demonstrates gravity and prudence."[33] Of course Guazzo is referring to spoken conversation and to

the importance of attentive understanding of the interlocutor's arguments, not to mention paying appropriate respect to the interlocutor.
Nonetheless, this formulation sets an important standard of receptivity,
which was reinforced by the decree of the Council of Trent obliging all
devout Catholics to listen to preaching as a duty parallel to that of attending liturgical rites in one's parish (see Tiacci 1999, 42). As we saw
in chapter 1, the skilled preacher's rhetorical power was esteemed both
for its ability to provide messages of transcendence and for the sonic
delight that careful listening would afford the devout. In the case of "apostolic preaching" to the highest ranks of the curia, including the pope
himself, careful attention to the nuances of the speaker ostensibly required absolute silence on the part of the listeners. A contemporary
account of a particularly esteemed apostolic preacher tells us that "the
[listeners'] attention is such that from such a crowd there is not a blink,
not a breath. Besides, if anyone were to move toward another's ear, the
latter would immediately stop him with authoritative gestures and command him to be quiet."[34] We can of course take this adulatory account
with some skepticism, but the writer's rhetorical construct is clear: the
well-disposed, noble *virtuosi* listeners are defending their ears from distraction and directing their entire focus to the anticipated transcendent
spiritual message.

Even Guazzo dwells on the sonic power of the voice as an important
conduit of meaning in discourse: "The delight that comes from spoken
reasoning, no less than that from music, is caused by changes in the
voice.... Variation in vocal quality gains *grazia,* and just like a many-
stringed instrument, elevates/relieves the listener and speaker alike. Such
variation must be made discreetly, according to the time and quality of
the words and the diversity of statements and reasoning" (Guazzo 1993,
1:90). The need to control and assess the sonic quality of the voice that
Guazzo describes is certainly in keeping with the exhortations to prudence and awareness as markers of the well-born and self-aware *virtuoso*.
Indeed, Uberti observes that while the most powerful prayer is silent (in
the heart), the voice can be of use in "counterpoint," as it were, with internal prayer:

> It is sufficient that private prayer be made to God with the heart, and the
> voice is not necessary [here Uberti mentions the example of Anne, mother of
> Samuel in Kings]. . . . It is nonetheless very useful also to pray with the voice,
> which—as an exterior sign—excites interior devotion, and since [the voice]
> was given by God to man as his unique gift, it is dutiful for it also to join
> in the praises of God; and since it is moved by the *affetto* of the heart, it is

appropriate that it accompany the heart in its prayer and keep the mind from wandering elsewhere. (Uberti 1630/1991, 130–31)

In this case, the voice engages in a sort of "discourse" with the heart, keeping the mind steady on grasping the evanescent (but more powerful) heart-based *affetto*/devotion. In a similar way, perhaps, *discourse about music* could "concretize" the heart-based *affett*ive response to music's transitory power and create a way to fix some aspect of the transcendent experience in memory.

This "concretizing" of experience through discourse may have provided part of the impetus for an extended discussion of musical expression that appears to have taken place among the members of the Accademia degli Umoristi in the 1620s and 1630s. The discussion seems to have initially materialized in 1623 through competing praise of two renowned female singers of the time, Adriana Basile and Francesca Caccini, driven by the poet Giambattista Marino, who was at the time leader of the Accademia.[35] It reached its peak with the publication in 1639 of a volume of poems—the *Applausi poetici*—in praise of Basile's daughter Leonora Baroni, also a prominent singer. Baroni had recently been named as an honorary member of the Umoristi—the only woman, apparently, to have been given that honor.[36] Many members of the Umoristi had probably attended the regular evening events—dedicated to music making, but also to discourse and poems about music and related subjects— hosted by the singer and her mother in their household, since according to a contemporaneous account they were "nowadays attended by the foremost gentlemen and *virtuosi* of this [papal] court; which makes this equal to any of the most famous academies that honor our Italy."[37] In his contribution to the volume, the Umoristi member Domenico Benigni (who was closely connected to the Baroni household) incites his fellow academicians: "Sacred swans of Apollo, for whom the CLOUD, which falls from the heavens, distills golden dew on the Tiber, let the wave of your sea be offered to [Baroni]."[38] The *Applausi* as a whole is a compendium of elaborately indirect descriptions of sophisticated responses to sound.

In her overview of the volume, Estelle Haan provides some key examples of the rhetorical approach in the *Applausi,* and here I offer a select few, referring the reader to her discussion for a more complete account:

Carlo Eustachio, for example, states that the harmony of her voice and her words do not seem to be of an earthly quality ("L'armonia di tua bocca, e le parole/Non son cosa terrena à chi l'ascolta")... . Francesco Caetani [speaks of being astonished by the wonder of nature and perceiving the beauty of the heavens when viewing and listening to her] (*Applausi*, 142: "Io con stupor de la Natura accolto / Scorgo quanto ha di bel mole Celeste / Se ti miro LEONORA, ò se t'ascolto")... . Giovanni Bentivoglio says, . . . "Se canti, LEONORA, ecco ci sveli / Il concerto de' Cieli, a noi mal noto. / Co'l tuo canto gentil, tu sol far puoi / De l'armonia del Ciel fede tra noi." [If you sing, Leonora, you unveil for us the harmony of the heavens which is unfamiliar to us. With your sweet singing you alone can testify to us the harmony of the heavens.] . . . [Francesco Ronconi, *Applausi* 151, says,] "COSMO, cui diede il Cielo / Di LEONOR si spesso udir le note / Di, con qual' arte a si soavi accenti / Stanno le sfere immote / Perdon gli Augelli il volo, il corso i venti? / Tacito ti confondi? / Col silentio rispondi; / Perche tanti stupori altrui distingua / Non ha voci la lingua." [Cosmo, whom heaven has so frequently allowed to listen to the notes of Leonora, tell me what skill makes the spheres stand motionless, the birds lose their flight, the winds lose their course, at such sweet tones? Are you confused and silent? You respond with silence. [Your] tongue has not the voice with which to convey such great marvels to another.] Giovanni Bentivoglio tells the heavens themselves to be quiet and to pay attention to Leonora's sweet singing: "Se canti, e spieghi al Ciel note amorose / Degni sono del Cielo i dolci accenti; / Tacete, ò Cieli, ad ascoltarla intenti / Aure vinte tacete, e vergognose." [If you sing and unfold your amorous notes to heaven, your sweet tones are worthy of heaven; Be quiet, heavens, be intent on listening to her, be quiet, o breezes, conquered and ashamed.][39]

The *virtuosi* authors are trading metaphors of listening, heavenly sound, focus, and silence, providing individual perspectives but drawing knowingly on a shared vocabulary of transcendence. Leonora Baroni is the ostensible subject of each poem, but each poem is also (arguably primarily) about the poet's sensibility, delivered in an opaque language shared among peers (see, for example, Ronconi's poem, which addresses a fellow *virtuoso*, implicitly praising his inability to put his transcendent experience into sufficient words). This use of shared, almost commonplace, figurative language is analogous to that traced by Renato Diez (1986) in his examination of official accounts of sacred spectacles in early modern Rome. As Diez observes, authors of descriptive accounts develop and then draw on a "collective imaginary" that is both shared by and defining of the cultural sphere of the curia and its affiliated hierarchies throughout Catholic Europe. This allows the author of the description "to speak in a fashion that is apparently hermetic but in fact comprehensible without additional explanations" within that cultural sphere.[40]

The English poet Milton, visiting Rome in 1639 and associating with the Umoristi, was inspired to join the *discourse about music* with his own poetic praises of Baroni (which were not, however, included in the *Applausi*). Milton's contribution to the shared discourse of "proper listening" deserves an extended quote:

> To Leonora singing at Rome: Each person (believe this o peoples) has been allotted a winged angel from the celestial ranks. What wonder then if, Leonora, you have a greater glory, for your very voice proclaims the presence of God. Either God or certainly the third mind has left an empty place in the sky and secretly progresses, coiling its way through your throat. Coiling its way, it progresses, and easily teaches hearts that are mortal gradually how to grow accustomed to a sound that is immortal. For if God is indeed all things and is diffused through all things, it is in you alone that he speaks, while holding everything else in silence.[41]

Milton here draws on many of the ideas, metaphors, and assumptions that we have traced thus far. It is reasonable to read this poem as a gesture by the Englishman to associate himself with the prestigious cultural sphere of the Roman *virtuosi* of taste.[42]

Even if Baroni had been able to read its classical Latin grammar and perceive the embedded references, the neoclassical intellectual discourse to which Milton's encomium aspires was marked as proper to a category of individual—male, noble, curia connected—to which Baroni could by definition never belong. While Baroni was apparently named to the Accademia degli Umoristi (perhaps on the occasion of, or in some circumstance connected to, the publication of the *Applausi*), it is unlikely that she fully participated in their gatherings on a regular basis, or even that the academicians truly considered her a full member of their cohort. It is more likely that the membership was an honorific, and it could even be seen as a way for the members of the academy to co-opt Baroni's sonic power (following the discussion of Cusick [2000] above) and to defuse its potential seductive danger. Through the *Applausi* and through their election of Baroni to academy membership, the Umoristi demonstrated both their superior judgment and their ability to understand the singing of female singers as transcendent by "framing" Baroni's voice in terms of its effect on their disciplined sensibilities. Furthermore, the quasi-interactive, "dialogic" interplay of the poems in the *Applausi* reflects the kind of shared/collective *discourse-about* that characterizes the gathering of *virtuosi*: the Umoristi are talking to each other ("over Baroni's head," as it were—regardless of her ability to understand the references) about the effects the music creates in them. To use Szendy's (2008, 114) term, they are "listening to each other listen" and making it clear that they are doing so in a refined and controlled way (rather than sensuously).[43] Baroni's nomination to the academy is thus partly an acknowledgment of her superior status as a *virtuosa*—though that status is understood as such through the superior judgment of the Umoristi and thus ultimately reflects on their taste and understanding—but also a way of "domesticating" her: making her "one of the boys" (but not really) indicates that her sonic power is wrested from her sinful female body and absorbed into the spiritual high-mindedness (and classicizing approach) of the male community of listeners. The *virtuosi* of taste thus can make use of their "proper listening" strategies to detach sounds from the generating bodies of performers and claim sonic meaning as a function of their refined response and interpretation, just as they appropriate the messages of the visual artworks in their galleries, which become framed as expressions of their own cultural heritage rather than of that of the individuals who created them. Much of this process is communal, since the individual's status as a *virtuoso* requires shared performance and recognition of that status within the hierarchical framework of the cardinal courts (and their related satellites, such as the Accademia degli Umoristi). However, a necessary complement to the shared hierarchical frame is the development and display of individual perspective, the assertion of the interpretation/description crafted by the *virtuoso* as an integral part of the cultural meaning of the visual or sonic artifact. It is to a consideration of some facets of this individual engagement that we now turn.

In the first place, it is worthwhile to note that Guazzo (1993, 1:35) observes that "conversational discourse" can happen in solitude within a disciplined individual: "It must be understood that all these, and others who retire to their private studies and considerations, even if they are solitary with respect to the place, where they dwell alone, nonetheless are in conversation with the diversity of things that they consider in their minds." The ideal of self-reflection was, as we have seen, strongly connected to Jesuit teaching and practice; it was also another aspect of Augustine's teachings that was appealing to the early modern *virtuoso*.[44] Indeed, Mancini (1956, 318) emphasizes that only those with a "disciplined intellect" (the adjective he uses is *purgato*, which has further association with penance and atonement) shaped by reflection can truly understand the expressive *affetto* of an artwork: "If the [purpose of] the painting, in addition to resemblance, is to bring about the expression of some *affetto* and action . . . in that case one must consider two things:

first, the resemblance as discussed above, and second, the *affetto* and expression of actions. . . . Such issues cannot be understood by a rough intellect but rather by one that is disciplined and intelligent, which considers those things that involve imitation and expression of such an action, costume, and *affetto*." Collecting and reflecting on works and experiences would certainly have provided opportunities to whet the creative imagination and would also have allowed the *virtuoso* to refine his identification of—and *with*—individual artists' creative "hands" or styles, in the process forming his own personal creative "style" of collecting and interpreting. One of the consequences of this concern with identifying individual creative "fingerprints" can be seen in the growing concern with attribution of artworks that Spezzaferro (2001, 15) observes in Roman inventories during the third decade of the seventeenth century. This concern, according to Spezzaferro (17), "is important in this case not because it actually reflects the actual attribution but because, since the attribution is understood as such, it acts as an index of taste and judgment: as the index of a critical practice, of a way of thinking, of judging things, of building ideas about them . . . and of keeping them as a function of this [practice]." In other words, the truth of the attribution is secondary to the notion that attribution is valuable as a reflection of superior judgment, as a "discourse" between *virtuosi* of taste in which the artworks play a necessary but functional, secondary role.

An episode from the travel diary of Vincenzo Giustiniani, whom we have discussed at some length in chapter 3 as one of the more prominent and influential *virtuosi* of taste of his day, provides a specific example of superior discernment and its link to attribution:

> In the cathedral of Faenza there is a beautiful painting at the head of the left nave of the church, and while everyone was admiring it, Pomarancio [a renowned painter in Giustiniani's retinue] was asked if he knew by whose hand it was; and he replied, "I don't know the name of the painter who made it, but I know it's very beautiful." Then the marquis [Giustiniani], having observed it, said: "I think it's by [Dosso] Dossi, given the way in which it's painted." Pomarancio continued to observe it more attentively, and by accident he saw a few letters, which were Dossi's name, who had [indeed] painted it, and everyone was delighted by this, and especially Mr. Vincenzo [Giustiniani], because he thought it was no small matter that he had determined the author, when Pomarancio himself could not say who it was. (Bizoni 1995, 29)

While the absolute veracity of this report is of course suspect, since Bizoni's travel account seems to be specifically designed to illustrate the marquis's discernment and superior sensibility in a wide variety of contexts, nonetheless the rhetorical framing is significant. The artist Pomarancio can only speak generically to the "beauty" of the work, while the *virtuoso* Giustiniani (without any specific explanation, but presumably going beyond mere surface "beauty") is able to perceive the essence of the work and the individual hand of its creator. The fact that the painter of the work in question (Dosso Dossi) had died a half century before this episode may indicate that the expressive link between artist and noble *virtuoso* was most easily evoked by the latter in the absence of the former. This of course would allow the *virtuoso* to control the parameters of interpretation and define the expressive meaning of a work without any disruptive "backtalk" from the creator of the work in question. And indeed, the fact that Giustiniani can recognize a "masterly hand" more readily than Dossi is further evidence of his greater worthiness to evaluate great art.

When collecting/evaluating music, of course, the *virtuoso* of taste could not gain such helpful distance from the creator of sounds—at least until collecting of musical scores became a more common practice in the second half of the century. However, it was possible for the *virtuoso* to consider the different levels of agency in the musical process and to assign more importance (and thus postulate a more high-level connection) to the composer of the music and the author of the text than to the individual who made the sounds. After all, the authors of texts set to music were often noble *virtuosi* (or individuals who aspired to that association, and in any case less often members of the trade classes akin to musicians and painters).[45] By the late 1650s, the Jesuit historian and preacher (and later rector of the Collegio Romano) Daniello Bartoli could build on the metaphor of God as "composer" and man as "singer," observing that "singers do not see or know the artifice of their part; the composer, who organized it mysteriously and with attention to the whole, knows . . . parts are not formed as they are sung; rather they were first organized and harmonized together in the score by the composer alone."[46] To be sure, Bartoli's metaphor obviously draws from polyphonic practice rather than the solo song repertory on which refined "aural collecting" would likely have focused. Still, the importance placed on compositional oversight (and, by implication, understanding that oversight as a more meaningful determinant of the musical quality than the agency of the singer) may have influenced the more systematic attention to compositional attribution that Margaret Murata (1990, 1993) has noted in manuscript sources of Roman repertories in the second half of the century, contrasting with the relative prevalence of anonymous or unidentified works in earlier sources.[47] The lack of attributions may be an indication not only of casual status but also of an interpretive paradigm that did not yet consider the composer's agency as determinant and/or essential to the experience or recollection of the work as performed. If the sonic experience and its evocation were the emphasis for "aural collectors" up to about midcentury, identifying the composer may not have been particularly relevant.

Indeed, the "aural collectors" whose accounts we briefly examined in the previous chapter (especially Della Valle and Giustiniani) mostly mention names of performers, rather than composers, in describing the most contemporary repertories—perhaps indicating that the essence of the "new music" was especially associated with the immediacy of its power as performed. To be sure, several of the singers who were exponents of the style—Caccini, Peri, Puliaschi—explicitly invoked the need for their style of singing to be heard "in person" in order to understand its effectiveness, though on the other hand their claims to this effect in the prefaces to their books of songs must also be understood as attempts to publicize themselves and their "schools." However, Bizoni's comment (which we also encountered in the previous chapter) that Roman-style music (ca. 1607) "is more successful sung than written" would appear to reflect this perspective. Furthermore, given that Bizoni's account of Giustiniani's connoisseurship in Faenza is roughly contemporary with his statement about the essence of Roman song, it would seem that the *virtuosi* of the early decades of the century would have understood the "creative hand" for music to be connected to the performer.

Ultimately, in any case, the episode with Giustiniani in Faenza underlines the importance of active and trained receptivity for the meaning and relevance of an expressive artifact to be brought to fruition. When viewed by an uninformed layman—or even by a trained artisan such as Pomarancio—the painting is merely "beautiful"; it takes Giustiniani's intervention (and naming) for the full import of the work to be understood.[48] Here an extended quote from Maravall's summary of seventeenth-century perspectives on interpretation can help bring together several strands of what we have been exploring thus far:

> A difference exists, nonetheless, between mandate and persuasion, with persuasion demanding a greater participation on the side of the guided, requiring that he or she be taken into account and thus be given an active role. Did

Suarez, in his theology, not speak of "active obedience" in defining the position of the created being with respect to its creator? . . . One of the means that proved effective in reaching this objective—which can very well be exemplified in art, but also in other areas—consisted in introducing or implying and, to a certain extent, making the spectators themselves participants in the work, which succeeded in making the spectators almost its accomplices. Such was the result obtained by presenting a spectator with an open work that could come about in various ways. . . . Perhaps involvement comes about by turning the spectator into a coauthor, making use of the artifice by means of which the work changes along with the viewer's perspective. . . . The receivers of the baroque work, being surprised at finding it incomplete or so irregularly constructed, remained a few instants in suspense; then, feeling compelled to thrust themselves forward and take part in it, they ended up finding themselves more strongly affected by the work, held by it. In this way they experienced an incomparably more dynamic influence of the work being presented, with a much greater intensity than when other tacks were taken. (Maravall 1986, 74–75, 220)

The incompleteness or irregularity of a work was not, however, the only determinant of the recipient's active participation: as Colantuono (1997, 179) observes, in early modern Italy "the viewing and enjoyment of pictorial imagery was inextricably bound up with the activity of interpretative oratory," and "description is in itself a form of interpretation . . . [which] involves the copious invention of ingenious *concetti,* designed to mirror not only the physical appearance of the painting but even the moral discourse and human sentiments embodied in it" (141). Thus the cultivated individual—and especially the "professional" *virtuoso* of taste—would have understood such interpretative participation as a duty integral to the proper understanding of the artifact. Also at midcentury, the historian and rhetorician Emanuele Tesauro (1995, 462) would claim that

the vocal witticism [arguzia] is a sensible image of the archetype, and its pictures, which have sounds for colors and the tongue for a brush, please the ear too. But these images are sketched rather than finished, so that ingenuity understands more than the tongue speaks, and the concept of the listener supplies what is absent in the voice of the speaker. Indeed, wit loses its insight when a saying is too clear. Stars sparkle in the darkness but become dim in the light. And this causes the double pleasure of one who forms a witty concept and another who hears it. For the first enjoys giving life in another's intellect to a noble product of his own, and the second enjoys grasping by his own ingenuity what the ingenuity of another furtively hides, since interpreting a witty and ingenious emblem requires no less wisdom than composing it.

While the process of meaning formation is interactive and dialogic, both the creator and the recipient of the "product of the intellect" are responsible for its life—and arguably the recipient can imply a level of understanding that is deeper than that of the creator, while avoiding the taint of pride (or the danger of excessive novelty) by claiming the presence of the meaning as resident in the creator's work and merely "uncovered" by the recipient. This interpretative process is analogous to the Jesuit *Exercises* in building the individual's identity through response and reflection—again Maravall (1986, 169): "One who contemplates a painting or reads some *Empresas* or follows the lines of a building with one's gaze has to collaborate in finishing the work—or at least one's own experience of that work. In the same way, the human being—who is the singular, individual human being—has to proceed making his or her own self."

A particularly lovely image of the kind of experience that Maravall describes is given by two linked poems by Lelio Guidiccioni, whose writing on music we will consider at some length in the next chapter:

THE STATUE AND ITS VIEWER

As you watch, the stone glides into your heart. Unawares, for his part, the viewer glides wholly into the stone. From stone, the hard race of men draws matter to make it stiff. From there, the stone draws one soul out of many. What wonder that in viewing I become a stone, or that when viewed the stone makes itself soft?

THE SAME MORE BRIEFLY

The visitor is alive, the stone stiff. Through art's mastery, here the stone, there the visitor, it gains life, he grows stiff.[49]

Guidiccioni assigns agency in the second poem to "arte magistra," controlling art—but it is unclear (probably purposefully so) whether that art comes from the sculptor (who is unnamed, even as an anonymous "artist"—the closest Guidiccioni comes is the reference to the "hard race of men" in the first poem) or from the viewer, who is much more present and "agent" in both poems. In the first poem, the subjectivity slides from "you" to "the viewer" to "I." The discourse is between viewers and/ or between various perspectives of the poetic subject—here perhaps Guidiccioni is drawing on the interactive, dialogic *discourse-about* of the community of *virtuosi*. In the second poem, the discourse is between the visitor (*hospes* is also "guest," an interesting resonance) and the stone— but of course only the visitor can have agency, and certainly it could be the viewer's "masterful art" of interpretation and "active receptivity" that gives life to the stone. In any case, all but the viewer and the stone (and the abstract "arte magistra") are absent in the "dialogue" of the second poem, which encapsulates the interpretative power of the *virtuoso* through a further interpretation of the first poem—which is itself an interpretation of the transcendent experience of viewing a statue and "becoming one" with it, in a way analogous to the goals of identification with Christ fostered by Franciscan spiritual teachings and Jesuit exercise practice.

Development of an individual interpretative "voice" was, as we have seen, fully in keeping with the Jesuit tradition—which took it for granted that true individual insight would be entirely compatible with the ultimate truths of hierarchy embodied by the Church of Rome.[50] The process of collecting—and the concomitant discourse by which the *virtuoso* expressed and shared his insights on the transcendent qualities of the items collected—can thus readily be understood as an extension of the "self-training" of the Jesuit *Spiritual Exercises:* the emphasis was not so much on the objects themselves as on the discernment and evolving (growing) spiritual understanding of the *virtuoso*. Ultimately, the early modern *virtuoso* of taste saw it as his role to engage with a work or experience, considering his individual interpretation (and its development through discourse with his peers) a crucial step toward the determination of the fullness of meaning—and, more importantly, toward the articulation of a collective superior unvarnished *(purgato)* divine truth to which the experience or artifact had pointed him, thereby enacting his understanding of *recte sentire*. Projecting an ability to discern the transcendent potential of an artifact was significant in applying the principles of *recte sentire* and the prudence to discern the classical ideal in the process of aural collecting, whether in a specifically sacred context (for example, the multimedia sonic experience of the *Quarantore*, with its flow of music and preaching) or in an ostensibly secular one (such as performances by musicians during "cardinal circuit" events). Through a careful assertion of "active receptivity," guided by the prudence and self-control that marked his status and training, the *virtuoso* of (spiritual) taste could thus assert a deeper understanding and a more effective control over the musical "transaction" than the lower-class listener, and even than the (venal, lower-class, or even female) singer. Such active discernment had the potential to resolve long-standing concerns about the potential dangers that could ensue from the passive sensuality of musical experience, since that experience could safely be understood as masculine because of its inherent proactive control of meaning. This specific concern with the definition of noble masculinity—*virtù*—through "proper listening" is a topic for the next chapter, which will focus on one of the most prominent *virtuosi* of taste of the Borghese and Barberini *famiglie*, Lelio Guidiccioni.

CHAPTER 4

Noble and Manly Understanding

G[ian] L[orenzo]: How, then, should one who desires glory
behave?

    L[elio]: We have said it before: plan to travel on the old
road, but with new *virtù* and creativity. He who does not have
natural talent, and the discipline to study, let him not set himself
to the task. But he who has both those traits, let him come into
the shared forum, and let him give novel demonstration. . . .
One must go by the common way, and show with one's
bearing, with one's work, and with one's mastery how much
one disdains and leaves behind the commonplace.

—Cesare D'Onofrio, "Note Berniniane 1: Un dialogo-recita di Gian
Lorenzo Bernini e Lelio Guidiccioni"

In his role as poet and literary critic, and as artistic and cultural advisor
to the highest-ranking members of the Borghese and Barberini circles,
Lelio Guidiccioni was one of the most prominent and influential *virtuosi* in the early modern Roman curia. He is best known to musicologists as the dedicatee of Pietro Della Valle's "Della musica dell'età nostra" ("On the Music of Our Time"; ca. 1640), arguably the most detailed
contemporary account of seventeenth-century Roman musical culture.
Della Valle's essay has been widely excerpted, cited, and mined for information on early baroque practices. Scholars have not, however, addressed
Guidiccioni's own unpublished essay on music, part of a manuscript miscellany in the Vatican Library. Like Della Valle's better-known counterpart, Guidiccioni's essay discusses both ancient and modern music, and
the perspective of the informed listener rather than that of the composer
or musician. The essay, while central to understanding Guidiccioni's perspective on music as heard, is not his sole pronouncement on the matter: in a wide range of his writings, Guidiccioni is keenly concerned with

the power of sonic imagery and the ability of sound (whether strictly "musical" or not) to be an instrument of transcendence for the properly disposed listener. Furthermore, he is singularly interested in theorizing the place of *virtù,* the essence of noble masculinity, in the sonic-receptive "practice" of music—indeed, in using receptivity to transcendence through sound as a defining trait of a notion of *virtù* that is inextricably linked with Reformed Catholicism. Using Guidiccioni's work as a touchstone, this chapter will delve into the ways in which the emergent discourses of musical connoisseurship examined in the previous two chapters were placed specifically in the service of noble, masculine, and spiritual identity fashioning in early modern Rome.

Through his work on the sixteenth-century Italian nobleman (and warrior-singer) Giulio Cesare Brancaccio, Richard Wistreich (2007, 211ff.) has recently explored what he has termed the "performance of honour" in early modern Italian court culture. The concept of "virtù" (derived from the Latin word for man, *vir,* and used by several prominent Italian authors of the sixteenth century—most notably Machiavelli and Castiglione) was essential to the self-definition of the would-be male courtier.[1] The sixteenth century saw an extended debate over the proper nature of *virtù*—and especially how it was to be gained and demonstrated. Wistreich observes that proponents of the idea that *virtù* was primarily to be found in the supremely manly practice of arms argued that it "consists in the conquest of difficulty" (229) and that it was inherently a "soldierly" trait (235). However, as sixteenth-century court culture shifted its attention from the practice of arms to that of letters (and the models provided by Castiglione and Guazzo contributed strongly to this shift), those who still attempted to advocate for the close connection between *virtù* and the arts of war were compelled to take up "the profession of arms in the form of verbal and written discourse, which depended more and more on the recall and historicizing of past experiences" (229). The performance of noble masculinity—*virtù*—was increasingly tailored to the environment of the court and the noble *famiglia,* and certainly the *virtuosi* of taste whom we have encountered in the previous chapters embodied their *virtù* not through the control of weapons but through the control of knowledge and language. This would be all the more appropriate for a member of the curia in a "sacred court" such as that of the cardinal *famiglie,* for whom being a soldier of God required not physical but rhetorical "battle-readiness."[2]

Specifically to the musical ramifications of "performance of *virtù,*" the "feats of valor" in sound production once associated with the noble way of singing (modo di cantar cavalleresco) become associated with professional musicians at the close of the sixteenth century, leading to the paradoxical application of the term *virtuoso*—once reserved for noble masculine self-fashioning—to working-class musicians, even eunuchs or women. Certainly there was significant debate in the early modern courts—and especially in the noble *famiglie* connected to the curia— about the growing presence within noble and curial spaces of individuals not graced with noble birth, and thus the increasing difficulty of main- taining the kinds of family/class distinctions on which centuries of social order had been predicated.[3] Guazzo himself (1993, 1:126–32) suggested the existence of two categories of "seminobility," one derived by blood and the other by *virtù*; and while full nobility could belong only to those who had both qualities, legitimacy derived by blood could be lost over time if a family began to lose *virtù*. While Guazzo does not explicitly state that blood nobility could be *gained* by actions—that would have been a supremely disruptive claim within what was still a stable blood- related hierarchy—he clearly takes the side of the "nobility of letters" in the arms-versus-letters debate and refers explicitly to their power to trig- ger transcendence: "The honor of those who know good letters is not so great as the dishonor and shame of those who do not know them. . . . [Letters], by raising [man] from the mud and out of the dross of the common people, assist him in climbing to honor, to dignity, and to the contemplation of heavenly and divine matters" (Guazzo 1993, 1:151). Thus, in Guazzo's formulation, the "seminobility" that can be gained by the masculine performance of self—*virtù*—as embodied in the knowl- edge of letters is the more powerful of the two, the more closely tied to the divine and transcendent (and thus by definition the more permanent and perfect). Guazzo's reference to the "common people" strongly implies the ability to rise to superior class status through the nobility of letters. As Amadeo Quondam remarks in commenting on Guazzo's project, "True nobility is reached through constant work on oneself. The *institu- tio* of a gentleman is perennial, is never a given; it requires careful updating, and especially the study of an art as difficult in its fulfillment as it is hidden in its display" (Guazzo 1993, 1:liii). The parallel with the self-*Bildung* achieved through Loyola's exercises is striking. Thus *virtù* was as essen- tial to the self-definition of the nobleman as it was important to constantly cultivate and define in opposition to the "common people." Giulio Man- cini, whom we encountered in previous chapters as a crucial exponent of the perspective of the *virtuoso* of taste on the visual arts, used his role as physician to the Barberini (and thus as a *virtuoso* in the understanding of the physical body and its meanings and messages) to pen a treatise on "dishonor" that argued that the physical deformations and ugliness of the indigent populace were outward demonstrations of their interior spiritual deficiency, as well as their inability to serve the *patria* (unlike the physically able upper classes) (Olson 2005, 95–96). Physical beauty, intellectual understanding, and spiritual elevation were thus simultaneous indices of the legitimacy of the upper classes. In Mancini's formulation (usefully designed to reinscribe the essential social component of the discriminatory work of a *virtuoso* of taste), *virtù* manifested itself not just in superior sensibility and self-regulation but also, and perhaps more importantly, in the individual's aptitude for transcendence.

We can then understand why a problem arose when—while the term *virtuoso* continued to be primarily connected to noblemen and their masculine "performative self-fashioning"—by the early decades of the new century its use as a descriptor for the very different "performative" actions of the professional musician (certainly not noble, and in some cases not even "masculine," or at least problematically so) had gained wide currency in Italian discourse. We will see below that Guidiccioni was very conscious of the dangers of "relinquishing" the notion of musical *virtù* (and the masculine, hierarchical stability that it entailed) to those who did not have the status to deserve such a label. Thus his attempt, as we will soon see, to recast *virtù* as a receptive/interpretative rather than sonically performative act.

Guidiccioni's name has appeared frequently in musicological literature, but almost in every case in citations to Della Valle's essay "On the Music of "Our Time" ("Della musica dell'età nostra"), which was dedicated to Guidiccioni.[4] Historians have generally characterized Guidiccioni as a somewhat grandiloquent poet and apologist for the Barberini, documenting his involvement with the rhetorical support of the glorification of the Church Militant and the parallel apotheosis of the Barberini pope Urban VIII. In retrospect, some scholars of the Catholic Reformation have seen the Barberini effort as "a dying ideology," pointing to the repression of Galileo and other luminaries whose work can now be characterized as progressive as indications of a conservative, almost regressive philosophical retrenchment; see, for example, Newman (1994). However, the rhetorical agenda of the Barberini papacy provided a crucial space for artistic production: many scholars have ably explored the opportunities that this provided for artists, architects, and musicians.[5] Guidiccioni clearly found a comfortable space within that agenda, but his rhetorical career was well established before he came into Barberini service, and his preeminent place in the growing discourse of the *virtuosi of taste* in early modern Rome deserves a closer look.

Born in 1582 in Lucca to a family of the lesser nobility, Lelio Guidiccioni received his early training in the latter years of the century at the Jesuit *collegio* in Rome.[6] His primary teacher was the renowned Jesuit rhetorician and playwright Bernardino Stefonio (1562–1620): Guidiccioni acknowledged Stefonio as a central influence on his thinking and intellectual approach (Lucchesini 1831, 46). Stefonio was one of a number of leading Jesuit authors who built on the power of Loyola's *Exercises* to expand the rhetorical message of the Society.[7] Stefonio and his associates at the Collegio Romano focused on rhetoric as a crucial marker of decorum, of spiritual and social refinement (Battistini 1981, 89). They taught on the basis of a two-stage *imitatio*—first the incorporation of classic models and then their transcendence and integration into the individual student's rhetorical "tool kit." As Fumaroli (1978, 823) observes, "After the apprenticeship [using strict Ciceronian methodology], it was up to the *ingenium* of each individual . . . to find his own expression, combining the 'loci' of Catholic culture that had become innumerable, bending them to forms adapted to the nature of the orator, to the circumstances, to the public." These principles, as well as the underlying notion of finding an individual spiritual path within an acknowledged hierarchy, were clearly formative for the young Guidiccioni.

Initially connected to the powerful Florentine cardinal Sacchetti, by the first decade of the seventeenth century Guidiccioni had gravitated to the cultural circles of Scipione Borghese Caffarelli, whom Pope Paul V had appointed Cardinal Nepote in 1605. Guidiccioni served Cardinal Scipione Borghese in a diplomatic capacity for a number of important events: for example, as his representative at a court funeral in Savoy (1605), at the wedding of Cosimo II Medici in 1608, and again in Florence in 1610 at the birth of Ferdinando the Younger (Criscuolo 1998a, 373). In 1608, Guidiccioni was one of the founding members of the Accademia degli Umoristi. He was also a crucial figure in the establishment of the tradition of *villeggiatura* by Cardinal Scipione Borghese in the first decades of the century, helping to shape the multifaceted experience of transcendent leisure for the cardinal and his guests; we will return to some specific aspects of that cultural work below.[8]

As his career progressed, Guidiccioni continued to gain esteem in the eyes of the leaders of the Roman Church. After the death of Paul V in 1622, he was entrusted with delivering the funeral oration, as well as editing a volume commemorating the pope's funeral celebrations. From this time one can document a strong and lasting connection between Guidiccioni and the sculptor Gian Lorenzo Bernini, who had been commissioned to create the statuary for the papal funerals: Guidiccioni appears to have acted as mentor and "cultural broker" for the younger up-and-coming artist.[9] Guidiccioni was also involved in sponsoring a number of other prominent artists of the time, perhaps most notably Guido Testa, who like Guidiccioni came from Lucca (Cropper 1984, 12–13) and was influenced by the ideals of neoclassicism advocated by Guidiccioni, but also the Gentileschi family, since he appears to have served as one of the witnesses for the wedding of Artemisia Gentileschi and to have granted her a substantial dowry.[10]

By now established as a leading *virtuoso* of taste—art connoisseur, poet, and orator—Guidiccioni was frequently called upon to display his knowledge and to model his *gusto*. For example, when Ferdinando II Medici visited Villa Borghese in 1628, Guidiccioni was asked to guide the grand duke through the "sculptures and paintings of which that villa is full."[11] More broadly, as Ehrlich (2002, 162) observes, throughout his association with Cardinal Scipione Borghese, "Guidiccioni's ceremonial duties included escorting guests of Scipione or dignitaries en route to the pope on the final leg of the journey through Latium to Rome; he may well have guided visitors from Rome to Frascati." Guidiccioni's own art collection was substantial; one of the first guides for Roman tourists, Totti's *Ritratto di Roma* of 1638, mentions it alongside the more famous collections assembled by the cardinal families.

At the death of Scipione Borghese in 1633, Guidiccioni came into the service of Antonio Barberini the Younger, Cardinale Nepote of Pope Urban VIII; from this position he continued to sponsor the career of Bernini and to build his own fame as an orator and poet.[12] Even before this official appointment to Cardinal Antonio, Guidiccioni had long been associating with the extended Barberini *famiglia*, since Scipione Borghese was a close ally of the new pope.[13] Arguably his most noteworthy contribution to the Barberini cultural-spiritual project was the remarkable *Ara maxima Vaticana*, a presentation oration for the 1633 inauguration of Bernini's *baldacchino* over the tomb of St. Peter in the Roman basilica, the opening of which we will examine below.[14] Antonio Barberini acknowledged Guidiccioni's importance with several benefices, most notably a canonry at Santa Maria Maggiore. Even as younger *virtuosi* were gaining standing within the Barberini *famiglia*, Guidiccioni was chosen to deliver the oration at the unveiling Bernini's statue of Urban

VIII on the Capitoline Hill in 1640, an unprecedented occasion of public intersection between the pope and the ruling families of Rome (Nussdorfer 1992, 182 n. 48). In his will—which was witnessed by the cardinals Giulio Sacchetti (who was being groomed as successor to Urban) and Antonio and Francesco Barberini, testifying to his place in the curial hierarchy—Guidiccioni carefully assigned many valuable items to his successors, not the least of which were his own unpublished writings, including the essay on music that we will address shortly.

Much historiography on Guidiccioni has characterized him as conservative, doctrinaire, or pompous. For example, an essay on a "recited dialogue" between Guidiccioni and Bernini (from which the opening epigraph of this chapter is taken) dwells on the putative progressive outlook of the latter to the detriment of the former: "Lelio's lines, prolix and tremendously boring just like all his writing, reveal their author as fixed on positions that are flatly conservative; we find him always ready to 'distinguish' and dispute, inflated with rhetoric and unclear, undistinct ideas" (D'Onofrio 1966, 128). Much has also been made of a contemporary's account of Guidiccioni being struck mute, unable to deploy his vaunted rhetoric, in front of visiting Medici princes, and of that same commentator's suggestion that Guidiccioni was mistaken about the attribution of some of his most prized paintings. This does not, however, take into account the fact that the stories come from a selection of semisatirical writings by an individual who could be characterized as a rival *virtuoso* and who also acknowledged that Guidiccioni's poetry—specifically a panegyric description/praise of a singer, Leonora Baroni—was "so pure, so elegant, so witty, so charming, that I truly can say that I have never seen anything so elegant or polished in that genre."[15] Shortly before his death, Guidiccioni was featured as one of the primary interlocutors in one of the most important "cultural manifestos" of the Barberini papacy—the *Aedes Barberinae* of 1642, a published description and explication of the contents of the new Barberini palace—which Fumaroli (1978, 832) characterizes as "the essence of Rome" in its intersection of classicism and rhetoric.[16] While Guidiccioni was by no means the only *virtuoso* of taste who contributed to the Barberini project, the significance of his contribution to that endeavor remains to be fully appreciated.

Guidiccioni's interest in music has primarily been measured by his ostensible role as foil for Della Valle's advocacy on behalf of modernity. It has been easy enough to take Della Valle at his word in characterizing Guidiccioni's perspective as "conservative"—even though Della Valle himself dwells only on specific aspects of modern music that Guidic-cioni finds problematic, rather than characterizing the latter's perspective as hostile to modern music as a whole. Guidiccioni's specific mention in his will of several prized musical instruments (for example, a harpsichord described as having been called "the joy" by Frescobaldi) has been noted (see, for example, Hammond 1994, 79–80, 299 n. 12). This testamentary mention would appear to vouch for his abiding interest in music, which he may have developed during his association with the active musical life in the *famiglia* of Cardinal Scipione Borghese, as well as through his interactions with the Barberini circles.[17] Indeed, these instruments may have held value as "treasures" because of the memories of sonic experiences that they could evoke. Their value appears to be linked in the will to their connection with specific musicians rather than to their potential to create particularly effective sounds; thus they apparently function symbolically rather than practically—as what Ago (2006, 124) calls "semiophores," raised to a special rank of "messengers of the invisible" by the "sacrifice of [their] utility." But while music was clearly a concern for Guidiccioni, his interest in the effects of sound and in the power of "proper listening" were more broadly framed, and it is to examples of this wider active-listening approach that we will turn before considering Guidiccioni's *discorso* on music at some length.

In her examination of Cardinal Scipione Borghese's use of the pastoral landscape as a social-political rhetorical framework, Tracy Ehrlich describes the role of Guidiccioni in both presenting and modeling the "proper" response to the crucial sonic component of that landscape, and her description bears an extended quote:

> During these banquets [at the Villa Mondragone in Frascati] the court poet Guidiccioni often recited his *in Tusculanam Amoenitatem,* a panegyric that he had composed for Scipione. Guidiccioni's verses resound with the "lowing of cattle and the songs of herdsmen," who extol the bittersweet charms of nymphs. The shepherd Aminta "sits beside burbling brooks." . . . Aminta "tills his fields alone, and cultivates the silent woods." . . . Guidiccioni's words were reinforced by a set of Latin epigrams inscribed on plaques over the tall openings of the portico. The epigrams made permanent what was ephemeral in Guidiccioni's performances. . . . Scipione called upon visitors to participate in the landscape in a novel fashion: the act of viewing was meant to induce pastoral reverie. . . . To view real land, in this case that of the Roman Campagna with its sheep and long-horned cows, as if it were idyllic landscape, requires an act of imagination and mental reconstruction. . . . In order for visitors to the Mondragone to understand this new way of thinking, Guidic-

cioni had to explain it to them. . . . Guidiccioni's soothing words encouraged viewers to embrace a vision of harmony. Surely the fields were less pleasing for the peasants who looked up at the villa from below. (Ehrlich 2005, 160–62)

The "vision of harmony" that Ehrlich describes was also clearly an "audition of harmony," and beyond Guidiccioni's systematic use of sonic imagery cited above we should also note the "recited-out-loud" nature of the panegyric pastoral verse, with its potential to connect both to the long and continuing tradition of *cantar versi* (recitations of poetry sung to simple bass/chordal formulas, many of which—the *ruggiero*, the *romanesca*, and so on—were being expanded and mined for expressive resources in early modern Roman musical circles) and to the perhaps-fading but still present association of Guarini-style pastoral genres with the polyphonic madrigal. While Ehrlich does not mention musical activities as an element of the Borghese "pastoral project," the documented presence of Borghese-household musicians at Mondragone could have provided the opportunity for reinforcement of the pastoral message through sung pastoral themes. Just as important, however, was Guidiccioni's role in establishing the nonhuman elements of the "soundscape"—or better, the sophisticated interpretation of such elements—as essential aspects of the refined pastoral "way of thinking/feeling" (we might justifiably use the term *aesthetics* in a context such as this). Guidiccioni was thus both providing his own sonic commentary on the sonic space of the "real" Roman countryside and giving his listeners the tools to engage in "proper listening" that would make the sounds of that countryside a transcendent soundscape of "pastoral reverie."

Guidiccioni's pastoral concerns at Mondragone were ostensibly secular, though, as Ehrlich observes, Cardinal Scipione was keen to characterize the *villeggiatura* as a specifically Roman endeavor, and thus by extension almost paraspiritual in nature (or at least in potential). Another of his concerns with the expressive power of sound and the listener's responsibility to understand it in its full subtlety, however, was firmly grounded in spiritual matters. If we are to judge by the extent of Guidiccioni's own correspondence and other writing on the subject, this was a topic very close to his own heart. The subject was preaching, and most specifically the preaching of one extraordinary individual, Girolamo Mautini da Narni, general vicar to the Capuchin order and *predicatore generale* to the Holy See. Mautini seems to have played a powerful role in Guidiccioni's thinking about the power of sound and the listener's responsibilities to engage properly (*recte sentire?*) with that power.

Girolamo Mautini da Narni (1563–1632) was a renowned Franciscan orator whose manuscript "method" on how to craft an effective sermon appears to have been widely circulated at the turn of the seventeenth century. Narni is credited with having initiated a "modern style" of preaching (Tiacci 1999, 99) that was quickly adopted by the preachers of his order.

Mautini was first called to the role of *predicatore apostolico*—private preacher to the Holy See and the curia, by invitation of the pope—Pope Paul V Borghese—in 1608–12.[18] Guidiccioni, as a high-ranking member of the *famiglia* of Cardinal Scipione Borghese, heard Mautini preach during this appointment. His admiration for the preacher was probably sparked by that experience, since the first drafts of the "letter" that he wrote in Mautini's praise (on which more below) date from that time. Mautini was again called to preach to the curia in 1621–23, and there is evidence that Guidiccioni heard him again during those years and that the two began a correspondence. By that point Mautini had risen to the highest administrative ranks within the Franciscan order and was able to obtain from Urban VIII (upon his election to the papal see) a new general house for his order—also obtaining the backing of the new pope's brother, Antonio Barberini the Elder, a high-ranking member of the order (Criscuolo 1998b, 299–300). The new house was built quickly adjacent to the Church of the Immaculate Conception, with the first stone laid by the pope himself in 1626 and the completion of the house marked by an apostolic visitation by Urban in 1629, flanked by his Franciscan brother and powerful cardinal-nephews (Antonio Barberini the Younger and Francesco) and many other members of the curia.[19] When Mautini died in 1632, Guidiccioni responded with several commemorative initiatives. First, he appears to have sponsored the production of a copperplate engraving of Narni's portrait, a copy of which he gave as a gift to Cardinal Antonio Barberini (before his official association with that cardinal's *famiglia*, but perhaps as a preparatory gesture for such an affiliation, which took place the following year) with a dedication that played on the dual "impression" of Mautini's sermons on paper (which Antonio Barberini had facilitated) and of Mautini's words in the cardinal's heart (Criscuolo 1998b, 313). Guidiccioni also wrote an epigraph for Mautini's tombstone and prepared for print a final revision of a descriptive "letter" about the power of Mautini's preaching that he had been crafting and revising for the better part of two decades. That letter—

which, as Criscuolo (1998a, 380–81) observes, is really a sort of *discorso*, performative in its rhetorical gestures and possibly designed to be read out loud—abounds with sonic references. This is of course understandable for a statement in praise of an orator, but it nonetheless reveals Guidiccioni's interest in the power of sound and his perceived duty to address and even model the process of listening to that sound.

In other writing mourning Mautini's death, Guidiccioni observed: "A once-fiery tongue is now frozen . . . a heavenly instrument, which ravished souls, enflamed *affetti*, and, preparing [the listener] for grace, opened up glory. . . . It is said that the habit of the Capuchin speaks and resonates; but how much more sonorous it is in this individual, whether living or dead; for it seems to me that, if only he were touched, he should bring forth sound, as if an instrument made [organizato] of heavenly metal."[20] Guidiccioni's terminology is always very carefully chosen, and his use of the verb *toccare* in the last statement goes with the term *organizato* and the metaphorical reference to "metal" in what is arguably an allusion to performance on the organ (and perhaps even the *toccata*, signature genre of Frescobaldi, whose music and performing approach Guidiccioni knew well, as Della Valle himself attests). Crucial, also, is the reference to Mautini's tongue and voice as an "instrument," which Guidiccioni suggests operated its transcendence-triggering power through sonic rapture rather than a reasoned verbal process. Indeed, the wonder of Mautini's body is that it seems apt to produce heavenly sound. Guidiccioni further suggests that in responding to the sonic power of Mautini's voice, the attentive listener was facilitating the flow of divine grace and opening the possibility for mystical union with the divine.

In his "letter" describing Mautini's preaching, which was first drafted around 1611 and was repeatedly revised until Mautini's death in 1632, Guidiccioni likewise dwells at length on the performative and especially sonic aspect of Mautini's spiritual power:[21]

> The sonorousness of his voice has never been heard in others, it is not fully bronze nor fully silver, it shatters the air from afar and disperses opposing opinion, but in such a way that it soothes with thunder and sweetens with lightning. . . . He speaks with pauses as much as with words. Every one of his motions and his glances works effectively. . . . In excited actions he is fearsome, graceful in calm and composed ones. . . . A turn of his eye, a lift of his hood, his gathering or extending his body, with all of which (gravely) he accompanies the *affetti* of his discourse, configure others' spirits as he wishes. If he becomes heated in admonishing, out of the small pulpit comes a tempest as from a military machine. If he sweetens and comforts, there is no song more dear to the ears than his speech. All in all, in his presence, words,

and actions, he is venerable, sublime, and penetrating, and altogether sweet, graceful, and lovely.[22]

When we briefly dwelt on this passage in chapter 1, we considered the terminological similarities between this account and contemporaneous descriptions of extraordinary singers of the "new music"; Guidiccioni employs the same language of *meraviglia* in response to sonic expressive power. But Guidiccioni goes further, in closing his "letter," by specifically considering his role as both recipient and describer of sonic power: "And if Your Highness were here to listen to him, I am certain that, along the same lines, you would not desire anything more. But where the corporeal presence of the first is lacking, often the narrator can fill in, speaking expressly of matters with exquisite grandeur, that is to say with due dignity."[23] Guidiccioni's term *il primo* ("the first") is ambiguous; it could refer to the first-person presence of the (semifictional) recipient of the "letter" or to Mautini himself. What is certain, however, is that Guidiccioni is the "narrator," providing the "exquisite grandeur" and "dignity" necessary to make his own account "fill in" adequately for a direct experience of the sonic power of Narni. Indeed, Guidiccioni refers to his account as "speaking," so that he is still drawing on the image of oral delivery though in fact relying on the written word (but again, this "letter" may well have been designed as a delivered speech, as many of Guidiccioni's literary contributions certainly were). In any case, Guidiccioni claims for his descriptive account the ability to convey the power of Mautini's sounds, specifically because of his ability to summon up a descriptive discourse of "exquisite grandeur" combined with "due dignity"— all of which stems implicitly from his superior receptive understanding, his *recte sentire*.

Guidiccioni reiterates his discursive ability to engage with sound at the very end of the "letter," when he suggests, "Let us concede that Mautino's sermons disappear once they have left his mouth, just as happened to Virgil's verses; but we must likewise concede that, just as Virgil's verses are on paper, thus may Mautino's sermons be in their own way."[24] Guidiccioni's choice of Virgil is not in any way casual: not only does it bring Mautini's preaching into contact with classical antiquity, positing the sermons as "modern Christian classics," it also inserts Guidiccioni's own agency as "interpreter" of both (since Guidiccioni was well known by this point for his translations of and commentaries on Virgilian verse) and as an "ideal listener" who can successfully engage with sounding rhetoric and convey its essential power through his *discourse-about*.[25]

Such a focus on the sonic power of Narni's preaching was still, however, an engagement with human sound as a medium for transcendence. Guidiccioni's next exploration of sonic power, which appears to have come shortly after his completion of the final draft of his tribute to Narni and in close connection with his transition from the service of Cardinal Scipione Gonzaga to that of Cardinal Antonio Barberini the Younger, concerned a sound that required still greater receptive refinement.

In 1633, Guidiccioni published a collection of his Latin poetry, and its keystone was a tribute to the newly completed *baldacchino,* the elaborate bronze covering that Gian Lorenzo Bernini had designed for the high altar of Saint Peter's Cathedral. While the *baldacchino* was certainly a reflection of Barberini grandeur (and indeed became a sort of embodiment of excess for those who later decried the actions and policies of the Barberini), it was also, Guidiccioni argued, a reflection of the power and glory of the True Church. Guidiccioni chose to locate that power in the sonic potential of the structure and in the importance of "hearing" that potential as an earthly embodiment of divine sonic power and glory and as a path to spiritual transcendence. And in this effort, Guidiccioni was aiming at verbal evocation of the spiritual sublime—to be achieved, as Fumaroli (1978, 828) paraphrases Leone Allacci (librarian to the Barberini, writing in 1634), not "through cold, fault-free, scholarly, predictable perfection, but rather through the unexpected qualities of demonic invention, seizing from those qualities the earthly diffraction, the light of *Logos.*" Fumaroli's paraphrase of Allacci addresses Bernini's approach, but Guidiccioni, a close associate of the artist, likewise appears to draw from that notion of the sublime in his "listening guide" to the *baldacchino:*

> Whoever sings of Memnon's image, and of the bronzes touched by the first rays of the dawn that give forth in the East sounds with unvarying music, . . . [let him go forward and halt his steps beneath the center of the dome]. . . . Immediately from the bronze statues of angels he will hear in his shaken heart airy voices and secret utterance, while the rays bestow on the gold a clear sun that enlivens the tawny metal into sounds. And these words he will drink in with a gulp of his stricken breast. So great is the power, so life-filled is the burning image.[26]

The opening gesture is clearly drawing from epic (even explicitly Virgilian) rhetoric, addressing those who would "sing of" the colossus statues of Memnon that famously guarded the temple of Amenhotep, one of which was reputed, during the Roman imperial era, to "sing" with oracular power. Guidiccioni is weaving a complex imagery of singing and song, claiming new and greater Christian-oracular power of the *baldacchino* against the heathen oracle—and note that the term he uses to describe that power is *virtus,* the Latin cognate of the noble-manly *virtù.* The individual who would praise (and listen to) ancient oracles can be instead enraptured by the (manly, noble) sonic power of the Christian message—but only if he is properly disposed and ready to hear that message: "Such sounds with their sweet measures and with fourfold voice, as if addressing the whole world in its four quarters, the images [of the *baldacchino*] utter, sounds unequaled and matched to the mind, that harmony gives. Do you see them at first glance as breathing but not perceive them with your ear as speaking? Do you not see the angels flashing in the shining sun? Indeed, you will receive their warnings deep in your breast—if earthly senses do not dull your mind, and your heart of clay."[27] Those who have the ears to hear will hear—but only those whose mind can transcend earthly concerns, those who know how to "feel/hear correctly" in their inner heart. Guidiccioni posits—indeed, models—a sort of protoaesthetic spiritual synesthesia as the goal of the individual confronting the *baldacchino* and understanding it as providing a path to spiritual understanding and transcendent connection with the divine. His metaphors are overwhelmingly sonic, dealing not only with the power of implicit speech but also with that of the resonating bronze four-columnar-part polyphony of the Bernini monument.

Here, then, we have Guidiccioni applying his neoclassical philosophy (which is articulated in the epigraph to this chapter, in a statement of purpose that is all too helpfully set up by Bernini himself): walking in the rhetorical and expressive paths of antiquity, constructing an individual contribution that is fully compatible with the hierarchies of faith, as any good Jesuit-trained religious would do, he reinterprets and refigures the known in search of its deepest meanings, its transcendent possibilities. And his efforts are manifest in a call for "proper listening" as the central metaphor of the effort to transcendence.

Having explored the sonic concerns inherent in some of Guidiccioni's most important literary endeavors, we can now turn to his essay on music, which is contained in a manuscript miscellany in what appears to be the author's own hand, currently housed in the Vatican Library's Barberini collection. On the flyleaf of the manuscript is Guidiccioni's remark that "in these notebooks are gathered [my] least foul efforts, which should be revised and better corrected, and collected, so that they will not be wasted."[28] Three dates appear on this page: 1619, 1624, and 1635. Several essays follow on a variety of literary, artistic, and spiritual topics; the writing in most of the essays is very legible, and several essays (including the one on music) include marginalia that correct or amplify on the "fair copy." It seems clear from the quality of the manuscript and Guidiccioni's own indication in the continuation of the flyleaf comments that these are essays intended for wider distribution, perhaps for print: "For my remembrance [or: so that I might be remembered]. Those that are in fair copy can pass with a correction. Within the others more light needs to be lit, and sickle and file should be employed."[29] It seems likely that this was one of the manuscripts of his work that Guidiccioni recommended be prepared for publication in his will. Whether these essays were or were not widely circulated in their final form, it is likely that they reflect Guidiccioni's conversations in the Roman intellectual circles in which he had been an active participant (including the Accademia degli Umoristi, of which he was a founding and long-standing member) and that their contents can provide significant insights into the perspectives of the emerging group of *virtuosi* of taste of which Guidiccioni was an important exponent. Given the importance attributed to Della Valle's "Della musica dell'età nostra," a parallel discourse on music written by Della Valle's more highly placed dedicatee deserves our scrutiny.

The essay on music is among the "cleanest" in the collection, but the marginalia are also considerable, and it is tempting to speculate that the revisions might have been occasioned by discussions with Della Valle and other *virtuosi* in the Barberini sphere (and more generally by the development of musical understanding through "aural collecting"), because they tend to expand on specific musical memories or experiences. The essay is dated October 15, 1632, at the end, but it is unclear whether this date refers to the "clean copy" or to the revisions and annotations, which would seem to postdate the "clean copy" since they are in a different ink, though the hand does appear to be the same.[30]

The Appendix provides a full translation of the essay into English, since to my knowledge it has never been discussed or edited since Guidiccioni's day. The discussion that follows dwells on a few aspects of the essay that can provide particular insight into the issues that we have been exploring thus far.

While ostensibly coming to the defense of the elevated nature of the musician's art (the opening gesture is a justification of the term *virtuoso* to describe a musician against an unnamed skeptic), the essay is ultimately a celebration of the listener/recipient as the validator of musical *virtù*. Replete with classical quotations, as any Barberini humanist's writing had to be (drawing especially on Virgil, the focus of Guidiccioni's literary criticism), the essay also provides reinforcement from sacred sources, not only biblical and patristic documents and lives of the saints, but also—subtly interwoven—doctrines and practices of the early modern Church Militant.

Guidiccioni begins by reflecting on the use of the term *virtuoso* to describe a singer, arguing in favor of the legitimacy of the word *virtù* to describe musical excellence. This is not a casual choice of opening strategy: through an extended discussion of the variety of legitimate uses of the word *virtù*, and returning again and again to the spiritual aspect of the term, he gradually appropriates this most humanistic of terms—central to Castiglione's notion of the courtier, and thereafter to the self-definition of the Italian nobility in the sixteenth century. In Guidiccioni's formulation, *virtù* becomes an indicator of spiritual direction; no longer merely the mark of a proper courtier, it is the primary indicator of a champion of the True Church.

"In the broad sense," Guidiccioni argues, "we honor with the name [*virtù*] every art that, nobly undertaken, brings honor and fame to the Artisan." This use of the term *artisan* (especially capitalized) is a clear reference to God the Maker, to whom all the arts bring honor. Quickly, however, Guidiccioni also establishes a hierarchy of arts, placing at the top the "speculative arts," then the intellectual ones, and gradually the more manual (making it clear, for example, that painting and sculpture are more noble because they require less physical exertion than other "artisan" arts—as demonstrated by the older master's being "esteemed more highly and securely" than his younger and more physically able apprentices). The notion of *virtù* in the arts is thus associated most highly with the creativity of the intellect, especially where connected with spiritual contemplation: Guidiccioni posits spiritually informed connoisseurs like himself at the top of the hierarchy of the *virtuosi,* and the rest of his essay is designed to display how his spiritual perspective on music embodies a *virtù* greater than that of the practical musicians he is ostensibly defending.

Early in the essay, Guidiccioni posits music as "numbered among the most noble and liberal arts, perhaps all the more clearly noble than its companions, as the strength of its power is most manifest." Here Guidiccioni begins a customary humanistic disquisition on classical sources that speak to music's power; but this statement itself is important because it dwells on the "nobility" of music. Since the whole essay is written from the perspective of the recipient, the noble effect of music is implicitly a measure of the worthiness and sensibility of the listener. Indeed, a number of allusions in this passage to the appropriateness of specific kinds of music for different classes of individual, though certainly drawn from well-worn passages in Aristotle, appear designed to reinforce the principles of "proper listening" in a way analogous to the passages by Bonini and Uberti examined in the previous chapter.

Not surprisingly, at the end of his extensive and obligatory allusions to Greco-Roman classicism, Guidiccioni guides us back to spiritual teachings, and his message again comes from the listener's perspective: "And the soul, which animates the universe, has its origin in music. Thus the human soul, conscious of having heard music in heaven, delights in earthly melodies, remembering the heavenly ones" (fol. 32). Note that the notions of earthly delight and of remembering are very present, pragmatic allusions to contemporary musical experience; Guidiccioni is drawing on the emergent tradition of auditory connoisseurship to ground his spiritual message.

Guidiccioni continues his tour through classical justifications of music by making the customary visit to Pythagoras and musical proportion, then quickly moves back to the spiritual realm. This section of the essay resembles many discussions of *musica mundana* and *musica universalis* from previous generations, though the metaphors used are arguably subtly more pragmatically and theologically oriented, less rooted in the discourse of music theory. Guidiccioni, after all, was not a musician, and probably would not have relished the complexities of the subject to the degree that Zarlino or Galilei (or even Guidiccioni's fellow Barberini protegé Giovanni Battista Doni) would have.[31] As Guidiccioni dwells on the manifestations of musical proportion in the properly balanced human, his examples are concrete rather than abstract: "The aforesaid could be defended by deducing it from a similar theme; by way of various examples, we call harmony in a beautiful woman the [combination of] beauty, grace, and honesty; in a valiant warrior, vigilance, boldness, and caution; in an orator, authority, persuasion, and fire; in a poet, movement, benefit, and rapture; in a prince, prudence, justice, and magnificence" (fol. 33). Moving up the hierarchy of *virtuosi*, Guidiccioni is reaffirming the majesty of the ecclesiastical court, placing himself (as the poet) closest to his prince—and sowing the seeds for a more direct evocation of rapture in a later part of the essay—but also clarifying the importance of combining contrasting elements to create harmony both within the individual and among the hierarchy. The metaphors here are fully compatible with notions of "concerto" that musicians were exploring in Guidiccioni's day, and of which the author could certainly have been aware—to mention just one, it is likely that Guidiccioni would have been familiar with the reference made by his fellow Barberini *famigliare* Agostino Mascardi, in the description of the first public ceremony celebrating the election of Urban VIII, to the musical performance that embodied the "*concerto* of *virtù* and *affetti*" in the new pope's soul.[32]

Moving away from the abstract concept of harmony, Guidiccioni begins to enumerate the various effects caused by musical sound: "Nature derives such pleasure and delight from sound that it has inserted a wondrous desire for it in poisonous animals, so that even their inanimate poison refuses to exit the human bodies that it has entered if it is not first satisfied with the sound that it desires. . . . And when the air changes from a terrible storm to a pleasing disposition, all the animals, cheering up, show their pleasure with song" (33v–34). Shortly afterwards, he asserts,

> Truly admirable is the force of music. Even though the swaddled child has little faculty of reason, still his cries cannot be soothed and he cannot be settled down to sleep without music. And the shepherd, who is simple, and the farmer, who knows little, and the wanderer, who is tired, and the one in pain, who has no joy, also feel this effect, since their only consolation and relief comes from song. What need is there for me to say here that which everyone knows, what powers warlike sounds of all sorts have on armies fighting at sea or on land. We read that powerful nations entered battle with song and gained in ferocity from the incitement of music. And that Alexander the Great raged, and changed his movements as the sounds varied. I myself know that Alessandro Carlo Farnese claimed about three of his servants, perfect performers on various instruments, that his laughter or weeping was in their hands. I also know that an Englishman greatly condemned by Pope Gregory XIII, having obtained with powerful resources [the opportunity] to present himself to His Holiness to argue his case, kneeling among many of the pope's familiars and bringing out a double lyre [?], sang the *Miserere* so sweetly to the beauty of its sound, that he astonished their spirits and moved them to tenderness, and softened to clemency the heart of the pontiff, which had been turned to harshness? (34–34v)

Here, also, Guidiccioni progresses from classical to religious authority, and from the effects of sound in nature (the singing of birds after a storm) to song's simple influences (the soothing of swaddled babies and of "the shepherd, who is simple, and the farmer, who knows little"—note the analogy with the distinction made by Bonini addressed in the previous chapter) to the effect of music on more noble spirits. Indeed, the final paragraph translated above is the longest marginal addition in the essay: in revising and expanding his *discorso*, Guidiccioni clearly decided that moving beyond the commonplace of the musical concerns of Alexander the Great through the addition of a pragmatic "for instance" of sophisticated reception by his (near-) contemporaries would be important to underline his argument. Thus he brings us up the hierarchy of understanding (and spiritual knowledge) to the musical receptivity of two prominent individuals in post-Tridentine reform: Cardinal Alessandro Farnese, whose "laughter and weeping was in [the] hands" of the instrumentalists who served him, and Gregory XIII, induced to clemency by hearing a Miserere sung to the accompaniment of a string instrument.[33] Again Guidiccioni's examples trace a route from the lower to the higher, and from the most abstract and historically distant to the present: the image of powerful solo singing to chordal self-accompaniment would have resonated very clearly with his contemporaneous readers, since such was the prevailing performance practice, especially for cardinals' private pleasures, spiritual or otherwise.

But Guidiccioni does not leave this connection to chance; emerging from his narrative, he addresses his reader explicitly and brings him into the collective sensibility of the connoisseur class: "Truly there is no well-organized person living among us who has not—by the work of the great *virtuosi*, which nature or art has not been stingy in providing to our time—felt within himself the strength of rapture, movement to pity, and stimulation of the *affetti*" (34). In closing the rhetorical sweep of his marginal addition, Guidiccioni thought it important to clarify the crucial role that the "well-organized" individual has in the proper understanding and appreciation of the power of the musical event. (Recall here also the use of the term *organizato* in the discussion of Narni above.) While the phrase acknowledges the work of the performing *virtuosi*, it does not name any of them (just as the instrumentalists and "Englishman" mentioned in the preceding passage are also unnamed) and instead centers on the experience of the listening *virtuoso*; and it is to that experience—and eventually to its spiritual importance—that Guidiccioni now turns.

As Guidiccioni progresses again from low to high, from the natural to the supernatural, his metaphorical language continues to draw from practical terminology of music making in early modern Rome. He first describes the sound of a river coursing through grass and rocks, using the terminology of the contemporary "new music," then dwells on his experience of the sounds created by the waves on the shores of the Amalfi coast (see Appendix, p. 147). This passage is similar to one in Gratioso Uberti's *Contrasto musico,* which follows:

> In the very beginning music was, according to some, invented by the wa-
> ter ... and it seems to me quite reasonable that men, even in their original
> primitive state, upon enjoying the burbling of the waves, the whispering of
> the winds, the chirping of the birds, happened upon the idea of imitating the
> waves, the birds, the winds with their voice, and hollow wooden and metal
> instruments, and strings, and their breath, at a time when poetry had not yet
> been invented. . . . If someone is tired from travel, if he sits by a stream, he is
> without a doubt comforted by its murmuring; if he rests in a shady place, he
> is certain to be consoled by the chirping of the birds; if he stops in an open
> place, he is sweetened by the whispering of the breeze: and still no words are
> heard, no stories are understood, no fables are comprehended. It is thus not
> a reprehensible thing that, when many sing together, the words (which are
> characteristic of poetry) are not understood precisely; because it suffices to
> hear the melody, which is characteristic of music. . . . He who wishes to hear
> words well should listen to one who is speaking, or reading, because in those
> cases the voice is continuous; but the singer's voice stops and changes, and is
> now high, now low, now fast, now slow. . . . Sweetness in song does not con-
> sist of presenting words and letting them be understood, but in the beauty of
> the voice, in the variety of sound, now low, now high, now slow, now orna-
> mented. (Uberti 1630, 81–83, 85)

However, while Uberti uses the example of "water music" explicitly to disassociate the power of music from the effects of words, Guidiccioni's argument is more subtle: since a listener (by implication a sophisticated one) can perceive the beauty of sound in inanimate objects (and evoke it through his well-trained memory, as Guidiccioni does with the description of the sounds of the Amalfi waves), and since it is clear that the listener's discernment is much more responsible for meaning than the inanimate waves, that superior discernment can then implicitly be understood as similarly responsible for attributing meaning to sounds that are made by other individuals. We might also consider the parallel between this "appropriation" of the idyllic soundscape and Guidiccioni's efforts to posit a transcendent pastoral soundscape at the villa of his Borghese patron, discussed above.

Guidiccioni also uses contemporary musical metaphors to rehearse the well-worn image of "musica humana": "Man, as a small world, [is] a dissonant consonance composed perfectly of soul and body, of intellect, sense, reason, and appetite: in sum, a double *concerto,* well tuned with the lower part subordinated to the upper one; and this music is well tuned when the heavenly *maestro* does not pause and does not withhold his supernatural assistance, but beats [fa la battuta] with the internal movements and infuses the sound and voice of his grace [et infonde il tuono, et la voce della sua gratia]" (38–38v). *Concerto, battuta, tuono, voce, gratia* were all terms that had pragmatic currency in early modern Roman musical circles, both for musicians and for their patrons (the last term, *gratia,* is especially important to Della Valle in his "Della musica . . ."); here Guidiccioni is bringing them as metaphorical aids to the understanding of the relationship between the well-"harmonized" individual and the divine. The harmony of creation is here expressed through the descriptive terms that were the vocabulary of the patrons and connoisseurs of musical experience, rather than the more "technically specialized" (indicative of artisan expertise, and thus socially suspect) terminology of musical and mathematical theory.

As he builds to the climax of his *discorso,* Guidiccioni dwells on the glory of Rome as provider of spiritual marvels through music, explicitly mentioning instrumental music (and metaphors based on that tradition) alongside vocal music (remarking, among other things, that the tenor *viola* is able to "create tenderness and overwhelm beyond compare").[34] Guidiccioni's reference to the tenor voice as most "natural" may be a well-calculated gesture (despite his initial rhetorical statement defending a singer as legitimately *virtuoso*) to implicitly characterize both female and castrato voices as "unnatural." The wordplay on "viola—overwhelm" (*viola—violenta*), which is also presented within a rhetorical oxymoron (literally "creates tenderness / does violence to"—my translation attempts to convey what seems to be a positive use of the term) is likely inserted here to set up the passage on Saint Francis that provides the culmination of the essay, discussed below. The grammatical subject here is the instrument, but the "real" subject-agent (the individual who feels the tenderness and violence/overwhelming) is of course not the inanimate instrument but rather the listener.[35]

Guidiccioni's account of the story of Palestrina as savior of polyphonic music at the Council of Trent puts a somewhat different spin on the priorities of the decision makers:

> And when the Tridentine decrees were already written, that polyphony should be banned in churches because of those who were abusing it, it became clear what force operated in those fathers' spirits through the music sent by that famous man, because of whom Palestrina is famous. When [the music] was played on the same day that the ban was to go into effect, *it ravished their affetti, changed their minds, and modified their wills; so that the sung expressiveness erased the written law* . . . and no more was said of the decree, allowing song to be used forevermore. (39v; emphasis mine)

In this account, the decision to keep polyphony despite the controversies raised by the Council of Trent is portrayed as stemming from the (noble, highly educated, and spiritual) listeners' rapture, rather than from the clarity of the text setting or from Palestrina's technical mastery of uncluttered counterpoint (criteria that eventually became central to musicians' mythology of the Pope Marcellus episode).[36] Guidiccioni thus finds an effective strategy to keep agency in the hands of the spiritually enlightened council members rather than in the craftsmanship of a professional musician. Indeed, the subject of the episode is not Palestrina himself (who is named only tangentially, as a product of his native city) but the music—which is given the miraculous ability to ravish the *affetti* of the Tridentine councillors. While the music ostensibly has independent agency, the ultimate subject is the discretion and sensibility of the councillors—an image of receptivity to transcendence that is analogous to the examples we have encountered in the preceding chapters (and we will momentarily see how Guidiccioni makes that resonance even more explicit in the closing passages of his *discorso*).

The one thing that noble *virtuosi* miss most when traveling to faroff lands, Guidiccioni tells us, is the sound of polyphonic music from the Roman churches. This is understandable, he continues, because the pleasure and transport brought about in the listener by spiritually appropriate music comes from divine providence. It is likely that Guidiccioni is here referring to Della Valle, who famously traveled through the Orient (even taking a Syrian wife) and published extensive memoirs of his travels.[37] The specific mention of organ playing further suggests that this is the passage of the *discorso* most clearly connected with Della Valle, since it resonates with the latter's allusion to Guidiccioni's assessment of Frescobaldi ("[Frescobaldi,] whom Your Excellency has confessed has made you astonished and quite often moved you,") in one of the passages of Della Valle's "Della musica dell'età nostra" that addresses Guidiccioni most directly.[38] Guidiccioni is here again focusing on the "appetite" of noble listeners ("prudent and sensible gentlemen"), which he claims requires sating through spiritually conceived sounds ("organs and church music"). The music and instrument are again disembodied, clearly placing the interpretative agency on the recipient.

Briefly reporting on musical transport in the Old Testament, Guidiccioni then dwells at length on the musical transcendence provided by God to his saints, especially Magdalen and Francis. This account of transcendence, which was briefly quoted in the epigraph for chapter 1, is worthy of an extended quotation:

And when God wants to highly favor one such as Francis, or Magdalen, he sends his musicians to have them hear those pieces [canzoni] that make them lose their senses. O venturesome Magdalen, you who poured at the feet of your Lord that precious oil, and those most precious tears; in order to return to you in this life an infinite gift in exchange, he commands that the ensemble of his singers be given to your senses. It is royal courtesy for an earthly prince to allow those he loves to hear the worth of his musicians. Thus the King of Glory makes a gift of his delights, and I could list many in this regard, but I turn to you, most blessed winged spirit, as you prepare to restore and comfort the languid and lovesick Francis with your song; ah, hold back the *accenti,* no longer play that harmonious instrument, which in being too lively brings him death and in lifting him too high oppresses him. Have mercy in stopping the course of so much mercy. If one more note comes out, it will relieve him of all life breath. If you wound that thin string one more time, you will cut the string of his life; nor can you handle that sweet bow again, for he will remain slain by its arrows. Thus Francis states when the music ends: the sensation of one more sound would render him senseless. This is how much music is prized in heaven: no greater riches are sent from above to those who are most beloved on earth. (40v–41)

Guidiccioni's description of Francis's transcendent musical experience, in its length and passion, greatly exceeds any previous descriptive moment in the essay: it is breathless, evocative, and arguably the climactic moment of the *discorso.*

The image of Francis responding with ecstasy to a violin-playing angel is, of course, exactly the one discussed at some length in chapter 1. Given Guidiccioni's extensive knowledge of both classical and contemporary art, it is almost unimaginable that he would have been unfamiliar with the iconographical tradition that, as we saw in that chapter, appears to have been especially widespread during his formative years. Indeed, he is likely to have been familiar with both of the depictions of the episode that we examined in chapter 1: Guido Reni probably painted his contemplative Francis for Scipione Borghese, in whose *famiglia* he was recorded as living shortly after the presumed date of the work, and the Domenichino fresco for the Merenda chapel was completed at the behest of patrons who moved in the "Tuscan-nation-in-Rome" circles to which Guidiccioni was closely connected at the time of its completion. In any case, Guidiccioni's excursus is the most extended gloss on the image that I have encountered, and its complexity and passion mark it as a keystone of his understanding of the power and worth of music.[39]

As Guidiccioni closes his discussion of music, he reiterates its connection to spiritual fulfillment and understanding. Gone are all the classical references, gone are the remarks about nature and even those about specific musical effects. The two long last sentences of the essay provide a parallel construction praising light and music as inextricable gifts from God:

> Light shines, and likewise shines music; both born at the beginning of the world, with the divine Word, *fiat lux,* which brought about the creation of heavens, and angels—the latter singing glory to God by their office, the former resonating through music by their very nature, according to the above reasoning. And both join together and make glory; both seem to me foreshadowed in the shining birth of the King of Glory, in which shepherds, as it is said, were uplifted by song, and the kings were guided by the star; both symbols of and arguments for heavenly splendor, the more one shows itself as such, the more the other reveals itself as such; and he who understands this, and does not want to be a Tiger, having a well-disposed spirit, can draw enjoyment from it. (41v)

It is entirely likely that this metaphor is purposefully Barberinian, since elsewhere Guidiccioni used metaphors of light to praise his most important patron.[40] With a nod back to his use of Virgil to expand on the subtlety of Orpheus's art (earlier in the essay he had quoted the *Georgics* to describe the musical demigod as "soothing tigers"), Guidiccioni closes with a final return to the importance of the listener, and specifically a well-disposed listener: his final phrase neatly encapsulates the transition from a defense of musical practice to an exaltation of musical experience. To the very last, Guidiccioni focuses on connoisseurship: rather than ending with a reiteration of the putative *virtù* of the performing musician with which he had opened his essay, he has implicitly transferred the subject of musical *virtù* to the "well-disposed" listener.

In the previous chapter we considered how a formulation of the role of the *virtuoso* of taste was central to the emerging project of spiritual and protoaesthetic connoisseurship. Indeed, Guidiccioni's choice of a consideration of the nature of *virtù* as an opening gambit (and as a recurring topic throughout the essay) is not at all casual: by reinforcing the hierarchy of the arts that can be considered *virtuose,* he is reasserting the primacy of the abstract and intellectual arts, embodying the "*virtuoso* listener" as he moves through the evocation of various memories of sound, and through it all emphasizing the spiritual connection and control that sets apart the noble connoisseur.

Despite a temptation to characterize the Barberini political and artistic agenda as conservative and retrospective (and indeed to project a conservative outlook onto Guidiccioni through the Della Valle essay), the viewpoint outlined in Guidiccioni's *discorso* is arguably one of progressive optimism. The question of the advantages of ancient versus modern models, which had occupied musicians and theorists in the previous generation, is here resolved in favor of modern music. Furthermore, the rationale is constructed around the listener's discernment, with the central notion of *virtù* safely assigned to the noble connoisseur rather than to the artisan performer. In keeping with the neoclassicist ideals that he had developed extensively in his other reflections on art and spiritual expression, Guidiccioni is drawing on established models but injecting them with new meaning through the cultivated insight of the individual *virtuoso* of taste—here embodying the kind of approach that he advocated in his dialogue with Bernini, encapsulated in this chapter's epigraph.

We can now understand Guidiccioni's argument with Della Valle not as a rejection of modern music—which Della Valle himself acknowledges Guidiccioni enjoys, at least in some of its components—but as an assertion of parameters of taste that do not match Della Valle's own. And indeed, Della Valle was a strong advocate of another facet of Barberinian musical neoclassicism: the one championed and theorized extensively by Giovanni Battista Doni, which involved extensive and complicated recreations of interval patterns and musical practices based on classical Greek models, and an advocacy of their use for the goal of greater musical expression. Doni (with the encouragement and support of Della Valle) had instruments built to his specifications, developed new theoretical systems and performing techniques, and convinced a small group of musicians (and, it would seem, an even smaller number of listeners) to experiment with his recreations.[41] While Doni maintained his enthusiasm for the approach systematically, Della Valle was more candid about the limited ability of these experiments to move the emotions of their listeners, observing that it was a constant struggle to advocate for the new approach against composers who were concerned about writing music that would not be heard and musicians who did not want to reconfigure their technique to suit the experimental approaches. Guidiccioni may have considered the Doni/Della Valle model pedantic or at least overly concerned with the "mechanics" of musical production; his own focus on the listener—both concerning superior judgment and the goal of musical experience as a path to spiritual transcendence—is evident from these pages. Thus, characterizing Guidiccioni's outlook on music of his day as "conservative" seems to do little justice to the complexity of his approach. Yet it is true that Guidiccioni's project is conservative in one crucial and, as it turns out, long-lasting way: it claims interpretative and ultimately creative primacy for the noble connoisseur, reinforcing the emphasis on a listener's "correct" understanding of the nature of music and paradoxically downplaying the creative impetus exerted by the performers who pioneered the various strands of "new music" in the early seventeenth century. Guidiccioni, after all, mentions no performers by name, while he does refer to several specific listeners. In a sense, he has further abstracted his "gallery" of musical experiences from the examples we considered in chapter 2. The individual creating the sounds is no longer defining the uniqueness and meaning of the musical event; instead, that role is clearly taken on by the listener. And perhaps this is as it should be—at least from the perspective of the elite *virtuoso* of taste—since in Guidiccioni's framework the listener is ultimately the one whose perception of (and response to) the sound event creates that event's meaning.

Guidiccioni's perspective on the primacy of the well-disposed listener for the definition of musical worth and the crucial role of sound in opening a path to transcendence does not seem to have taken significant hold in Italian musical circles beyond midcentury. Such a perspective does, however, resonate strongly with French court culture in the ensuing decades, and in closing we will briefly visit the possible reasons for the similarities between the spiritual, protoaesthetic approaches to "correct listening" and some facets of the development of musical aesthetics in the *grand siècle*.

Envoy

From Gusto *to* Goût

But what can truly distinguish the honest man [honeste homme] from the one who is trivial and vulgar, better than his remarkable education in the knowledge of beautiful things? Discrimination [sçavoir] is a distinction that separates men from men, those who are *galant* from those who are coarse, the able ones from the foolish, and those who have merit from those who have none.

—Michel De Pure, *Idée des spectacles anciens et nouveaux*

In Rome, in contrast to what will take place in Paris, there is no antithesis between classicism and the baroque: a single musical beat coordinates order and inspiration, the transcendence of the beautiful and individual genius.

—Marc Fumaroli, "Cicero Pontifex: La tradition rhétorique du collège romain et les principes inspirateurs du mécénat des Barberini"

Lelio Guidiccioni died on July 7, 1643. As we saw in the previous chapters, it was his wish—explicitly expressed in his will—that some of his most prized possessions (not only items that he had collected in embodying his role as *virtuoso* of taste but also those writings through which he had modeled the *virtuoso* receptivity to transcendence that he had so carefully cultivated) be made more widely available, both for the benefit and glory of the Barberini *famiglia* and for the edification of the spiritually minded *virtuosi* who would follow him.

Unfortunately for Guidiccioni's potential legacy, Urban VIII Barberini died barely a year later, on July 29, 1644. The complex cultural apparatus established by the Barberini quickly unraveled: while every transfer of papal authority was disruptive to the political balance and authority of the cardinal *famiglie* in early modern Rome, the death of Urban VIII brought about what was arguably the most dramatic sequence of events in Catholic religious politics of that century.[1] Crowds gathered to attack statues of the deceased pope, angered by the economic crisis they perceived to have been caused by Urban's expansionist military strategies, and probably abetted by *famiglie* that saw an opening for much-desired "regime change." While the Barberini had built a strong alliance within the network of cardinal *famiglie,* they were outmaneuvered in the subsequent conclave—the longest and arguably most contentious in more than a half century—which resulted in the election of Innocent X Pamphilij, from a family with Spanish backing that had clear suspicion of the Barberini cultural project, perceived as overly Francophile. Accused of corruption and financial mismanagement, former cardinal-nephews Antonio and Francesco Barberini fled Rome—taking shelter under the protection of a former member of their *famiglia,* Cardinal Giulio Mazzarino (a.k.a. Jules Mazarin), regent of France, who had arrived too late at the conclave to convey the French veto against the Pamphilij candidate but could at least provide a safe haven to his patrons.[2]

The arrival of the Barberini in France was arguably just the most striking result of a long-standing and multifaceted political connection between the Florentine nation (both at home and abroad) and the Parisian court. Duke Ferdinando I Medici had been an important intercessor for the conversion of Henri IV in the early 1590s and his successful negotiations with Pope Clement VIII (also from the Florentine nation) and of course had then married his niece Maria to the new king of France. In the early years of the new century, the relationship between the Medici and the Bourbons became more strained (and indeed political turmoil arose between Maria and her son Louis XIII, who was advised by Richelieu), but key families of the Florentine nation in Rome maintained and reinforced their allegiance with the French crown. Most notably, Clement VIII's appointment of the young Maffeo Barberini as papal legate to Paris began a long-standing amity between the up-and-coming future Urban VIII and the leaders of the House of Bourbon (as well as the cardinals Richelieu and later Mazarin, who were immensely influential as their chief advisors). While Urban VIII eventually also cooled to what he perceived as excessive demands—largely in terms of liturgical and church-administrative autonomy—from Louis XIII and Richelieu, perhaps also engaging in an attempt to avoid appearing too anti-Spanish in his policies and outlook, the Barberini cardinal-nephews (and particularly Antonio, eventually appointed as cardinal protector of France) continued to champion the French cause within the Roman curia.[3] Conversely, Mazarin arguably drew his "court model" from his experiences as a *famigliare* of the Barberini in Rome, since there are parallels between the social-political structures established at Paris and Versailles and those in place in the Roman curia of the first decades of the century.[4]

The Jesuit ascendancy that we have examined as central to new ways of thinking about "receptive agency" was also crucial to early modern France under the early Bourbons. Henri IV invited the formation of Jesuit schools in Paris in the early years of the century, and through their publication of spiritual contrafacta of *airs de cour*—crucial to the sonic sensibility of the court of Louis XIII—they provided young French noblemen with a ready resource for understanding musical sensuality as compatible with spiritual understanding.[5]

We saw in the preceding chapters that one of the most important cultural institutions in the Barberini ascendancy was the Accademia degli Umoristi, and that institution was also important to the close connections between the Florentine nation in Rome and the French court. As Alemanno (1995, 101) observes: "Even from a more strictly political point of view, the Accademia degli Umoristi appears to be in sync with the pro-French orientation followed by the papal curia in the first third of the seventeenth century. This tendency is confirmed by the presence of significant individuals such as Flurance de Rivault and Nicolas Fabri de Peiresc, as well as by the visit to the Accademia in 1620 by the ambassadors from France, Venice, and Savoy, in whose presence Girolamo Aleandro recited a poem in praise of King Louis XIII of France." Flurance de Rivault had been welcomed as the first "foreign" member of the Umoristi upon his visit to Rome in 1610. He was a minor nobleman who had traveled to the Levant (like Della Valle) and had authored a number of learned books, including a treatise on "self-embellishment" (*L'art d'embellir*) dedicated to Maria de'Medici (which, incidentally, used the beauty of music as a structuring device; see August 1965, 128). On his return to Paris, Rivault became a professor of mathematics (in 1611) and then, in 1612, the chief instructor and counsellor of state to the young Louis XIII. Rivault proposed to the king (with a parallel appeal to the regent Queen Maria; Yates 1947/1988, 277) the creation of an academy in Paris with a structure and purpose analogous to the

Umoristi and even published "a plan for an academy in France and its introduction at court" (Gravit 1935, 513), though the idea did not come to fruition under the watch of Rivault, who died in 1616. Richelieu resurrected the idea of a "French Academy," but under his watch the Académie Française focused on language (more closely modeling its goals on the Florentine Accademia della Crusca) rather than on the variety of topics envisioned by Rivault. Marin Mersenne was also important to the effort to create French academic discourse in the second quarter of the century, though in his *Harmonie universelle* of 1636 he expressed disappointment with the absence of music in French academic efforts, looking back nostalgically to its pride of place in the Baïf Académie de Poesie et Musique of the previous century (perhaps not coincidentally, another enterprise that flourished at a time of close French-Florentine connections).[6]

While the Académie de France appears not to have taken upon itself the kinds of broad cultural goals that characterized the meetings of the Umoristi, some have argued that the salon culture that was an integral extension of the French court was the "institution" that embraced the *virtuoso* interaction that had been fostered within the Roman curial court, transforming it—especially under the guidance of the influential Madame de Rambouillet, who also had Roman ties—into a more "sociable," mixed-gender model and "exporting" it back to Rome in the following decades.[7] As two final connections between Roman and French academy (and salon) culture, one might point to Giambattista Marino, who prior to his tenure as *principe* of the Umoristi was court poet to Louis XIII from 1615 to 1623 as well as an important presence in the salon of Madame de Rambouillet, his work widely lionized and imitated by poets connected with the Parisian court (Rizza 1973, 71ff.), and to the Palazzo Mancini, where the Umoristi had been founded and had met for the first decades of their existence, and which passed to the ownership of Mazarin (through his family connections by marriage with the Mancini) and eventually to the Academie de France in Rome (Dietrich 2005).

Mazarin's efforts to integrate what he saw as the best (and most powerful) cultural and artistic/creative resources from his native Italy—and more precisely, from the Florentine-Roman circles in which he had received his cultural and spiritual formation—have been documented at length, especially concerning his collecting of visual artworks.[8] Already before the Barberini exile, Mazarin worked to "collect" musicians from Rome as well, particularly in the service of reinforcing international Catholicism; writing to Cardinal Antonio Barberini to express a desire to provide support for the embattled Charles I of England in 1636, he stated, "I want to be . . . the one who brings the Berninis and the Cortonas and the best musicians, so they may erect statues and make pictures and write melodies to celebrate the glory of such a [great] king."[9] When Antonio and Francesco Barberini fled to Paris, several of the prominent musicians who had been associated with the Barberini enterprise quickly followed: Leonora Baroni in 1644—indeed, she was in Paris when Urban VIII died—and Atto Melani and Luigi Rossi later in the decade.[10] Rossi's vocal compositions appear to have been especially influential in French court culture around midcentury (see, for example, Ruffatti 2006, 291), and it is entirely likely that the discourse of musical connoisseurship that had circulated around Rossi's music in the Roman circles of *virtuosi* (see Holzer 1992, with particular reference to Della Valle) would have been another Barberini-inspired influence surrounding that diffusion.[11] Indeed, Ruffatti (2006, 289–99) observes that a 1678 article in the *Mercure Galant* indicates that "the king [Louis XIV] and the public had the greatest esteeem for the Roman vocal style of the first half of the seventeenth century" and that Le Cerf de Vierville, in making his argument in favor of French musical style in 1704 (and in opposition to what he considers the "Italian" style), characterizes Rossi as embodying a "French" sensibility—providing yet another example (alongside Mazzarini/Mazarin and Lulli/Lully) of an Italian (indeed, a Florentine/Roman) playing a central role in the cultural definition of the French *grand siècle*.

There were also paramusical "sympathies" between the French court and the Barberini *famiglia,* both before and after exile: Giovanni Battista Doni, whose perspective on musical "neoclassicism" we briefly examined in the previous chapter, was a Barberini *famigliare* who also had significant contacts with French musicians and theorists (most notably Marin Mersenne, on whom more below). Doni's ideas influenced Nicolas Poussin, who is credited (as eventual "First Painter in Ordinary" to Louis XIII) with bringing a number of Barberini-influenced artistic ideals into French pictorial practice before the Barberini exile and appears to have been very interested in music and its surrounding discourse (see, for example, Hammond 1996, 82–85).

The French nobility's resistance to Mazarin's Italophile cultural policy—primarily under the political movement known as the Fronde—is also well documented. Mazarin was fortunate to maintain the support of his young ward Louis XIV, who was able to quash the Fronde uprising and ultimately clear Mazarin of the charge of "Italian interference" with the French cultural heritage. But certainly the substantial "importation" that

Mazarin engineered of cultural resources from Italy, especially in the wake of the Barberini fall from power, had a lasting impact on the collecting habits and possessions of the French court. For example, Jonathan Brown (1995, 207) examines the importance of Mazarin's successor as minister to Louis XIV, Colbert, in following and expanding his predecessor's mentorship of the collecting habits of the young king. Brown further observes that the central and northern European market became significantly more active through these initiatives, leading to a increasing need for expert "tastemakers" to advise the French nobility. These *connoisseurs*— the term is of course French—included those, such as the Dutch physicist Christian Huygens, who first explicitly theorized about absoluteness in beauty coupled with "authenticity" in attribution (208)—and did so without reference to the moral message of the subject or the status of the beautiful as manifestation of the divine.

One of the individuals who most dramatically shaped the young Huygens's perspective on music was Marin Mersenne, whose influence on the complexities of French discourse on music in the *grand siècle* is of course significant to a degree that can only be adumbrated in a brief closing chapter such as this. Mersenne's early Jesuit training places him in the same spiritual-intellectual frame as the Roman *virtuosi* whose ideas we have explored in previous chapters, and indeed his interest both in spiritual self-discipline (with his earliest work being a set of "spiritual exercises" of sorts) and in the power of transcendence through auditory experience (by means of spiritual-rhetorical expression in general, whether preaching or music—and he specifically associated the two in a letter to Huygens) reflects several of the concerns of his Roman contemporaries, with whom he had extensive correspondence.[12] With the Roman *virtuosi* Mersenne shared a suspicion about musicians' ability to judge effectively the quality of their art, suggesting in the *Harmonie universelle* that individual musicians had too limited a set of preferences or approaches to be able to understand the perfection of melody, arriving at effective melodies "haphazardly, by chance, as they themselves confess."[13]

While Mersenne and other early French intellectuals from the generations closest to the Tridentine reforms (for instance Montaigne, and later Sarasin and La Mothe de Vayer) built their theories of sensation and enjoyment from assumptions of correspondence between beauty and the understanding of divine universality, as discourses concerning an "epicurean ear" became more systematic in midcentury France a transition becomes evident from a spiritually framed conception of pleasure to what Manuel Couvreur (2006, 84) terms "worldly epicurianism" (épicurisme mondain) in the writings of a younger generation. Michel de Saint-Evremond, writing around 1647, focuses on "delicate" individuals without whom "*galanterie* would be unknown, music would be rude, meals improper and crass" (quoted in Couvreur 2006, 85.) Descriptions of such individuals' qualities and actions are analogous to the ideals of self-control and "receptive agency" that earlier authors connect to spiritual practice, but the transcendent dimension of enjoyment now reflects back on class identity and individual distinction, no longer underpinned by religious engagement. We are well on the way to self-sufficient theories of taste both reinforced and gently mocked by Molière in his *Bourgeois gentilhomme* a quarter century later.

The model of courtly behavior that had developed under Henri IV and Louis XIII in the first half of the seventeenth century drew very explicitly—both in direct translation and in paraphrased reinterpretation—on the seminal Italian courtly texts (Castiglione, Guazzo, Della Casa) of the late sixteenth century (see, for example, Lorenzetti 1996). However, the centralized nature of the French court of the *grand siècle* allowed for a substantially more systematic implementation of courtly behavior and expectations than was possible (or perhaps even desirable) among the more fragmented and competing courtly *famiglie* on the Italian peninsula. The relevance of this phenomenon to musical "tastemaking" in the later seventeenth century has most recently been explored by Don Fader (2000; 2003), who observes,

> The idea that 17th-century French concepts of *politesse* are intimately connected to taste and ultimately to criticism has been well established in literary studies for some time. One of the main foci of interest in this regard has been the concept of *honnêteté*, a code of *politesse* held by "les honnêtes gens," a heterogeneous group only vaguely synonymous with "the court" or "the aristocracy," for it included courtiers, members of the *noblesse de la robe* and *noblesse d'épée*, as well as worthy commoners. Often referred to simply as "le monde" or "les mondains," *les honnêtes gens* figured in court life from the time of Louis XIII and in the salon culture of such influential *ruelles* as the Hôtel de Rambouillet and the gatherings around Madeleine de Scudéry. At their best, *les honnêtes gens* embodied a flawless grace and pleasing manner that in turn required a perfect but completely invisible self-control. This self-selecting society, whose aim was mutual recreation of its members through conversation, gave rise to a quasi-aesthetic set of values often summed up as "l'art de plaire" (the art of pleasing). (Fader 2003, 6–7)

While "worthy commoners" could be part of the *honnêtes gens,* suspicion of "professionality" was strong, and this manifested itself with respect to music in two ways. First of all, speaking of music using "technical" terms was considered off limits; again quoting Fader (2003, 14), "When an *homme du monde* (a member of polite society) speaks of the arts, he should do so in the language of *honnêteté* rather than in technical jargon which flaunts his knowledge in the manner of a (lower class) artisan, and does not please." This perspective is absolutely analogous to the self-conscious avoidance of technical language in the earlier Italian *discorsi* on music that we have encountered in the preceding chapters.[14]

However, an important difference between the aesthetics of *honnêteté* and the concerns of Jesuit-inspired and spiritually grounded authors—both Italian and French—of the earlier seventeenth century lies in the purpose of the discourse: pleasing is an end in itself rather than a means to persuading. Indeed, no better than the artisan was the pedant, whose "emphasis on argument (i.e. oppositional exchange) made him unwelcome in *mondain* society which stressed the pleasing, rather than the convincing, of others" (Fader 2000, 16). As Fader (2003, 16) continues, "*Mondain* judgment does not proceed from study or vast knowledge of the classics as it does for an academician, but rather from 'bon sens,' common sense or natural good judgment." While the *mondain* notion of "bon sens" is similar to the notion of *gusto* that we have explored above, and while it likewise enacts and reinforces the social status of the individual who manifests it on the basis of long-standing experience, the emphasis is now entirely on comportment rather on an outside ideal of knowledge, and on dialogue as a social phenomenon rather than as a site for display and negotiation of spiritual understanding.

The second manifestation of "professionality" that was rejected by the proponents of *honnêteté* was related to the extreme display of musical ability—what we might today term "virtuosity." Again Fader (2003, 8): "In the late 17th century, the more harmonically complex and virtuosic Italian sonatas and cantatas described as invading Paris were thus (initially, at least) regarded with suspicion. This style's perceived flaunting of compositional 'learning' and virtuosity grated against basic standards of *politesse*, which emphasized the concealment of effort, knowledge, and 'artifice' behind a pleasing and 'natural' courtly facade." Through this institutionalized suspicion of virtuosity, French *mondains* provided a response that would have pleased Guidiccioni in some ways, since they rejected the sonic power of the vocal professional, establishing their cultivated and elevated taste as the determinant of quality and "true meaning." On the other hand, the *mondains* refused the noble spiritual masculinity

that Guidiccioni wanted to posit as ideal (*virtù,* as opposed to virtuosity)—
their *honnêteté,* shaped as it was by mixed-gender secular sociability, provided a very different ideal of engagement with sound, one that preferred
subtle gesture to transcendent transport. After all, the central role of the
lute and theorbo and eventually on the *style luthé* on the harpsichord) at
the French court relied on their nature as "instruments of rest destined
for serious and tranquil pleasures, whose languishing harmony is enemy
of all action, and only demands sedentary listeners."[15] Careful listening
was important to the *honnête homme,* but it had to happen in stillness
and had to avoid disrupting the listener's balance, whether internal or
external.[16] The powerful, drastic disruption into transcendence that provided the climax of Guidiccioni's *discorso* on musical *virtù* was here
rejected and replaced by a different and more gnostic notion of control,
one that established a greater distance between the listener and the "musical object" to be aurally contemplated.

As the century progressed, it was the French who took it upon themselves to theorize and systematize the notion of the *virtuoso* of taste—
beginning with parameters that had arguably been picked up by French
visitors to Rome who became acquainted with its culture in the early
seventeenth century (the reader will recognize in Fader's summaries above
a number of the themes that we have encountered in the preceding chapters).[17] However, the cultural context in Paris was significantly different
than in Rome: the most important feature was the lack of the religious
imperative in the northern capital. To be sure, Paris was a Catholic city
(though the agreement reached by Henri IV with the papacy on his conversion allowed significant flexibility in the relationship between Galli-
can practice and papal authority, and Louis XIV was to take full advan-
tage of that flexibility in establishing his model of absolutism). However,
the French nobility was not a clerical nobility: it did not draw its identity from a spiritual mission. Thus, if a *virtuoso* of taste in Rome chose
(or was compelled) to draw his images of transcendence from spiritual
models, in compliance (willing or not) with the Jesuit mandate for indi-
vidualism through hierarchical obedience to the church, his *mondain*
counterpart in Paris (and later Versailles) had no such incentive or obligation. Transcendence could instead be understood as an independent
goal, reflecting on personal status and *sensibilité,* and on human interaction rather than connection with the divine. However, the language of
self-mastery and of the controlled expression and reception of emotions
that characterizes the ideals of *recte sentire* in the Italian spiritual elite

has direct parallels with—and may well be a source for—the discourse of *grand goût* in mid- to late seventeenth-century France.[18]

Under Louis XIV, classicist French writing—the beginnings of what may be described as "aesthetic theory"—claimed that "Rome was no longer in Rome," building on the Roman neoclassicism of the second quarter of the century but systematizing it within a temporal framework. French writers claimed the classicism of empire away from those (such as Guidiccioni) who had postulated a classicism of Roman religion.[19] Furthermore, Fader (2000, 9) observes that the *mondains* of the French court likewise theorized a "classicism" of sociability, positing "that the natural moderation and good judgment of *les honnêtes gens* made them the ideal audience whom Aristotle had assigned the role as arbiters of 'the natural' in the arts." The creation of a discourse to codify this righteous role of cultural arbiter would occupy the *honnêtes gens* and their associates in central and northern Europe for the coming century.[20] For example, Matthew Riley (2004, 10ff.) traces the gradual "secularization" of transcendent attention from Descartes through Malebranche to German theorists of Enlightenment aesthetics (from Leibniz to Wolff to Baumgarten, and eventually to Forkel and Koch in the mid–eighteenth century and beyond), whereby self-discipline and focus are ultimately subordinated to the pleasure and enjoyment that should be the transcendent goal of the arts (perhaps music foremost among them).

Indeed, when early eighteenth-century visitors to Rome describe sacred artworks, their descriptions address "aesthetic" considerations of color and form, pronouncing on the "masterwork" status of works and discussing key characters of attribution, in a language designed to indicate adherence to social understandings of "mutual pleasure"—while descriptions from even half a century earlier focus on the content and spiritual message of the work, its functionality to the goal of sacred transport.[21] Abstract artistic "transcendence" is here beginning to supplant concrete spiritual transcendence as European sensibilities move into the rejection of religious thought—or at least its reappropriation into more diffuse Deistic models—that characterizes the northern European Enlightenment.

With respect to musical patronage, Margaret Murata (1990, 277–78) has postulated an important shift in models of Roman "collecting" in the last decades of the seventeenth century: "In 1690, I propose, for a non-musician, scores collected as objects served as a kind of surrogate for live-in musicians (*musici di casa*). . . . Collecting scores was a relatively inexpensive and passive form of having music, or showing interest in a fashionable but expensive occupation of current culture. . . . As both singers and the image of singers were de-cameralized, proprietary interest in music materialized in the library." Murata's insight is crucial not only in economic terms but because it underlines a broader shift in "collecting practice": by focusing on collecting musical scores as paper traces of musical events—and indeed as "works" associated as much with compositional as with performing practice, since Murata also demonstrates the significantly greater attention to compositional attribution in the cantata manuscripts of the later seventeenth century—the Roman elites no longer relied on "aural collecting" and its dialogic display by the *virtuoso* of taste. The term *virtuoso* had now been effectively transferred to the performing musician, and the responsibility for musical meaning creation or agency had been shifted to the music professional (with the controversies now resting on performers' "excesses" with respect to the written score). French practices of sociability had also proven influential on the Roman court of the last quarter of the *Seicento,* and new perspectives on neoclassicism were emerging under the patronage of Christina of Sweden and the Arcadian movement. Much of the Barberini cultural project had been left behind, arguably present in Rome by the end of the century only through its (at least partly secularized) French reflections.[22]

It is not possible to demonstrate a direct and self-conscious line of influence from the theorists of the early Italian *Seicento* (for example, Guidiccioni), who posited spiritual transcendence through "proper receptivity" to beauty as divine manifestation, to the theorists of aesthetics of the French Enlightenment a century later, whose systematic concern with artistic transcendence was framed in secular—or at least, nonclerical spiritual—terms and relied on the ultimate independence of the artwork from a functional frame.[23] Indeed, the extensive observations on music by Descartes and Mersenne were doubtless crucial resources for mid- and late seventeenth-century French authors who sought to build systematic criteria for understanding the perception of beauty in music, and it is difficult to determine how independent these authors' conclusions were from discussions of similar issues that were contemporaneously of concern in Italian (and especially Roman) circles.[24] Still, the analogies between the discourses of transcendence from these two disparate cultural contexts are in keeping with the systematic contacts that took place between the Florentine-Roman cultural sphere and the French court during the second quarter of the century.[25]

. . .

Guidiccioni's descriptions of musically triggered transcendence lie at an intersection of Small's nuanced concept of various modes of "musicking" and Abbate's proposed distinction between a "drastic" and a "gnostic" mode of engagement with music. The spiritually informed listening practice (thus the "musicking") that we can glean from the writings of Guidiccioni and other early modern Italian "active listeners" is actively unconcerned with perception of musical detail, with the kind of evaluation of musical specifics that can be gained only through critical distance. Rather, it postulates an attention to the processes of response to sound and its ability to create immediate connection to the interlocking concepts of the divine and the beautiful. This kind of "musicking" fits Abbate's "drastic" mode quite well. While the drastic immediacy of the experience involves a loss of selfhood and thus of control, such a relinquishing of control to the divine is less problematic than a relinquishing of control to a lower-class individual—indeed, it is a marker of spiritual competence and standing within the religious hierarchy. Since this immediacy is framed as functional, integrated into religious fruition, it cannot fully survive the transition into a *mondain* discourse of individual (though socially marked) taste. Thus, while the appeals to the power of drastic engagement (and to the concept of music as transcendent and fully understandable only by those who have a proper orientation toward it) continue to shape the emergent discourse of musical aesthetics in the later seventeenth century, the processes whereby individual judgment may be determined and shaped become increasingly more gnostic, more concerned with identifying specific sonic antecedents for the listener's response. Another "gnostic" aspect connects to the increasingly socially shared nature of the idealized musical experience: while for the Roman *virtuosi* of taste of the earlier seventeenth century the definition of social status was framed within an ideal of spiritual direction (with the connection to the divine at the top of the hierarchical pyramid), for the later seventeenth-century French and North European *mondains* social status was contained within a secular frame. Thus, returning to Szendy's idea (2008, 142) of an "irrepressible desire to listen to listening," we might suggest that while for Guidiccioni it is most crucial that God be taking note of one's listening practices, in the later systematic development of listening aesthetics it is the social action of "listening to listening" among worldly elites that creates the discursive power of "listening as musicking."

Our continuing exploration of the "normalization" of musical listening as a path to aesthetic transport could well benefit from further consideration of how a seventeenth-century model of listening as spiritual practice may have provided a framework for the "sacralization" of musical experience in the centuries to come, even as the focus shifted from a drastic union with the uncanny divine to a gnostic attention to human perception.

Lelio Guidiccioni, "Della Musica"

Transcription and Translation

from Rvat Barb. Lat. 3879

Editorial notes: the transcription is diplomatic; the original text (which appears to be a clean copy) is in roman type, later corrections and/or added marginalia are in *italics,* and words that were canceled in the later corrections but are still legible are marked in ~~strikethrough~~ type. Words that are unclear in the original are marked in {curly brackets}. Editorial comments, including folio numbers, are in [square brackets]. All translations are mine (including the secondary sources cited by Guidiccioni) unless otherwise indicated. Individual folia in the original are separated to facilitate comparison.

[fol. 1] In questi quaderni sono raccolte le fatiche meno scontie, le quali bisogna rivedersi, et meglio correggere, et ponere insieme, per non haverle buttate.

In these notebooks are gathered [my] least foul efforts, which should be revised and better corrected, and collected, so that they will not be wasted.

[three dates: 1619, 1624, 1635]. Per mio ricordo. Quelle, che sono ridotte in netto, con una correttione potranno passare. Nell'altre s'ha da accender piu lume; et usar falce, et lima.

For my remembrance. Those that are in fair copy can pass with a correction. Within the others more light needs to be lit; and sickle and file should be employed.

[fol. 29] Troppo austero, et ristretto a'rigorosi termini filosofici, fu chi {riportò} poc'anzi, la lode data ad un {ecc.mo cantante}, con titolo di

Too austere, and limited to rigorous philosophical terminology, was the one who objected a little while ago to the praise given to an excellent singer

virtuoso. Noi, per non ci lasciar distogliere dal proposito, con cui in quella occasione fu cominciata a lodar la musica, diciamo che NIUNA cosa è tra noi più bella, che la Virtù, la quale per tanto, ovunque si trovi, genera Amore, insin dove l'odio regna. S'ama un brutto, et difettoso, et mostruosamente disconcio, per la bellezza della Virtù. I grandi s'inchinano alle virtuose conditioni de' Vili, e'l capital nemico è forzato amare, et ammirare la virtù eminente nell'avversario. Anzi per essere la Virtù d'assai più bella, et più potente, che la bellezza, le compartisce il suo essere, et le usurpa l'operatione, principalmente l'attrarre, et il necessitare ad amare. Intanto di lei più bella, che tra lor due son di mezzo non pochi gradi, et oggetti del nostro amore, sottoposti à quel primo; et supremo della Virtù, da cui venendo à basso, se ne discendono molti prima, che si giunga all'infino della ~~corporea~~ *muliebre* bellezza; come salendosi, segue à punto il contrario. Dunque sotto la Virtù viene amata la gratia, cosa spiritale, et sublime; di noi quanto meno si sà la definitione più s'intende la forza. Et essa con l'aria, et con i movimenti suoi; donde traspare il raggio dell'Anima ben composta, rapisce altrui con modo assai superiore à quello della beltà. A lei suc-

[fol. 29v] cede il gentil costume, spiraglio manifesto dell'animo alla Virtù rivolto. Segue la maestà de i sembianti, et delle maniere, il vivace spirito, il parlar saggio, l'accorto giudicio, il tratto cortese, il portamento leggiadro, l'honesta giocondità, la dolce mansuetudine; cose tutte di tal momento, che si ritrover-

by using the title of *virtuoso*. In order not to let ourselves be distracted from the purpose for which on that occasion we had begun to praise music, let us say that there is no more beautiful thing among us than *virtù*, which, wherever it may be found, generates love, even where hatred reigns. One can love an ugly man, with defects, and monstrously dirty, because of the beauty of his *virtù*.[1] Great men bend down to the *virtù* of lowly men, and the harshest enemy is forced to love and admire the eminent *virtù* in his adversary. This because *virtù* is much more beautiful and powerful than beauty itself, and it indeed usurps beauty's own influence—principally, to attract, and to compel to love. [*Virtù*] is even more beautiful [than beauty] because there are several degrees and objects of our love between the two, all of them below the supreme place of *virtù*, coming down from which one goes through several [degrees] before arriving at the lowliness of female beauty; and rising in the reverse order, likewise. Thus below *virtù* we love grace, a thing spiritlike and sublime; the less we can define it, the more we feel its power.[2] [Grace] with its way [aria] and its movements, from which the ray of a well-shaped and settled soul can be perceived, ravishes in a way that is highly superior to that of beauty.

Below [grace] follows gentle demeanor, manifest outlet of the soul directed to *virtù*. Below that follows majesty of appearance and of manner, a lively spirit, wise speech, careful judgment, courteous behavior, a graceful manner, honest cheerfulness, sweet calmness—all things of such importance that one will find them

anno nelle *moderne* Scuole, e
{*modeste*} *carte del* {*prodigioso*}
Petrarca, più esaminate, e dibattute,
che la pura bellezza. Di cui son tanto
più degne, quanto il loro amore è più
nobile, più humano, et più lunge dal
risco d'incorrere nel ferino. Adunque
non contenendosi la beltà nel primo
grado delle cose belle, et sopra lei per
tanti altri sormontandosi alla Virtù,
idea del perfetto, regina dell'Universo,
vita dell'anima, et anima della gloria,
apparisce quanto ella sovrasti al bello
si variamente sparso nelle creature.
Ma doppo haver detto di lei queste
cose universalmente et in genere;
inoltre si amplia questa generalità col
ridurla, et applicarla ad un altra
generalità; Benche qui non si piglia
solo per virtù, la morale, la specula-
tiva, e l'heroica, ma largamente
s'honora di questo nome ogni

more extensively examined and
debated in modern schools, and in the
modest writings of the prodigious
Petrarch, than pure beauty is. They are
more worthy of this, since love of
them is more noble, more human, and
further from the risk of turning
toward a feral sentiment [than is love
of beauty]. Thus since beauty is not
contained in the first degree of
beautiful things, and since *virtù* can be
placed so far above it and above other
things—as it is the idea of the perfect,
the queen of the universe, the life of
the soul, the soul of glory—it may be
seen how much [*virtù*] triumphs over
beauty, which is so scattered among
creation. But having said these things
about [*virtù*] generally and universally,
we might amplify this generalization
by reducing it and applying it to
another generalization. For here I do
not take *virtù* to mean only the moral,
speculative, and heroic kind; in a
broad sense we honor with this name
every

[fol. 30] arte, che nobilmente
esercitata rende honore, et chiarezza
all'Artefice; ogni habito, dico,
lodevolmente drizzato ad abbellire, et
ornare il mondo, che si nomina
dall'ornato ò consista detto habito
nelle operationi dell'intelletto, come
avviene dello speculare, o
l'essercitarlo s'appoggi all'uso degli
instrumenti corporei, come le facoltà
ratiocinative, principalmente
Eloquenza, e Poetica, ò discenda alla
prattica dell'attioni virtuose, come le
cardinali, et simiglianti virtù; ò sia
habito attivo con retta ragione, che
non dependa dall'opera delle mani,
come son l'Arti più nobili, dette
liberali; ò finalmente sia bisognoso
dell'uso manuale, circonscritto da
regole non fallaci, à nobiltà, et

art that, nobly undertaken, brings
honor and fame to the Artisan; every
habit, I say, directed in a praiseworthy way to embellish and decorate
the world, whether the ornament
derives from (or the habit consists of)
intellectual work, such as the
speculative, or its exercise relies on
the use of bodily faculties, such as the
faculties of reason, principally
eloquence and poetics; or [whether it]
comes down to the practice of acts of
virtù, such as the cardinal and similar
virtues; or active habit with true
reason, which does not depend on the
work of the hands, as in the case of
the more noble liberal arts; or finally
[whether it] needs manual labor,
governed by true laws, for the
nobility and the enlargement of the

propagatione del publico bene. Io non sono per ragionar di quest'ultime, trà le quali nel vero, non sò, s'io m'inducessi a ripor la Pittura, e Scoltura (che dell'Architettura è certo, che non vi hà luogo), parendomi esse altrettanto conformi alle liberali, quanto diverse dalle Mechaniche. Poichè, se nell'arte Mechanica si richiede il vigore, et l'opera della mano, nelle due,

[fol. 30v] che son dette, è manifesta la diversità, in guisa, che più tosto invecchiando, et indebolendo l'artefice, si perfettiona l'artificio, et il magisterio s'avanza. Et se per altro l'ingegno del vecchio maestro non perde, esse raffinano, et ne viene egli stimato migliore, et più sicuro, che i giovani, a lui molto superiori di forze. Mà lasciando queste, tra l'Arti nobilissime, et liberali è numerata la Musica, forse tanto palesemente più nobile delle sue Compagne, quanto è più manifesta la forza del suo potere. Et qui noi per honorarla con la supposta latitudine, la chiamaremo Virtù, come à punto un gran Musico vulgarmente si chiama un gran Virtuoso. Aristotile [in margin: Bol. Lib. 8 e.5. (?)], ricercando se la musica è nel numero delle cose gioconde, mà necessarie alla vita, come il sonno, et il cibo, ò delle honeste, et virtuose, come quelle, che instituiscono il costume, ò delle utile per l'attiva, et che conducono alla prudenza; et, per dire co'i suoi termini, se pertiene à solazzo, à disciplina, od à misura d'attione, conclude, che

[fol. 31] abbraccia tutt'e tre le ragioni; et aggiunge, che contiene in se le due parti, onde consiste la felicità, che sono l'honesto, e 'l

public good. I will not discuss these last [manual arts], among which I am not sure whether I would place painting and sculpture (certainly architecture does not belong among these), because they seem to me as similar to the liberal arts as they are different from the mechanical. Because if in the mechanical arts one requires force and manual labor, the two

arts just mentioned [i.e., painting and sculpture] are different in that the older and more feeble the artisan becomes, the more his artistry and mastery improves. And if the old master's ingenuity does not otherwise fail, [his art] becomes more refined, and he is esteemed more highly and securely than young men who are stronger than he is. But leaving aside these, Music is numbered among the most noble and liberal arts, perhaps all the more clearly noble than its companions, as the strength of its power is most manifest. And here, in order to honor it with the aforesaid latitude, we will call it *virtù*, just as a great performing musician is in common parlance called a great *virtuoso*. Aristotle, reasoning whether music is to be numbered among the pleasant things necessary to life, such as sleep and food; or among the honest and *virtù*-bearing ones, such as those that teach customs; or among the actively useful ones, which bring one to prudence—to use his terms, whether [music] pertains to solace, discipline, or action— concludes that

it embraces all three reasons; and he adds that it contains within itself the two parts of happiness, that is to say the honest and the pleasurable; that it

voluttuoso. Che piace a tutte l'età, et à tutti i costumi, et che, secondo Museo, il canto è dolcissima cosa a i mortali. Che per darne giuditio, non è necessario impararla, con l'esempio de' i Laconi, che senza apprenderla ottimamente la giudicavano. Che conferisce alla quiete, desiderato fine delle fatiche; che è rapto dell'anima, il quale rapto forma i costumi. Che insegna rallegrarsi con rettitudine, amare, et odiare con buona elettione, compiacersi di mansueti costumi, et d'opre laudevoli che sono in lei rassomigliate, la vera natura dell'ira, della mansuetudine, della fortezza, della temperanza, et de' i lor contrarij, et che mutando noi l'animo co'l sentir queste somiglianze, siamo tanto maggiormente gl'istessi verso le rassomigliate verità, come chi si rallegra in mirar l'effigie, l'istesso farà nell'effigiato. Prova dapoi, che nell'armonie sono l'imitationi dei costumi, onde si veggono i movimenti. Perche la Lidia mista fà piangere, la Do-

[fol. 31v] rica compone gli affetti, et è costante, e virile; la frigia rapisce l'animo, et l'infiamma alla guerra, et in un certo modo la pone fuori di sè. L'eolia tranquilla i moti; l'ionica è florida, et dilettevole. Parimente i ritmi, overo numeri, altri contengono gravi costumi, altri concitati, alcuni rendono più violento, altri più liberale. Comanda dunque, ch'ella s'insegni alli giovani, non però lasciando di consolare chi non l'impara; con l'esempio di Giove, il quale non suona la cetera. Purche non vi sia solo quel senso di gustare la musica in commune che si nota in

is pleasant for all ages and all customs, and that, according to Museo, song is a very sweet thing to mortals. [Aristotle further suggests] that in order to judge it, it is not necessary to learn it, giving the example of the Lacoons, who could judge it excellently without learning it; that it brings quiet, a desired end of labor; that it is a rapture for the soul, and this shapes custom. [He says] that it teaches [one] to be joyful with rectitude, to love and hate with good judgment, to delight in calm habits, and in praiseworthy things that are portrayed in it, [such as] the true nature of rage, gentleness, strength, temperance, and their opposites; and that as we change our souls by hearing these semblances, we are likewise inclined toward the represented truths, just as one who rejoices in viewing a portrait will do the same [when viewing] the person represented. [Aristotle] then proves that in [different] harmonies there are the imitations of the tendencies [of the people] from which they come. Hence the mixed Lydian [mode] makes one weep; the Dorian

composes emotion and is constant and virile; the Phrygian enraptures the soul and inflames it to war and to some degree places it outside itself. The Aeolian soothes emotion; the Ionian is florid and delightful. Likewise rhythms or meters: some reflect grave tendencies , others excited ones; some make one more violent, others more generous. [Aristotle] therefore directs that [music] be taught to youths, but does not leave out consolation for those who do not learn [to perform] it, giving the example of Jupiter, who does not play the *kithara*. As long as

certi animali, et nel Volgo de gli idioti vecchi, et de' i putti. Ei insomma, a chi la biasma, od in qualche parte la diminuisce, sì come Socrate, sensatamente risponde; nè altro di vile ammette in lei, se non l'artificio per i contrasti de'i giuochi, et l'uso degli instrumenti, come in specie fù detto di quelli, che scontorcono la faccia; onde Diana si nascondeva sonando la cornamusa. Di che non hà quì luogo il ragionamento. Concludendosi per suo detto, che l'huomo tiene

one does not display merely that sense of common delight in music that we see in some animals, and in senile elderly common people, and in babies. In sum, [Aristotle] responds sensibly to those who blame or somewhat disparage [music], such as Socrates; he does not see anything lowly in it, except for the artifice of competition in games, and the use of instruments, specifically those that distort the face; thus Diana hid while playing the *cornamusa*. But our discussion does not concern those. We can conclude with his saying, that man has

[fol. 32] certa attinenza con l'harmonia, poiche molti sapienti hanno detto, che l'anima era harmonia; altri, ch'ella haveva harmonia. Onde afferma Platone, che la musica è trovata per cavar da noi la consonanza dell'anima. Et l'anima, onde è animato l'universo, prende origine dalla Musica. Et però l'anima humana, conscia d'haver udito musica in Cielo, si diletta delle terrene melodie, con la ricordanza delle celesti. Pitagora, il quale tra'Greci inventò la musica dal battere de' i martelli, dall'ineguaglianza delle corde, et dalla disparità delle cannuccie dice, ch'il Mondo è aggiustato alle musiche ragioni. Vuole, che chi si sveglia dal sonno, subito senta musica, per ben comporsi alle attioni. Et alla cantatrice ordinò, che usasse lo spondeo, tardo di modi, et grave, per frenare il furor de' i gioveni. Quindi fu da i Lacedemoni ributtato il Chromatico, come effeminato. Mà che la musica di Chirone addolcisse in Achille i fieri costumi, il dimostra Homero. Et vuol Tolomeo, che la Musica si sia inserita alle cose del Cielo, et serva a placare i Numi. Non si vedeva in Tebe

a certain affinity with harmony, because many wise men have said that the soul is harmony; others, that [the soul] had harmony. Thus Plato maintains that music was designed to bring out of us the soul's consonance. And the soul, which animates the universe, has its origin in music. Thus the human soul, conscious of having heard music in heaven, delights in earthly melodies, remembering the heavenly ones. Pythagoras, who among the Greeks invented the music of hammers, of inequality of strings, and of the different sizes of reeds, says that the world is regulated by musical ratios and reasons. He suggests that one who wakes from sleep should immediately listen to music, so that he may be well disposed to action. And he told one singer to use the spondee, slow and serious, in order to curb a youth's frenzy. The chromatic [genre] was rejected by the Lacedemons as effeminate. Homer demonstrates that Chiron's music sweetened Achilles's fierceness. And Ptolemy believes that music is included in heavenly matters and that it serves to placate the gods. One could not find in Thebes

[fol. 32v] statua di Pindaro, ma sì di Cleone cantore, nel cuoi seno gettato l'oro da alcuno, che fuggiva il saccheggiamento della Città, vi fù ritrovato doppo 30 anni. Socrate già vecchio imparò di cetera. Et qual prova maggiore che appresso gli antichi, la Musica insegnasse buoni costumi? Dice Strabone, che gli elefanti s'inteneriscono al canto, et al suono de i timpani. Plutarco, che i Cervi à quello de i Zufili; et altri, che solo le Tigri s'inaspriscono con la musica. Ond'il Poeta, volendo sublimar la Virtù del canto d'Orfeo, disse più, che non pare à chi nol considera: Mulcentem Tigres. Et veramente questa Eufonia misurata di numeri, et modi con raccoglimento di unità, et missione di Voci pari, et dispari, che si chiama arte musica, è tanto nobile, che considerandosi il mondo Archetipo, si troverà altro non essere, che una equal sinfonia dell'istessa natura in tre suppositi realmente distinti, mà con tal convenienza, che niuno d'essi è dispari ad alcuno; et però sono tanto concordi, l'intendere, il volere,

a statue of Pindar, but there was one of Cleon the singer; and when someone abandoned his gold there while fleeing the sack of that city, it was still found there thirty years later. Socrates learned to play the *kithara* as an old man. And what greater proof is there that music taught good customs among the ancients? Strabo tells us that the elephants become gentle when hearing song and the sound of drums. Plutarch [says the same] about deer and the sound of panpipes; and others say that only tigers become more fierce with music. Thus the Poet [Virgil], wanting to show the sublime nature of the *virtù* of Orpheus's song, said more than might be apparent to those who do not ponder it: "Soothing Tigers."[3] Truly this measured euphony of numbers, and modes in which individuals are gathered and then dispersed in close-spaced or scattered voices, that is called the art of music is so noble, that considering the world as an archetype, one will find that it is nothing other than an equal *sinfonia* of nature itself in three parts, which are distinct but [are coordinated] with such ease that none is unmatched to the others—and these concordant [parts] are understanding, willing,

[fol. 33] et l'operare. Anzi Dio sommo Padre, à guisa di sovrano musico universale, ha posta nell'Universo tanta harmonia, che tutte le cose vi stanno disposte in misura, numero, et peso. Veggasi, come ogni intelligenza con mirabil'ordine agita la sua sfera; come rallegra l'anima il corpo con l'harmoniosa sua convenienza seco in tutte le parti. *Et quando per naturale, ò violenta offesa, le impedisce esercitarse in esso le sue armoniche*

and acting. Further, God our highest Father, acting as the sovereign universal musician, has placed so much harmony in the universe that all things are disposed in measure, number, and weight. Let us behold how every intelligence moves in its sphere with wondrous order; how the soul cheers the body with the harmonious existence in all of its parts. And when it is prevented by some natural or violent accident from exercising its harmonious effects in

operationi, subito subito se ne parte.
Musica proportione hà la volontà
con gli oggetti precogniti, l'intelletto
con ciò ch'intende, la memoria con
ciò che rammenta. La Verità signora
del mondo, gode anch'essa di questo
nome, essendo adequatione della cosa
all'intelletto. Non si dice un huomo
di questa nobilissima Arte manchev-
ole, quando con le sue operationi ò
dall'obligo naturale, ò dalle regole del
giudicio dell'utile e dell'honesto
traligna. *Et ben potria difendersi il
ditto, e dedurla da simil tema,
chiamando* per cagione di variati
esempi, armonia in vaga Donna la
bellezza con gratia, et con honestà; in
prode guerriero, vigilanza, ardimento,
et avvedimento; in Oratore, autorità,
suadela, et concitatione; in Poeta,
moto, giovamento, et rapimento; in
Principe, prudenza, giustitia, et
magnificenza. Mà queste son musiche ra-

[fol. 33v] tionali, mi sarà detto. Sì
veramente; et per ciò ne fo io grande
stima, perchè sono secondo ragione.
S'ammette con gratia in ben composta musica qualche nota falsa. Sò,
che queste, son musiche metaforiche;
mà se in figura vagliono tanto, che
faranno in essenza? Hora, se vogli-
amo per miglior concordia abbassare
la voce, et parlar della musica, et sua
efficacia secondo [illegible erased] *il
fatto*, non ci manca il suono della
tromba che inanimisce, et accalora il
cavallo; quel de' i timpani, che ferma
la seditione dell'Api; quel di Torpan-
dro, et d'Arione, che guarisce le
infirmità; quel di Pitagora, che
secondo Cicerone, mutando tuono
raffrena il giovane infuriato; quel de'i

[the body], [the soul] immediately
departs it. The will has musical
proportion with the objects it desires,
the intellect with that which it
understands, memory with that
which it remembers. Truth, mistress
of the world, also has this name [i.e.,
harmony], since it consists of the
matching of the thing with the
intellect. Do we not call a man
lacking in this most noble art
[harmony] when he departs—either
concerning natural obligations or
concerning the rules of judgment—
from useful and honest conduct? The
aforesaid could be defended by
deducing it from a similar theme; by
way of various examples, we call
harmony in a beautiful woman the
[combination of] beauty, grace, and
honesty; in a valiant warrior,
vigilance, boldness, and caution; in
an orator, authority, persuasion, and
fire; in a poet, movement, benefit, and
rapture; in a prince, prudence, justice,
and magnificence. But these are
musics of reason,

one might say to me. Truly yes; and
because of this I esteem them greatly,
since they follow reason. We gratefully accept some false notes in a
good composition. I know these are
metaphorical types of music; but if
they are so worthy in the abstract,
what will they do in their essence?
Now, if we want to lower our voice
to gain more concord, and speak of
music, and its efficacy according to
fact, we have the sound of the
trumpet that animates and stirs the
horse; that of the kettledrum, which
stops the swarming of bees; that of
Torpander and Arion, which heals
illness; that of Pythagoras, who,
according to Cicero, restrained an
infuriated youth by changing mode;

sacri metalli, che fuga gli spiriti delle procelle, e' tempeste; quel della sacra Lira, che scaccia i Demoni. *Et l'armonia delle voci apostoliche sanò il mondo; in omnia D[omi]no exivit sonus eorum.* E'l suono della tromba neomenia da Dio... *[a half dozen illegible words]* ...*{interpretato?} in armonia da gli Oracoli, e Profeti e dopo {Evangelisti}.* Tanto si diletta la Natura, et gode tanto del suono, che à gli istessi animali velenosi vi ha insirita meravigliosa vaghezza; et l'istesso lor veleno inanimato, nega uscir da quei corpi humani, ov'entrò, se non resta prima sodisfatto del suono, che desidera. *Alla quale assiduo {giudicio}, se il suono non basta, aggiungesi il ballo.* Et quando l'aere passa da un horrido temporale à

that of sacred metals, which dispels the spirits of storms and tempests; that of the sacred lyre, which dispels demons. And the harmony of the voices of the apostles healed the world: "In all of God's creation their sound went forth."[4] And the sound of the trumpet at the [time of the] new moon [illegible] as harmony by the Oracles, the Prophets, and later the Evangelists. Nature derives such pleasure and delight from sound that it has inserted a wondrous desire for it in poisonous animals, so that even their inanimate poison refuses to exit the human bodies that it has entered if it is not first satisfied with the sound that it desires. And if in their judgment sound is not enough, they add dancing. And when the air changes from a terrible storm to

[fol. 34] lieta constitutione, tutti gli animali di ciò rallegrandosi, ne dan segno col canto. Hinc ille avi: um concentus in agris, et lata pecudes, et ovates gutture coevi, dice il Cantor Mantovano, i cui detti a me sono di sì grata harmonia. Chi non vede, che il Rosignolo prigioniere, od altro simile uccello, sentendo il suono di dotte corde, non può tenersi, che col suo canto non gli risponda? Anzi chi non sà, che l'istesse corde si rispondono l'una all'altra in diversi, et lontani instrumenti, mentre accordatele al medesimo tuono, et percossane una, si muovono tutte due? Ammiranda nel vero è la forza della musica. *Et per molto, ch'il fanciulletto in fasce manchi dell'uso del senno; pur niega co'suoi pianti acquetarsi, et comporsi al sonno senza la musica.* E 'l pastorello, ch'è semplice, e 'l zappatore, che poco sà, e 'l viandante, ch'è pien di stanchezza, et l'addolorato, ch'è voto di gioia,

a pleasing disposition, all the animals, cheering up, show their pleasure with song. "Thus those birds: as a consort in the fields, with the wide-scattered cattle, and the lambs all [sounding] from their throats at once," says the Mantuan Bard, whose sayings are such enjoyable harmony for me. Who cannot notice that a caged nightingale, or some other bird, hearing the sound of learned strings, cannot keep itself from answering with its own song? Or who doesn't know that those same strings answer one another in different, separate instruments, that when they are tuned to the same pitch, and one is struck, they both move? Truly admirable is the force of music. Even though the swaddled child has little faculty of reason, still his cries cannot be soothed and he cannot be settled down to sleep without music. And the shepherd, who is simple, and the farmer, who knows little, and the wanderer, who is tired, and the one in

pur provano questo effetto, che l'unica lor consolatione, et allevia-mento è il cantare. *Che mi bisogna qui dire ciò che sà ognuno, qual forza hanno i guerrieri suoni di varie sorti, ne gli eserciti combattenti in mare, od in terra. Noi leggiamo che Nationi formidabili entravano nella pugna col canto, et acquistavano ferocità dall concitatione della Musica. Et che Aless{and}ro Macedone infuriava all'istessa, et cangiava moti al variar de'suoni. Non sò io, che Alessandro Carlo Farnese*

[fol. 34v, insert continued] *affermava di tre suoi domestici, perfetti maneg-giatori di diversi stromenti, che in lor mano stava il suo ridere, o piangere. Non seppi già, che un Inglese, gran contumace appresso Papa Gregorio 13mo, ottenendo con poderosi mezzi, di presentari a dir sue ragioni a S{ua} S{anti}tà, quivi inginocchiato frà molti familiari dell'istesso Pontefice, trahendo fuori una lira di due ordini, con la suavità d'essa unì cantando sì dolce-mente il salmo del Miserere, che indurò di stuporegli animi à tenerezza com-mossi, ed inteneriti ad usargli clem-enza il cuor del Pontefice à durezza rivolto? Certo che non vive trà noi ben organizzata persona, che per opera de' sommi Virtuosi, de' quali Natura, od Arte non fù col nostro secolo scarsa, non habbia in se sentito la forza de' rapimenti, de' moti pietosi, et dell'agitatione de gli affetti.* [fol. 34r continuation] *Se tali son dunque gli effetti del Canto, et del suono, à ragione i saggi poeti considerandogli in se medesimi, sopra la lor condi-tione gli sublimarono; facendo Anfione col suono della lira dar*

[fol. 34v] ~~note, et~~ *legge, et sito all dure pietre, onde* ~~h~~*armoniosamente*

pain, who has no joy, also feel this effect, since their only consolation and relief comes from song. What need is there for me to say here that which everyone knows, what powers warlike sounds of all sorts have on armies fighting at sea or on land. We read that powerful nations entered battle with song and gained in ferocity from the incitement of music. And that Alexander the Great raged, and changed his movements as the sounds varied. I myself know that Alessandro Carlo Farnese

claimed about three of his servants, perfect performers on various instru-ments, that his laughter or weeping was in their hands. I also know that an Englishman greatly condemned by Pope Gregory XIII, having obtained with powerful resources [the opportu-nity] to present himself to His Holiness to argue his case, kneeling among many of the pope's familiars and bringing out a double lyre [?], sang the *Miserere* so sweetly to the beauty of its sound that he astonished their spirits and moved them to tenderness, and softened to clemency the heart of the pontiff, which had been turned to harshness? Truly there is no well-organized person living among us who has not—by the work of the great *Virtuosi*, which nature or art has not been stingy in providing to our time—felt within himself the strength of rapture, movement to pity, and stimulation of the *affetti*. If these are thus the effects of song and of sound, righfully the wise poets, considering them. exalted them above their condition; since Amphion, with the sound of his lyre,

gave law, and position to the hard stones, by which he harmoniously

construsse le Tebane mura; Arione ammollir gli scogli, et render compassionevoli i crudi regni marini; et Orfeo figlio di Calliope, allettar gli animali più fieri, le Tigri, i Serpenti, ad ascoltare il suono delle sue corde; arrestare il corso de' i fiumi, sveller dal suolo le dure quercie; et udito ne' i regni di Morte, ritrasse mercè di vita, sospendere i tormenti infernali, et rendere il céntro dell'impietà, pietoso del suo rammarico. Che? Non dice il Poeta, cantando rumpitur anguis? Non dice: carmina vel Coelo possunt deducere Lunam? Sono dunque in tutto maravigliosi gli effetti del canto. Che oltral'esser medicina à diversi mali, come habbiam detto, cresce, et rende soavi i beni della vita, lusinga i generati amori, desta i guerrieri spiriti, consacra gli Heroi, nudrisce gli affetti contemperandogli, eccita religione, et honora Dio. Che però nel apparir doppo le tenebre quel gran dono, che Dio fece al mondo, che non potendosi

[fol. 35] mirar senza lume fà egli lume a se stesso; io dico il Sole, dal cui moto attuale, luce essentiale, et calor virtuale, hanno vita, et conservatione tutte le vite, et hà governo, et sostegno questa gran machina; Nel suo apparir, dico, la terra non sapendo in più degno modo, et ringratiamento, rappresentar le divine laudi, in ogni parte dell'hemisfero sveglia ad un tempo istesso tutti gli uccelli à cantar varie canzoni con uniforme garreggiamento. Et questa è ben altra musica matutina fatta al Sole, della favolosa, che fà il Sole percotendo co' i raggi, quasi con plettro, nella statua di Mennone. Ma che dirò? Non

constructed the walls of Thebes; Arion softened the rocks and rendered compassionate the cruel kingdom of the sea; and Orpheus, son of Calliope, induced the fiercest animals, tigers and snakes, to listen to the sound of his strings; stopped the course of rivers, and tore hard oaks from the ground; and being heard in the kingdom of death, brought back the mercy of life, suspended infernal torment, and made the center of unholiness pity his grief. What? Does the Poet not say, "By singing the snake is burst asunder"? Does he not say, "Songs can bring the moon down from the sky"?[5] The effects of song are thus marvelous in every way. For besides acting as medicine to several illnesses, as we have said, [Song/ Music] increases and makes sweet the goodness of life, pleases growing love, awakes warlike spirits, praises heroes, fuels the emotions and tempers them, stimulates religion, and honors God. When, after the darkness, that great gift that God gave the world, since it [the world] could not

be viewed without light—itself gives light: I mean the sun, from whose actual motion, essential light, and virtual heat all lives are derived and preserved, and this great machine is governed and sustained. At its appearance, the Earth—not being able to present the praise, and thanks to God, in a worthier way—awakens all at once in every part of the hemisphere all the birds to sing various songs in uniform competition. And this is an entirely different morning music performed for the sun from the one that the sun creates by striking with its rays, as if with a plectrum, the statue of Memnon.[6] But how shall I say it? Do the fragrant trees of the

garreggiano *con* gli stessi uccelli *infra giorno* gli odoriferi alberi delle selve, l'un susurrando con l'altro, allhor, che Zefiro spira, con tacite note di scambievole melodia? Et la sottil canna palustre, non men docile, che pieghevole, sibilando là intorno alle rive del limpido fiumicello, non rende all'aria quel suono, che da essa riceve? Et, lasciando il canto onde' *anche* lodano il lor Fattore l'acque sopra il Cieli; non suona il rio trascorrendo per l'herba, con varietà di passaggi, et note sostenute, ed interrotte, ò dall'

[fol. 35v] egualità del suo corso, ò dalle minute gemme, che si nudriscono nel suo seno? Mirabil cosa m'occorse vedere in estiva stagione, con assiduo godimento di sì belle opere di natura, in un sopramodo dilettevole boschetto, là dov'io con lunga educatione, appresi, se parte alcuna appresi già mai, del canto soave delle muse. Essendo stato rapito il nido con suoi teneri figli ad uno scaltrissimo Rosignolo, egli, gran maestro del canto, fermatosi di continovo sù diversi rami, distesi sopra un loquacissimo ruscelletto, che ~~con lamentevoli accenti~~ irrigando tutta la Villa, in quel luogo sopra ogni altro si rendea riguardevole, et grato; con lamentevoli accenti, et pietosi modi, indefessamente dolendosi, participava col rio le sue eterne querele; ne in prova, mai venne fatto ad alcuno di discacciarlo dal luogo, ò desviarlo dal pianto, che giorno, et notte perpetuava *con incredibile ansietà, senza pensiero alcuno di cibo, ò d'acqua*; in guisa, che havrebbe svegliato Amore, et pietà nell'istessa fierezza; credo, intanto, consolandosi, in quanto dalle pietose onde sentiva soavemente compiangersi al suo

woods not compete with the birds themselves during the day, whispering one to the other, when Zephyr blows, with quiet notes in an interchanging melody? And the thin reed of the swamps, no less docile than flexible, hissing around the banks of the limpid brook, does it not answer the air with the sound that it receives from it? And putting aside the song by which the waters above the heavens praise their Maker, does the brook not sound, as it runs through the grass, with a variety of *passaggi*, and notes sustained and interrupted,

either by the smoothness of its course or by the minute gems that are nourished in its breast? I happened to view a marvelous thing in summertime as I was enjoying all the beautiful works of nature, in a most delightful woods, where through a long course of study I learned—if I ever even learned a small part—the sweet song of the muses. Since his nest with its young offspring had been stolen from a very skilled nightingale, he, great master of song, continuously moving among several branches extended over a most loquacious stream, which, bringing water to the whole countryside, made itself esteemed and delightful above all in that place; with plaintive tones, and pitiful actions, grieving without pause, he made his eternal case to the stream. Nor could anyone, despite their efforts, chase him from that place or interrupt his crying, which he continued night and day with incredible anxiety, without thought for food or water; so that he would have stirred love and mercy in fierceness itself, meanwhile, I believe, consoling himself, since he was hearing sweet condolence in his pain from the pitying waves; and he

dolore; In che durò sempre, insino, che la sua vita, che tutta

continued in this, until his life, which was all

[fol. 36] era voce, nell'aria, ond'è creata la voce, intieramente si risolvette. Io penso, che gli Alcioni, di cui disse il Poeta: Littora et Halcyonem resonant; cántino volentieri nel lido del mare, non solo per la gioia della lieta stagione, ma anche per l'harmonia, che loro accompagna dal mare stesso, che in seni tranquilli io ho tallhora osservato tra innocenti scoglietti placidissimamente risuonare. Et notisi, senza varcare oltre i termini della costiera Napolitana, cominciando dall'antico ridotto Formiano, quando Nettunno giacendo posa nell'azzurro suo letto, et gli amorosi spirti de i soavissimi venti, increspando i liquidi suoi zaffiri, con canora proportione il lusingano; con qual leggiadria musica i placidi flutti, hora nel seno della sirena gorgogliando, hora di quà da Nisida, ò di là da Capri, in picciole cavernette rientrando, hora frangendo in folti, e schiettissimi scogli per angusto spatio della riviera d'Amalfi, dilettano in guisa col misurato, et dolce lor risuonare, ch'io là trahendo, con meraviglia del racconto, che n'hebbi, me ne partii con istupore dell'harmonia, che v'intesi. Nè stimai gran cosa

voice, resolved itself entirely into air, from which the voice is created. I think the Halcyons, about whom the poet said, "The shores resonate with the Halcyon," prefer to sing at the seashore, not only because of their delight in the beautiful season, but also because of the harmony that accompanies them from the sea itself—which I [myself] have observed resounding most placidly between innocent rocks. And let us note, without going beyond the coast of Naples, beginning at the old town of Formia, when Neptune lies calm in his azure bed, and the loving spirits of the sweet winds, rippling his liquid sapphires, delight him with singing proportion, with what musical grace the placid waves, now gurgling in the siren's breast, now entering small caverns either on the side of Nisida or that of Capri, now breaking through a narrow inlet against the thick and upright rocks of the Amalfi coast, delight so much with their measured and sweet sound that, after I went there marveling at the account I had heard, I departed with astonishment at the harmony that I heard there. Nor did I give great credence to

[fol. 36v] ciò, che delle Sirene animate gli antichi narrano; poiche le onde, et gli scogli senza anima, in luoghi determinati hanno virtù di rendere sì vago suono. Et dissi, quali saranno le soavità di Parnasso, ò del Cielo, se quelle del mare arrivano al segno di sì manifesta dolcezza? Hor sia chi pensi, qual animo sarebbe tanto abbattuto, che non si ravvivasse in mezzo alle morti di molti Cigni,

that which the ancients tell of the animate sirens, since the inanimate waves and rocks have the power/ability [virtù] to make such a lovely sound. And I said: What can the sweetness of Parnassus, or of heaven, be if that of the sea can manifestly be sweet to such a degree? Now let us think what soul would be so base that it would not be revived in the midst of the deaths of many swans,

che sol dovendo finir di vivere, cominciano il cantare, per terminar la Vita insieme col canto. Sarebbe empio il desiderio d'udirgli, andando congiunto col voler la lor morte; et io, che mai non udii quel dolce lor canto, se la natura gli fà con esso risplendere sol quando s'estinguono, temprarò un desiderio sì nobile d'ascoltargli; acciochè il lor merito non si converta in ingiuria; et quello, che di lor piace, non rechi *spiacevole* occasione *del lor morire* di farsi spiacere. Nè voglio intanto meravigliarmi, che di tale uccello, sicome anche della Lira d'Orfeo, il Cielo honori le sue costellationi; mentre il canto delle cose inferiori così gli piace, che insino all'infime Cicade, che tutto il lor vivere impiegano nel cantare, qua

[fol. 37] si per ciò divenute celesti, altro alimento non permette somministrarsi, che celeste. Vile, et {puro} animaletto è la Cicada per sè medesima; pretiosa è la Conca, et la Madreperla; et nondimeno si pasce di mattutina rugiada la Conca, perchè è pretiosa, et la Cicada grata è cantatrice. Ecco il prezzo del Canto, equivalente a' i tesori. Nè per altro cred'io, che tal canto, si come quello di simili animaletti, onde dì, et notte risuonano i prati, si formi con l'ale; se non perchè essendo l'ala instrumento da poggiare in sù, resti dalla natura mostrato, che l'harmonie di qua giù, son gradite, et sagliono al cielo, *et che il canto, quasi per se medesimo alato, vola all'immortalità.* La pompa funerale di Psiche, dal padre condotta allo scoglio del suo precipitio, resto ammirato, ch'il Cielo si movesse a pietà del suo caso, mediante la flebil musica di flauti, et naccari, che dolorosamente

who begin singing only as they end their lives, in order to finish life together with their song. A desire to hear them would be evil, joined as it would be with the wish for their death; and I, who have never heard their sweet song, if nature makes them resplendent with it only when they are extinguished, will temper my noble desire to listen to them, so that their merit will not be turned to injury and so that the feature for which they are pleasing will not bring the displeasing happenstance of their death. Nor should I be surprised that heaven honors its constellations with this bird, as it does with Orpheus's lyre; while it [also] likes the song of inferior beings so much, that it does not allow the lowly cicadas—which spend their whole life in song, almost

becoming heavenly because of this—to consume any food but that of heaven. In and of itself, the cicada is a lowly little animal; precious is the snail, and the mother-of-pearl; nonetheless the snail feeds on the morning dew because it is precious, and the cicada is a beloved singer. Thus is the price of song equivalent to treasures. Nor would I believe that such song, like that of similar little animals on account of which the fields resound day and night, is produced by the wings, were it not that, since the wing is an instrument that is to be held upright, it is shown by nature that the harmonies of this earth are valued and rise to heaven and that song, as if winged itself, flies to immortality. At the funeral celebrations of Psyche, when she was brought by her father to the cliff of her sacrifice, it was remarked that heaven moved in mercy of her situation, through the feeble music of

l'accompagnava. Et per molte comparse meravigliose, ch'io m'habbia veduto in finti combatti-menti, niuna m'ha più commosso, che udire in Giostra, in mezzo à varie foggie di machine, et armi, comparire un Cavalier lugubre con musica di lamentevoli zufiletti; ò in

flutes and castanets that grievingly accompanied her. And among the many marvelous illusions that I have seen in mock combats, none has moved me more than to hear in a joust—in the midst of [the sounds of] various sorts of [stage] machinery and weapons—the arrival of a lugubrious knight to the sound of lamenting pipes; or [to hear], in

[fol. 37v] mezzo à trasparente marina, cantar la Sirena ò Venere, od Anfitrite; od aprendosi teatro voraginoso, sentire il Canto propor-tionato delle infernali Deità; ò per mezzo di machina hor celestiale, hor terrena, godere in somma gli effetti, che in mille modi ne rappresentano le Scene; alle quali però assegna Aristotile questa parte conve-nientissima del musicale apparato. Già non hanno l'intiero lor condi-mento frà noi l'adunanze virtuose, se non le condisce la musica; et sino di quei saggi adunati ne' i Campi Elisi, il nostro Poeta dice, che stavan sù per l'herba, Vescentes, laetumque choro Paeana canentes. Ma noi pure à guisa delle musiche dissonanze, che talhor passano dalle più basse voci alle più sovrane, senza toccar quelle di mezzo; dalla bassezza del centro *ove ci siamo ridotti*, ripigliamo la voce alle celesti sommità. Qual fantasia non si stanca, et non vien meno sotto la dolcezza dell'imaginata harmonia naturale, immensa, et perpetua, che formano girando intorno, le soavissime, e trasparenti machine celestiali? Io ne vorrei dir due parole à mio senno, ma non le ritrovo. Soccorra ad un

the middle of a transparent sea, the song of a siren, or Venus, or Amphy-trite; or, upon the opening of a theater's pit, to hear the proportioned song of the infernal gods; or—in sum—delight, by means of a heavenly or earthly machinery, from the effects that are represented in a thousand ways on stage, to which Aristotle assigns this most suitable deployment of musical resources. Virtuous gatherings do not have their proper spice if music does not garnish them; and our Poet even says of those wise men gathered in the Elysian Fields that they were on the grass, "dining, and singing paeans in a happy chorus."[7] But just like musical dissonances, which sometimes go from the lowest pitches to the highest, without touching on the intermediate ones; from the lowliness of the point where we have arrived, let us raise our voice again to the heights of heaven. What fantasy does not tire and fail in the sweetness of imagining the immense and perpetual natural harmony that the sweetest, transpar-ent heavenly machinery makes with its rotation? I would like to say two words about it from my own imagination, but I cannot find them. To the rescue of a

[fol. 38] Lelio, che vegliando vede ben corto, uno Scipione, che sì alto

Lelio, who is so shortsighted while awake, may come a Scipio, who sees

vede, et intende nel sonno. Ecco
Africano parlante con le voci
dell'Arpinate, più dolci, ch'il suono di
soavissima Arpa. Quis, qui complet
aures meas, tantus, et tam dulcis
sonus? Hic est sonus, qui intervallis
coniunctus imparibus, sed tamen pro
rata portione distinctis, impulsu; et
motu ipsorum orbium efficitur: et
acuta cum gravibus temperans, varios
aequabiliter concentus efficit. Noi
vediamo chi parla, et pure in materia
da sollevarsi ad immagini tanto
nobili, vediamo ove resta, et di che si
contenta. Dunque ancor noi conten-
tiamoci di raggiungere, et ripigliare;
Ch'il mondo superiore, et i Cieli si
governano, et girano con harmonia;
L'inferiore è una concorde discordia,
et mistura de gli elementi; le Vite de' i
corpi animati sono una concordanza
de gli humori; l'huomo, picciol
mondo, una dissonante consonanza
di perfetto composito d'anima, et di
corpo, d'intelletto, et di senso, di
ragione, et d'appetito: in somma un
doppio concerto bene accordato di
portione inferiore subordinata alla
superiore; la qual musica allhora

and understands so loftily in his
sleep. Here is Scipio Africanus
speaking with the words of the
Arpinate [Cicero], sweeter than the
sound of the most delightful harp.
"What is this, that fills my ears, such
a mighty and sweet sound? This is
the sound created by the coming
together of unequal intervals,
distinguished by rational proportion;
the motion of those spheres brings it
about and, tempering the high with
the low, creates a variety of balanced
intervals."[8] We can see who is
speaking, and even though he is able
to lift himself to such noble images,
we can see where he stays, what he
contents himself with. Thus let us
also be content to reach this, and
repeat it; that the upper world and
the heavens are governed by and turn
with harmony; the lower world is a
concordant discord, a mixture of
elements; the lives of animate bodies
are a concord of humors; man, as a
small world, [is] a dissonant consonance composed perfectly of soul and
body, of intellect, sense, reason, and
appetite: in sum, a double *concerto*,
well tuned with the lower part
subordinated to the upper one; and
this music

[fol. 38v] ben s'accorda; quando il
mastro superno non pausa, et non
sottrahe gli aiuti sopranaturali, ma fà
la battuta co' i moti interni, et
infonde il tuono, et la voce della sua
gratia. La bellezza dell'huomo è
proportione, et harmonia di colori, et
di linee: il suo allettante costume è
mistura harmoniosa di dolce, et
grave, d'honesto, gratioso, et
convenevole. Tutte le sue operationi
più lodate, il comporre, il dire, il
guerreggiare, il governare, hanno del
proportionato, et del metrico. Ma

is well tuned when the heavenly
maestro does not pause and does not
withhold his supernatural assistance,
but beats with the internal movements and infuses the sound and
voice of his grace. Beauty in man is a
proportion and harmony of color and
line; his pleasing manner is a
harmonious mixture of sweet and
grave, of honest, gracious, and
appropriate. All of his most praiseworthy actions, composing, speaking,
waging war, and governing, have
proportion and meter to them. But let

quà vagliami una dichiaratione, opportuna à più luoghi del mio discorso; che sebene Aristotile dice, che Musica est per melodia, et rhythmus; et Cicerone dà alla Musica, numeri, voci, et modi; tuttavia nel mio applicar di musico significato, talhora intendo il traslato, et non il proprio; talhora il partiale, et non l'integrale; per esempio, bastandomi, che ove non siano Voci, vi siano numeri, et modi. Et ordinariamente intendo il totale, proprio, et assoluto significato. Col qual senso camina il detto Peripatetico, che tutti i moti naturali, i numeri, e le cose fattte à misura, dilettano all'

[fol. 39] huomo, come si vede anco ne' i putti. Et in tutte le attioni, la consonanza, et contemperatione de' i contrarij, conservando proportione, diletta. Nè sol piace la musica a' vivi; ma è convenientissima a' i morti. Et per non dir delle altre nationi, Roma nel funeral de'vecchi usava la tromba, e de' giovani il piffaro; e i corpi s'accompagnavano alla sepoltura cantando; mentre l'anime eran credute tornare al loro principio musicale, ch'è il Cielo stesso; ò secondo Hirofilo, fù creduta l'anima [essere] armonia. Seguendo dunque oltre, aggiungo che tutte le Virtù fanno, et accrescono al mondo harmonia, non solo per risultanza de' i loro effetti, ma anche per il modo di produrli, che consistendo nella proportionata distanza frà gli estremi, fanno la parte di mezzo; adeguano potenza, et obieto, aggiustano eccesso, et defetto; et con dolce, equabile, et continuato tenore (voce à punto, che più commove, et unisce, perchè è più naturale, et ha

me make one statement here that is appropriate to several sections of my essay: that though Aristotle says that "music consists in melody and rhythm," and Cicero attributes number, voice, and mode to music, nonetheless, in my use of the term *music,* sometimes I mean the extended and not the specific; sometimes the part, and not the whole; for example, it is enough for me, if there are no voices, that there be numbers and modes. And generally I mean the total, proper, and absolute meaning. That is the sense by which the Peripatetic saying goes, that all natural motion, numbers, and things made according to measure, delight

mankind, as can be seen even in children. And in all actions, consonance—and the balancing of opposites, maintaining proportion—delights. Nor does music only give pleasure to the living, but it is most appropriate to the dead. Not to mention other nations, the Romans used the trumpet in the funeral of the old, and the *piffaro* in that of the young, and bodies were brought to burial with singing, while souls were believed to return to their musical beginnings, that is to say heaven itself; or according to Hierophylus, the soul itself was believed to be harmony. Moving on, I will add that all the *virtù* make and build harmony in the world, not only as a result of their effects, but also in the way these are produced, which, consisting in a proportionate distance between the extremes, create a middle part; they adapt power to the object, they adjust excess and defect; and with a sweet, equal, and continuous *tenor* (the range that most moves and unites because it is most natural

più dell'humano, il che è manifesto nella viola trà gli istrumenti, che sopra ogni paragone intenerisce, et violenta) arricchiscono il mondo del loro concento. Ma qual cosa mai s'usa in Terra di più pomposo costume, nè che più illustri la vera Religione, et saglia più grata al Divino conspetto, che in magnifico, e ricco Tempio, da cento maestre voci con grave, et dolce, et vaga maniera, concordamente cantansi le glorie del sommo Dio? Di questo pregio và Roma

[fol. 39v] altiera à ragione, di questo s'honora la nostra religione sopra l'uso di tutte l'antiche, ò moderne superstitioni. In questo solo, si com'io penso, noi contrastiamo più francamente, ch'in altro, a' quei secoli, da' i quali siamo in tante nobili arti sopravanzati. Et quando i Tridentini decreti erano già scritti, per doversi vietar nelle Chiese il canto figurato, colpa di coloro, che l'abusavano; ben apparve, qual forza havesse ne' gli animi di quei Padri la Musica, che inviata là dal famoso, per cui Pelestina è famosa, et usata in quel giorno istesso, che soprastava il divieto; rapì gli affetti, cambiò le menti, et mutò i voleri, per modo, che gli accenti cantati cancellarono le scritte leggi; le note d'aria, *come* ~~furon~~ più stabili, ~~et~~ annullarono le scritte leggi; et più non si parlò del decreto, perchè sempre s'havesse ad usare il Canto, *e tal silentio fù {palese segno della perpetuatione delle ecclesiastiche note}*. Là onde se mai alcuno prevaricasse, non può scusarsi, di non haver l'esempio lodevole innanzi. Io sò, che Signori prudenti, et sensati, nello stare lunghi anni, per loro affari, in Orientali

and most human; this is manifest in the *viola,* which among all instruments can create tenderness and overwhelm beyond compare) enrich the world with their consort. What custom on earth carries more pomp, or illustrates more clearly the True Religion, and rises more delightfully to the divine presence, than when in a magnificent, rich church the glories of the highest God are sung by a hundred masterly voices in concord in a delightful, sweet, and wonderful way? Rome

is justly proud of this distinction, our religion is honored by this above all ancient or modern superstitions. In this alone, I think, we surpass most clearly those centuries by which we are surpassed in so many arts. And when the Tridentine decrees were already written, that polyphony should be banned in churches because of those who were abusing it, it became clear what force operated in those fathers' spirits through the music sent by that famous man, because of whom Palestrina is famous. When [the music] was played on the same day that the ban was to go into effect, it ravished their *affetti,* changed their minds, and modified their wills; so that the sung expressiveness erased the written law; the airy notes, as the more stable of the two, canceled the written laws; and no more was said of the decree, allowing song to be used forevermore, and such silence was the clear sign of the continuation of ecclesiastical singing. Thus if someone ever strays on the subject [of composition], he cannot say that he does not have a praiseworthy example before him. I know that prudent and sensible gentlemen, who have spent long years doing business in the Orient,

[fol. 40] paesi, ove non partecipano di questo uso, di niuna cosa sentivano maggior noia in sì lunga assenza, et per niun desiderio più sospiravano Italia, et Roma, che per gli Organi, et musiche delle Chiese, mal soffrendo simil mancanza, benchè di tutte l'altre consolationi, et commodi si spogliassero. Nè questo può dirsi *appetito* humano *disordinato*, ò vile sentimento; perchè in quella gran notte, che fattosi Huomo, volle nascere infrà i mortali l'eterno Dio, in niuna cosa fù più sollevato il Paradiso, che in accompagnar la solennità della Terra, et de gli huomini col canto de' i Chori Angelici. Svegliò dal sonno i Pastori con la sua musica, et iniziò moltitudine di celeste esercito à cantar lode all'Altissimo. Davide à lui tanto caro, quando vuole segnalatamente honorarlo, chiama in aiuto con titoli gloriosi il salterio, et la cetera, ond' egli è maestro. Et è chi scriva, ch'ei fece i Trimetrii, et i Pentametri. Ch'egli inventò la cetra di dieci corde, il {Nablio} di dodici voci, et i Cimbali di bronzo grandi, et larghi. Nel vittorioso passaggio del Mar d'Egitto ove si trattava della salvezza

[fol. 40v] di sì numeroso popolo, Maria cantò con l'altre damigelle, le gratie sul Timpano. Et quando Iddio vuole altamente favorire un Francesco, una Maddalena, manda i suoi musici à far loro sentire quelle canzoni per cui smarriscono il sentimento. O' avventurosa Maddalena, che versasti a' i piedi del tuo Signore quel pretioso Nardo; et quel pretiosissimo pianto; egli per rederti in questa vita un cambio di prezzo infinito, rende al tuo senso il comandato concerto de' i suoi cantori. È regal cortesia, che un Principe della

where this custom is not in use, found nothing more bothersome in their absence, and wished to be in Italy and Rome for no other reason than for the organs, and church music, which they were unable to do without, even though they cast aside all other consolation and comfort. Nor can this be called a disorganized human appetite, or a lowly sentiment: because in that great night when the eternal God, making himself into Man, wished to be born among mortals, nothing stirred heaven more than accompanying the solemnity of earth and mankind with the song of the angelic choirs. [Paradise] woke the shepherds from sleep with its music, and a multitude of the heavenly host began singing praise to the Highest One. David, so dear to God, when he wants to honor him fully, calls to his aid with glorious titles the psaltery and the kythara, of which he is the master. And there are those who write that [David] invented the kythara with ten strings, the nablius with twelve tones, and the large and widely resounding bronze cymbals. In the victorious crossing of the Sea of Egypt, where the salvation

of such a large population was concerned, Miriam, with the other women, sang praises, accompanied by the drum. And when God wants to highly favor one such as Francis, or Magdalen, he sends his musicians to have them hear those pieces [canzoni] that make them lose their senses. O venturesome Magdalen, you who poured at the feet of your Lord that precious oil, and those most precious tears; in order to return to you in this life an infinite gift in exchange, he commands that the ensemble of his singers be given

terra faccia sentire à chi ama, il valore de'suoi musici. Così regala i suoi diletti il Rè della Gloria et di molti potrei far qui numero; ma mi rivolgo à te, beatissimo *alato* spirito, che col tuo canto prendi à ristorare, et confortare il languido, et innamorato Francesco; Ah, ferma gli accenti, non toccar più l'harmonioso instrumento, che per esser troppo vitale, à lui reca morte, et per troppo sollevarlo, l'opprime. Deh sia mercede, fermare il corso di tanta mercede. Una sol nota, che mandi fuora, trarrai da lui tutta l'aura vitale. Se ferisci più quella sottil corda, tronchi

to your senses. It is royal courtesy for an earthly prince to allow those he loves to hear the worth of his musicians. Thus the King of Glory makes a gift of his delights, and I could list many in this regard, but I turn to you, most blessed winged spirit, as you prepare to restore and comfort the languid and lovesick Francis with your song; ah, hold back the *accenti*, no longer play that harmonious instrument, which in being too lively brings him death and in lifting him too high oppresses him. Have mercy in stopping the course of so much mercy. If one more note comes out, it will relieve him of all life breath. If you wound that thin string one more time, you will cut

[fol. 41] il filo del viver suo; nè puoi maneggiar sì dolce arco, ch'egli non resti esangue alle sue saette. *Così riferisce Francesco al finir della musica: l'{animare un accento} di più, lo rendeva esanime.* Ecco, quanto si pregia la musica in Cielo, che ricchezza maggior *di lassù* non s'invia à ~~quelli~~ coloro, che più s'amano in terra. Combattono i valorosi Campioni, e s'affliggono, e scarnano, per giungere a Dio; et Dio si communica à loro, et quà giù gli rinforza, et rinvigorisce con quell'istesso, ch'è l'ultimo lor fine, et premio là sù. O' combattimento, ò premio! Anco i Cantori celesti vengono armati da combattenti, *come talhor si fa nelle Musiche notturne in terra, per sostenerle senza disturbo.* Et però si dice: multitudo celestis exercitus; per difendere, et propagare l'honore di quel Principe Supremo, che fa la Musica. Si che, per la parte di chi la fà, et di chi la riceve, vediamo di quanta importanza è la musica. Et se Dio tanto la stima, possiamo credere,

the string of his life; nor can you handle that sweet bow again, for he will remain slain by its arrows. Thus Francis states when the music ends: the sensation of one more sound would render him senseless. This is how much music is prized in heaven: no greater riches are sent from above to those who are most beloved on earth. Worthy champions battle, and afflict themselves, and mortify their flesh, to come unto God; and God communicates with them and gives them strength down here and reinvigorates them with the same thing that is their final goal and prize up there. What a struggle, what a prize! Celestial singers are also armed like warriors, as is sometimes done for nighttime music on earth, [when we bring armed escorts] to achieve it without disturbance. For it is said: "the multitude of the celestial army"; to defend, and propagate the honor of that Supreme Prince, who makes music. Thus we can see how important music is for those who make it

che secondo la nostra debolezza, gli
giunge cara anche da noi; sicome la
vuol sempre da gli Angeli, e da' i
Beati, che in gloria non intermettono
un punto, ne' per tutta l'eternità
intermetteranno la lor Divina
salmodia verso il santo de' i santi.
Ond'à ragione frà noi suol dirsi in
vulgar proverbio,

[fol. 41v] esser nato al Cielo chi è
nato alla musica; nè frà noi si
depinge, ò s'adombra il Cielo, et la
gloria, se non con la luce, et con la
musica; et frà gli arteficii, tanto vuol
dire una gloria dipinta, quanto uno
sfondato lucente d'Angeletti, che
cantano. Splende dunque la luce, e
splende la musica; *ambe nate nel
principio del mondo, con la Divina
parola, fiat lux; ch'importò la
creatione de'Cieli, e degli Angeli;
questi cantanti gloria à Dio per
officio; e quelli, risonanti in Musica
per natura; secondo la sopraddetta
opinione.* Et ambe insieme
s'uniscono, et fanno gloria; *l'uno, e
l'altro parmi adombrato nel lucido
nascimento del Rè della gloria,* dove e
i pastori, com'è detto, furon drizzati
dal Canto, e i Rè furon guidati dalla
Stella; ambi contrasegni di splendor
celeste; et *argomenti, che tanto più*
l'uno apparisce tale, tanto più l'altro
si trova essere tale, da chi conoscen-
dolo, et non volendo esser Tigre con
gli spiriti ben purgati sà trarne il suo
godimento. 15 ottobre 1632.
[Guidiccioni initials?]

and those who receive it. And if God
esteems it so greatly, we may believe
that according to our feeble abilities
he receives it kindly from us as well;
since he wants it perennially from the
angels and the blessed, who in their
glory never cease or pause throughout eternity in their divine psalmody
toward the holiest of the holy. Thus
with good reason we have a popular
proverb:

that he is born to heaven, who is born
to music; nor do we paint, or describe
heaven, and glory, without light, or
music; and among artists, a painting
of glory is equivalent to a light-
infused background of singing angels.
Light shines, and likewise shines
music; both born at the beginning of
the world, with the divine Word, *Fiat
lux*, which brought about the creation
of the heavens, and angels—the latter
singing glory to God by their office,
the former resonating through music
by their very nature, according to the
above reasoning. And both join
together and make glory; both seem
to me foreshadowed in the shining
birth of the King of Glory, in which
shepherds, as it is said, were uplifted
by song, and the kings were guided by
the star; both symbols of and
· arguments for heavenly splendor, the
more one shows itself as such, the
more the other reveals itself as such;
and he who understands this, and
does not want to be a Tiger, having a
well-disposed spirit, can draw
enjoyment from it.
15 October 1632.

Notes

INTRODUCTION

1. See, for example, Sohm (1995, 792). Sybille Ebert-Schifferer has specifi-cally suggested (with reference to Vincenzo Giustiniani, whom we will encoun-ter in chapter 2 in the context of his discussions of visual as well as musical connoisseurship) that such individuals "could seem a precursor to French aris-tocrats of the second half of the [seventeenth] century in their refusal, within the *Salons,* of any technical language (proper to a 'pedant,' but not to an 'honest man') and their preference for spoken language, simulated through the literary epistolary form" (1994, 104).

2. The two book-length studies that are most crucial not just to the present project but to any real understanding of Roman musical patronage in the first third of the seventeenth century are those by Frederick Hammond (1994) and John Walter Hill (1997).

3. All passages are from De'Rossi (1645/1989): Santa Maria dell'Orto "è benissimo tenuta, & offitiata, con musica, organi, e ricchi paramenti. . . . Vengono a gli 8. di giugno ad honorare questa Chiesa i Musici di Roma, cantan-dosi una Messa solenne per voto fatto alla Beatissima Vergine il 1584" (60). At Santa Caterina de'Funari, "vi è buona musica dall'istesse Suore devotamente cantata" (174). At San Lorenzo in Damaso, the Compagnia del Soccorso, insti-tuted in 1602, "Nelli giorni di Carnevale espongono con grand'apparato della chiesa, e dell'Altar maggiore il Santissimo Sacramento con oratione continua, sermoni, e musica eccellentissima di cose pie, cominciando il giovedì della Ses-sagesima, fino alla Domenica seguente" (221). At Santa Maria in Vallicella, Chiesa Nuova—Congregatione dell'Oratorio, "E v'è devota, e buonissima musica. In ci-aschedun giorno feriale, eccetto il sabbato, si fanno quattro sermoni di mez'hora l'uno; alla fine dei quali si canta qualche mottetto spirituale; e ne'giorni festivi doppo il Vespro si fà un solo sermone. . . . Si è poi questo instituto propagato in

molte città d'Italia, e fuori, e tuttavia và moltiplicando con frutto grande de'luoghi, dove s'introduce: non dependendo una Congregatione dall'altra, ma vivendo ciascheduna sotto l'Ordinario, conforme alle regole di S. Filippo [Neri], confermate da Paolo V. con Breve Apostolico. . . . Dal principio di Novembre sin'a Pasqua la sera fanno devoti Oratorij con buoni sermoni, e musica per lo spatio d'un'hora, e meza" (227–28). Services at Sant'Apollinare and the Jesuit Collegio Germanico "viene offitiata dagl'istessi Alunni [del Collegio Germanico], che assistono al Choro tutte le feste con musica eccellente" (262). The Chiesa and Compagnia del Crocefisso is "una bella chiesa, di bellissime figure ornata, dove i venerdì della Quaresima la sera i fratelli procurano, che uno de'più valenti Predicatori, che vada sù i pulpiti di Roma, ci faccia un sermone, accompagnato da esquisiti suoni, & eccellenti musiche" (291). At San Lorenzo in Lucina, "hanno spese molte centinaia di scudi in vasi d'argento, parati d'altari, e chiesa, organo, & altri abbellimenti, & ogni sabbato sera si cantano in detta chiesa con buonissima musica le Litanie, & altre lodi della Madonna, facendosi inanzi da uno delli stessi Padri un sermone in lode della Beatissima Vergine" (332).

4. Roger Freitas suggests that "the cantata would usually not have been considered equivalent to the old participatory tradition, a tradition which probably continued to exist alongside the newer styles: the social setting, however, seems to remain similar" (2001, 518 n. 43). As Freitas observes, the social context in which the elites establish their interpretative control over the meaning of "musicking" remains the same, even as the nature of that "musicking" changes to discourse on music. This situation is made more complex by the continuation of a tradition of amateur music making (which, at least in Roman circles, tended toward simple solo song with strummed *chitarra spagnola* accompaniment rather than polyphonic performance; see Gavito 2006) in parallel with the professional tradition, though there seems to have been a clear distinction in the minds of early modern elites between the expressive goals of participatory versus listening-based "musicking."

5. As Gino Benzoni (1978, 159) puts it in a discussion of the incorporation of Stefano Guazzo's *La civil conversazione* into early modern intellectual structures, "Wisdom comes through dialogue, knowledge is a multivoiced discourse."

6. Tim Carter has made an analogous argument about some aspects of the transmission of the "new practice" by musicians, suggesting, "The more one works with these songbooks the more one realizes that they are not so much neutral transmitters of information from composer to performer as iconic representations of specific or generalized performance acts that need to be handled as carefully as any other iconographical evidence from this period" (2000, 28). As I have suggested elsewhere, "The introductions' focus on singing technique and the visual depiction of vocal fireworks in the musical notation appear to be attempts to evoke the sonic effects of *meraviglia* experienced by the listener in the new style" (Dell'Antonio 2005, 118–19 n. 21). Thus the idea of evocation as reaching more effectively to the essence of the "new music" than "accurate" description is in no way exclusive to the listeners' *discourse-about,* though I will argue that a particular group of listener-tastemakers deploy it most systematically and effectively.

7. In describing the discourse surrounding the cantata in the mid–seventeenth century, Freitas observes that "In an environment that so valued the marvellous, to describe an experience simply as 'miraculous' may well have been a more potent laudatory technique than rational dissection" (2001, 526 n. 7).

8. Giovanni Baffetti's excellent summary of this phenomenon bears an extended quote: "The unstoppable expansion of the Jesuit order leads its ideology, across all fields of culture and knowledge, to expand and root itself deeply within the Catholic world, and especially in Italy, starting from the second half of the sixteenth century and for the entire century to follow. The direct means of this capillary establishment is constituted by the order's imposing doctrinal, philosophical, and scientific output, but no less a contribution is provided by the pedagogical influence of the company's colleges, which in the span of a few years become the most authoritative and visited sites for educating the elites. The spiritual directors for princes in European courts are Jesuits, as are the cultural leaders of the ruling classes, as are the authors of the works in which the values and ideals of the Counter-Reformation are fully established. . . . Following their founder's lead, in order to shape an intellectual and moral elite that could guide the reform movement within the Catholic Church—but could also aspire to gaining a hegemonic role with respect to lay culture, linking its fate to that of Catholicism—Jesuits postulated themselves as the heirs to a great tradition, but were also able to renew it, showing themselves to be sensitive and attentive to the needs of contemporaneous society, and ably capturing its vital centers. The attempt to integrate and conciliate the values of humanist lay culture with the renewal project launched by the Counter-Reformation constitutes what we might call, echoing Asor Rosa, the heart of Jesuit 'ideology' " (1997, 85).

9. However, in closing I will also argue that this approach (possibly because it may have been "transplanted" to France with the fall of the Barberini) appears to have been less developed in Rome in the ensuing years, perhaps making the new approach to material collection of scores a more prevalent phenomenon.

10. Indeed, this phenomenon may have fostered an increasing concern with compositional attribution. Murata herself implies this by noting the increased accuracy of (and in any case, concern with) composer attributions in the cantata anthologies of the later seventeenth century.

11. The special issue of the *Musical Quarterly* entitled "Music as Heard, 1300–1600," which includes several essays from a 1997 conference organized by Rob Wegman at Princeton, is an excellent example; see Wegman (1998), which provides an introduction to that issue. Of course Johnson (1995) and Weber (1997) (and the issue of *Early Music* in which it appears, dedicated to "listening practice") are crucial as well, as is the semifictional model of three ways of listening to a Haydn symphony featured in Lowe (2007, 78–98).

1. RAPT ATTENTION

The first epigraph, from Lelio Guidiccioni's *Discorso sopra la musica*, 1635(?), Cod. Barb. lat. 3879, Biblioteca Apostolica Vaticana, 40v–41, reads in the original: "Mi rivolgo à te, beatissimo alato spirito, che col tuo canto prendi à ristorare, et confortare il languido, et innamorato Francesco; Ah, ferma gli accenti, non toccar più l'armonioso instrumento, che per esser troppo vitale, à lui reca morte, et per troppo sollevarlo, l'opprime. Deh sia mercede, fermare il corso di tanta mercede. Una sol nota, che mandi fuora, trarrai da lui tutta l'aura vitale. Se ferisci più quella sottil corda, tronchi il filo del viver suo; nè puoi maneggiar sì dolce arco, ch'egli non resti esangue alle sue saette. Così riferisce Francesco al finir della musica: l'[animare un accento] di più, lo rendeva esanime." The second epigraph, from Lodovico Casali's *Generale invito alle grandezze, e maraviglie della musica* (Modena: Gadaldino, 1629), 151, reads in the original: "Venendo il Canto, e il Suono da un'intimo pensiero della mente, e da un impeto della fantasia, e da uno affettuoso diletto del cuore, e percotendo insieme con l'aere, già dirotto, e stemperato, spirito di che ode, il quale, è un nodo dell'Anima, e del Corpo, facilmente viene à muovere la fantasia, e diletta il cuore, e penetra fin dentro all'ultime parti della mente: onde penetrato, opera il suo effetto secondo la dispositione, e complessione di chi gusta, e gode l'armonia della Musica."

1. "Deve operare imitando con l'armonia gli affetti dell'oratione, acciò che nel cantare habbino diletto non solo il proprio compositore, ma parimenti gli cantori et audienti" (Banchieri, *Cartella musicale* [Venice: Vincenti, 1614], 166, quoted in Ferrari Barassi 1994, 340). This formulation is very similar to (and may be derived from?) the nearly contemporaneous description of *affetto* by Caccini in his second book of *nuove musiche*: "*Affetto* in the singer is nothing other than the expression of the words, and the concept that one is singing about, designed to move *affetto* in the listener through the power of different notes, of various expressive devices through varying soft and loud" (Caccini 1614/1978, xxxiii). The goal of a musical language directed "to expressing concepts in order to impress *affetti* on the listener" had been stated by Vincenzo Galilei in his *Dialogo della musica antica et de la moderna* ([Florence: Marescotti, 1581], 89, quoted in Ferrari Barassi [1994, 331]), and it is entirely possible that Caccini was drawing on his fellow Florentine's rationale. Banchieri's use of the term *oratione* may be connected to Giulio Cesare Monteverdi's famous formulation concerning the "seconda prattica" (that *oratione* should be mistress of *armonia* rather than its servant; for a discussion of this passage, see Cusick 1993a), but its resonance with the discussion of *oratione sacra* (preaching) that follows should also be noted.

2. On performing instructions, see, for example, Cima (1610/1986) [at the end of each partbook]: "To those gentlemen who would sing these *concertini* of mine for your pleasure . . . please sing them as they stand, with as much *affetto* as possible." Of the many reports of singers "ravishing the *affetti*," see, for instance, Isidoro Ugurgieri Azzolini, *Le pompe sanesi overo relazioni delle huomini e donne illustri di Siena e suo stato* (Pistoia, 1649, 2:432–33): "Some [nuns?], by playing some musical instrument, or singing sweet songs or sacred compositions, ravish the *affetti* of those who hear them. . . . Unique is Bargaglia at Ogni Santi, who—among the other instruments she plays—works miracles and creates wonders in playing the theorbo" (quoted in Reardon 2001, 192; my translation). For an interesting exploration of musical *sacri affetti* in the context of early seventeenth-century Rome, tracing the possible intersection of textual elements in sacred music of the time with Caravaggio's approach to spiritual *affetti*, see Ziane (2007). While there are arguably some shared characteristics among a

number of instrumental passages marked *affetto,* most notably the use of non-diatonic chromaticism or diminished intervals, attempts to "pin down" a reliably shared "musical language" denoting *affetto* have not been entirely successful. See, for example, Donà (1967), Kubitschek (1988), Franco Piperno's introduction to Marini (1617/1990, esp. xxvi–xxx), and Dell'Antonio (1997, esp. 281ff.).

3. Paleotti (1961, 215); see also Boschloo (1998, 47). For a discussion of Augustine's reconfiguration of Ciceronian principles of oratory in his *De doctrina christiana,* see McGinness (1995, 55).

4. "Affetto: passion d'animo, nata dal disiderio del bene, e dall'odio del male" (Accademia della Crusca 1612/1974, 25). For more on *affetto* more generally, see Spear (1998).

5. McGinness (1995, 82–86). Preaching as an inspirational practice was also adopted by Franciscan-inspired movements such as the Company of Jesus; we will return below to the importance of both the Franciscan and Jesuit orders, and of their interrelationship, for ideals of listening and transcendence.

6. Tiacci (1999, 45) documents the "popular success" of preaching in the post-Tridentine era and refers to occasional crowds of many thousands. For a systematic overview of Roman preaching practices following the Council of Trent, see also McGinness (1980).

7. Tiacci, for example, posits a "Capuchin school" of preaching characterized by "austerity, apostolic zeal, fervor, immediacy" (1999, 45). On the Franciscan preachers' goal of focusing on the "authentic message" and the direct example of the saint's life and teachings, see Giombi (1998, 155).

8. "La sua oratoria non vuole strabiliare, ma predisporre l'uditorio alla parola di Dio, alla meditazione delle verità che la Sacra Scrittura propone." Girolamo Mautini da Narni, *Modo di comporre una predica,* quoted in Tiacci (1999, 107).

9. Lelio Guidiccioni in an unpublished "discorso" on Girolamo Mautini da Narni, quoted in Cargnoni (1998, 333); my translation. We will return to both these individuals, and to this very passage, in chapter 4.

10. Building from a quote of this remark, Lina Bolzoni (1995, 78) observes that "likewise the [sermon's] *prologhino* serves to direct in some way the spirit of the listener, in order to create a kind of musical resonance with the preacher's words."

11. "La strada dell'affetto, & dell'amore, la quale più tosto nasce per mezzo delle inspirationi, che delle meditationi." Herp, *Breve direttorio per conseguire la perfezione nella vita* (Venice, 1597), quoted in Treffers (1998, 78).

12. For an excellent concise overview of Augustine's theories of understanding and relationship to the divine, see Furley (1999).

13. As Treffers (2001, 354) observes, "In the first quarter of the seventeenth century, the type of affective spirituality that was thought to have its seat in the heart played a central role. The more emotion a work of art could summon up, the greater chance the soul had of being transported to the heavenly spheres."

14. Indeed, Borromeo maintained that artistic evocations of the divine had privileged status for their ability to "allow the faithful access to the spiritual world in a visionary state" (Menozzi 1997, 37).

15. See, for example, Kendrick (1996, 450–51). Colleen Reardon has also noted a number of descriptions of Sienese nuns' engagement with music as a

means to trigger ecstasy (see, for example, Reardon 2001, 104–6). The examples cited by Kendrick and Reardon mostly involve music-making individuals reaching ecstasy by their musical performance. However, there are other musicians who dwell on the ecstasy felt by listeners—for example, Lodovico Casali, who concludes his account of listening to singing nuns in Modena by claiming that "at times for my pleasure/taste [gusto] I become transported, delighting in those virginal voices . . . as if they were live incarnations of heavenly angels" (1629, 103).

16. While Evangelical theory maintained the presence of faith from birth, the Church of Rome (especially after the Council of Trent) held that education—through catechism—was necessary to deploy faith in the soul. See Fumaroli (1998, 337).

17. "Le genti si parton dalle piazze, et dalle loro case per girsene al sacro Tempio, invitato da i concerti spirituali per mezzo delle Musiche disposti, e però oltra gli effetti universali, che sono hormai da tutto il Mondo conosciuti, che sono quelli di rallegrare i spirti nostri afflitti, et lassi, di racconsolarci l'animo, di sollazzarci, di renderci disposti, e di trattenerci con diletto, c'incita, et ci spinge anco alle devotioni, et a i tributi divini; perche mentre nelle Chiese si loda Iddio con canto dolce, et soave, le genti vi corrano, e correndovi acquistano mercede, essendo che non vi corrano mai indarno, ne mai se ne partano senza qualche acquisto" (Zacconi 1592, 6).

18. See Morelli (1993, 175–76) and the frequent references to musical practice in De'Rossi (1645/1989, esp. 60, 174, 221, 227–28, 262, 291, 332).

19. Indeed, accounts from the Collegio Germanico indicate significant pride in the musical "draw" of the Collegio's public worship services, which already by 1611 featured primarily professional singers and instrumentalists rather than relying on the musical ability of the students, as had been the case at the founding of the institution three decades prior (Culley 1970, 343–66).

20. Andrea Amici, "Diario cerimoniale della ss. Basilica Vaticana dall'anno 1602 a tutto il 1620," 354, quoted in O'Regan (1999, 131), my translation. As O'Regan observes, the organist for this event may well have been Girolamo Frescobaldi, who was the titular organist at Saint Peter's at the time and had a reputation for attracting and moving crowds equivalent to that of some of the "star preachers" discussed above. For a similar contemporaneous account describing musical events for a special mass at the cathedral of Como in 1618 as a foretaste of heavenly transport, see Longatti et al. (1987, 301–2).

21. See Fumaroli (1998, 266–67).

22. As Goldthwaite (1994, 98) remarks, "One of the chief reforms inspired by the spirit of the Council of Trent was to make the liturgy at once more accessible and more impressive in order to involve the worshipper more actively." For a discussion of the political/polemical nature of this choice, see, for example, Burke (1987, 181).

23. Burke (1978, 232) suggests that this was in direct response to "Protestant attacks on transubstantiation, the Mass, and the special position of the priesthood."

24. According to the religious historian Robert Bireley (1999, 108), "[Public celebration of the Eucharist] was both a profession of faith and a celebration of

the Real Presence, which called for expression not only in word but in external, bodily actions, in music, song, and dance. The greater the faith, the more joyful was the occasion." Christopher Black (1998, 17) provides a similar perspective: "A new emphasis on the sacrifice of Christ, the presence of the flesh in the bread of the Host, and most importantly its display for veneration by the laity had thus become the central platform for Catholic reformers."

25. From the introduction to the *Catechismo Romano* (approved at the Council of Trent, 1566), quoted in Cuaz (1982, 286).

26. "2: Donde provenga così eccelso dono di fede. Poichè la fede è concepita dall'udito, è evidente quanto sia necessaria all'acquisto dell'eterna salute l'opera fedele e il ministero di un legittimo maestro." *Catechismo Romano*, quoted in Cuaz (1982, 283).

27. While Ratti's settings are generally polychoral, the elevation motets tend toward reduced textures as well as less celebratory texts. It is interesting to speculate whether the distinction between *grand motet* and *petit motet* that developed at the court of Louis XIV in the third quarter of the 1600s—the former polychoral and concerted, the latter more circumscribed in both forces and mood—may have been influenced by Ratti's model, also given the Barberini influence on French court culture in the mid-1600s; on the latter point, see the Envoy.

28. On the link between sonic intensity and potential "evocation of spiritual fervour and devotion" in Frescobaldi's toccatas, see Silbiger (2005, 465–66).

29. See Bonta (1969; 1990).

30. Weil (1974) is still the most thorough examination of the *Quarantore*, especially from a visual standpoint, Oddly, Weil does not address the musical component of the celebration, which contemporary commentators seem to consider an essential aspect of the ritual; see also Weston-Lewis (1998, 162–63). On the early Roman years of the *Quarantore*, see Wazbinski (1994, 320ff.); and for an overview of the musical context of the *Quarantore* in early modern Rome, see Hammond (1994, 151–55).

31. Bishops often went to extensive trouble to secure popular preachers for the *Quarantore*, even competing with each other in ways analogous to maneuvers by princes' agents and later operatic impresarios to secure particularly renowned singers; see Delcorno (1998, 124).

32. As Hammond (1994, 155) observes, "Since the Forty Hours was essentially a prolongation of [the] moment of adoration [of the Host during Mass], Quarantore could employ the same repertory of motets as the Elevations: texts focusing on the presence of Christ in the sacrament, set in a highly expressive style designed to evoke the sufferings of the Crucifixion." As we have seen above, instrumental works were also considered appropriate for the elevation, and it is entirely possible that these were also integrated into *Quarantore* devotions, though there is less specific evidence to that effect. For example, an account of a celebration of the *Quarantore* in the main church of the Jesuits in Rome in 1611 specifies that "musicalia instrumenta, et vocum armoniae non defuerunt," though this may be referring solely to concerted vocal music rather than including instrumental practice. See Culley (1970, 85). Also, the composer and keyboardist Luigi Rossi is documented as directing a *Quarantore* in Santa Maria Maggiore

in Rome in 1635, but again this leaves open whether the repertory would have included *toccate* as well as motets; see Holzer (2001).

33. Quoted in McGinness (1995, 84).

34. For Siena, see the account of a 1622 *Quarantore* in that city transcribed in Reardon (1994, 188–89); for Bergamo, see an account described in Roche (1966, 305).

35. As Tiacci observes: "One of the essential instances of Capuchin sermonizing was that offered by the *Quarantore*. The Capuchins were not the first to approach that form of evangelizing, but rather made it their own and spread it through their preaching" (1999, 39).

36. On the link between Franciscan preaching and the *predicatore apostolico*, see Criscuolo (1998a, 65).

37. For example, the following version of the "music as comfort" story is from an early account of the saint's actions, the *Second Life* by Thomas of Celano (ca. 1246): "During the days when Francis was staying at Rieti to have his eyes cared for, he called one of his companions who had been a lute player in the world, saying, 'Brother, the children of this world do not understand the hidden things of God. For musical instruments that were once destined for the praises of God lust has changed into a means of pleasure for the ears. Therefore, Brother, I would like for you to borrow a lute secretly and bring it here so that with it you may give some wholesome comfort to brother body that is so full of pains.' The brother replied, 'I am not a little ashamed to do so, Father, because I am afraid men may suspect that I am being tempted to frivolity.' The saint said: 'Let us then forget about it, brother. It is good to give up many things so that the opinion of others may not be harmed.' The next night, when the saint was watching and meditating about God, suddenly there came the sound of a lute of wonderful harmony and very sweet melody. No one was seen, but the volume of the sound marked the going and the coming of the lute player as he moved back and forth. Finally, with his spirit fixed on God, the holy father enjoyed so much the sweetness in that melodious song that he thought he had been transported to another world. When he got up in the morning he called the aforementioned brother and telling him everything just as it had happened, he added, 'The Lord who consoles the afflicted has never left me without consolation. For behold, I who could not hear the lutes of men have heard a far sweeter lute'" (Habig 1973, 466–67). A later version of the story, which became the "approved" version circulated by Franciscan hagiography, is from Saint Bonaventure's "Greater Legend" (*Legenda maior*), approved in 1266, when all other accounts of the life of Francis were officially disapproved (and ordered to be burned) by the Franciscan order (Bonaventure's is a conflation/redaction of previous lives of the saint, including that of Celano) [ch. 5, pt. 11]: "Not only did all creation obey his slightest wish; by his providence God himself condescended to his will. On one occasion he was afflicted with a number of different ailments simultaneously and he longed to hear some music to keep up his spirits. The fear of giving scandal made it impossible to get anyone to play for him, but then an angel came in answer to his prayer. One night as he lay awake thinking about God, he suddenly heard the sound of a lyre playing a melody of incredible beauty. He could see no one, but the rise and fall of the music showed that the musician was walking back

and forth. With his spirit all intent on God, Francis felt such pleasure at the wonderful melody that he thought he had left this world and the friars who were closest to him were well aware that something had happened. They knew from various indications that he was often visited by God who comforted him beyond measure, so that he could not hide it from them completely" (Habig 1973, 669–70). This account may be the source/inspiration for the account from the *Little Flowers* discussed below. The story of Francis's own singing is from the *Mirror of Perfection (Speculum perfectionis),* which seems to have survived only in manuscript tradition, so it is unclear how widely known this story might have been: "Sometimes [blessed Francis] would pick up a stick from the ground, and laying it on his left arm, he would draw another stick across it with his right hand like a bow, as though he were playing a viol or some other instrument; and he would imitate the movements of a musician and sing in French of our Lord Jesus Christ. But all this jollity would end in tears, and his joy would melt away in compassion for the sufferings of Christ. And at such times he would break into constant sighs, and in his grief would forget what he was holding in his hands, and be caught up in spirit into heaven" (Habig 1973, 1226–27).

38. Marion Habig, editor of the Franciscan-sponsored *St. Francis of Assisi: Writings and Early Biographies,* refers to this source as the "most widely read book" about Saint Francis. The "little flowers" were originally redacted by an anonymous writer (probably a friar from southeastern Tuscany or Umbria) at the end of the fourteenth century; the text circulated widely in manuscript version, was first printed in 1476, saw seventeen editions before the end of that century, and continued to be reprinted well into the sixteenth century, though Habig maintains that it was "almost forgotten in the seventeenth [century]" before enjoying a resurgence in the eighteenth and especially nineteenth centuries (Habig 1973, 1285–88). Given the popularity of the iconographic episode that I discuss here well into the 1600s, Habig's conclusion about the seventeenth-century fortune of this collection might require revisiting.

39. "Essendo san Francesco molto indebolito del corpo, tra per l'astinentia, & tra per le battaglie de i demoni, & egli volendo con il cibo spirituale dell'anima, confortare il corpo, cominciò a pensare della smisurata gloria, & gaudio de beati di vita eterna, & sopra ciò pregava Dio, che gli concedesse gratia di assaggiare una particella di quel gaudio. Et stando in questo pensiero, subito gli apparve un'angelo con grandissimo splendore, il quale haveva una violetta nella mano dritta, & l'archetto nella sinistra. Et stando san Francesco tutto stupefatto nell'aspetto di quell'Angelo, esso menò una sola volta l'archetto sopra la violetta, & subitamente tanta soavità, & melodia addolcì l'anima sua, & solevossi si ogni sentimento corporale, che secondo che recitò poi alli compagni lui dubitava, che se l'Angelo havesse menato l'archetto, che per intollerabil dolcezza l'anima sua sarebbe partita dal corpo" (*Fioretti di San Francesco* 1576, 92v–93).

40. Prominent artists from the late sixteenth and seventeenth centuries who depicted some version of this episode include Gioacchino Assereto, Gérard Audan, Agostino and Annibale Carracci, Giuseppe Cesari (Cavalier d'Arpino), Domenichino, Domenico Fetti, Andrea Lilli, Paolo Piazza, Guido Reni, Francesco Ribalta, Raphael Sadeler, Carlo Saraceni, Bernardo Strozzi, and Francesco Vanni; the earliest of these works appears to date from about 1580, and the

period of greatest "density" for this theme was about 1590–1630. Askew (1969) provides an initial assessment of this tradition, and I have found quite a few additional instances, at this point approximately three dozen, drawing from Pigler (1974) and from a variety of other sources and encounters (for example, there is an otherwise unmentioned instance of the theme in a side chapel of Santa Maria Maggiore in Rome, by the hand of an unnamed artist). See also Radinò (1982). Arnauld Bréjon de Lavergne (in Galeries nationales du Grand Palais [France] and Palazzo Reale di Milano 1988, 74, 385–86) also remarks on the widespread popularity of the iconographic theme and suggests that Francesco Vanni's engraving from the last decade of the 1500s was the catalyst for its popularity throughout the Italian peninsula in the early seventeenth century.

41. "Dalle cronache di San: Francesco, mio particolare protettore, si racconta, come dilettandosi della Musica, gli vene un desiderio di gustar il suono di una Vivuola, che appresso d'un San. Huomo nomato F. Pacifico, suo caro compagno, si serbava . . . mà esso Padre ricusando, per buon rispetto, Iddio Sommo Provveditore di tutte le cose, che i servi suoi volentieri consola le mandò dal Cielo un'Angelo, che sonando una Vivuola, come era il desiderio di San Francesco con quella soavità, che comprender si può da man Celeste, consolò l'anima, e l'aflitto corpo del Santo Padre" (Casali 1629, 89).

42. Since the descriptive passage occurs within a broader discussion of the excellence of the *viole*—after all, Maugars's own instrument—we might not be surprised by the emphasis on its "sweetest and most charming" status. Maugars may also be drawing on Mersenne's claim that the instrument "contrefait la voix en tous ses modulations' and that 'il n'y a rien de plus ravissant." Marin Mersenne, *Harmonie universelle* (Paris: Cramoisy, 1636–37), 3:197, quoted in Ferrari Barassi (1994, 330).

43. Reni was closely associated with Franciscan spirituality in early seventeenth-century Rome; see Fumaroli (1998, 378).

44. For more on the Cappella Merenda and Domenichino's role in its decoration, see Carloni (1996).

45. Scholars have commented on Domenichino's exceptional and systematic interest in music; the most thorough discussion is in Spear (1982, 40–46). Meucci (1996) even characterizes him (somewhat tongue-in-cheek) as a "musicologist," arguing that the artist's *Madonna con santi Giovanni Evangelista e Petronio*, created around 1626–29 for the Bolognese community church of S. Petronio in Rome, provides a realistic depiction of angels engaged in what he characterizes as a new-style trio ensemble (violin, cornetto, viola da gamba, lute), and he goes so far as to suggest that various *pentimenti* and modifications to the angel-musicians' hands may even be depicting a specific chord. Whether this is the case or not, the depiction of the angelic ensemble in the Merenda fresco is more rudimentary, though arguably more dynamic.

46. While Gentili refers to the more common iconography of the violin-playing angel with Saint Francis, this painting is from 1688—substantially later than the tradition on which we are focusing here—and there does not seem to be a parallel tradition concerning the Magdalen in the early seventeenth century. On the other hand, a popular medieval hagiographic text *(The Golden Legend)* conveyed an image of the Magdalen, in her later years, being raised to heaven to

hear angelic music; we will touch again on this image in chapter 4. On intersections between visual iconography of the ecstatic Magdalen (without specific depictions of instruments or music making) and texts in sacred music of the earlier seventeenth century, see Ziane (2007, 176). Ziane briefly touches upon parallels with Caravaggio's ecstatic depictions of Francis, mentioning a text by Marino set by three separate composers (Cifra, il Verso, Dentice) in the early seventeenth century; in a footnote she tantalizingly refers to a significant repertory of Marinist texts on Francis set to music in that time frame but regrettably leaves discussion of the topic for a later date.

47. One example that would bear further analysis is that of Saint Cecilia, who is of course extensively associated with music in early modern depictions, especially after the foundation of the Roman Academy of musicians that bears her name in 1585. Some of these depictions do appear to emphasize the power of sound on the listener. See, for example, depictions of the saint by Guido Reni, which exist in a couple of different versions with the saint holding a bowed string instrument—either "da braccio" or "da gamba"—and perhaps draw on the image of the violin-wielding angel; for example, Bellori described one such version as "[Saint Cecilia] . . . who pulls a bow-stroke on the *violino,* turning her head and eyes to the harmony" ("[Santa Cecilia] . . . la quale tira un'arcata di violino girando la testa e gli occhi all'armonia"; Bellori, *Le vite de'pittori, scultori, e architetti moderni* [1673], ed. E. Borea [Turin: Einaudi, 1976], 12, quoted in Bini, Strinati, and Vodret 2000, 230–31), and it is easy to see the "arcata di violino" as analogous to the single all-consuming angelic bowstroke of the *Little Flowers.* However, many contemporaneous depictions of Cecilia do not draw on the images of listening explored above, so a full discussion of the various varieties of musical expression and reception embodied by Cecilia in early modern iconography will await another day.

48. See, for example, Maravall (1986, 90ff.).

49. As Giovanni Baffetti observes, "The Jesuits quickly understood that the mission of disciplining souls had to be paralleled and supported by a capillary cultural 'reconquest,' which had to be put in place 'in the field' through education, especially of the ruling classes. . . . Ignatius of Loyola and his followers furthermore set for themselves the objective of creating an intellectual elite *ex novo,* one dedicated to study and research, in order to ensure high cultural prestige for the order, and then guaranteeing—through teaching—the growth and transmission of that cultural heritage" (1997, 34).

50. Indeed, before the canonization of Loyola and other early Jesuit saints (which came in 1622, after a long and purposeful "canonization drought" following the Council of Trent), Franciscan devotion was seen as crucial to the new spirit of reform at the end of the sixteenth century, especially among the upper classes. See Treffers (2001, 353ff.). Franciscan devotion, particularly mysticism and "Franciscan affective spirituality," was crucial to the militancy of the first decades of the Catholic Reformation; several new saints canonized in the first decades of the seventeenth century (Carlo Borromeo, canonized in 1610; Filippo Neri, Francis Xavier, Ignatius of Loyola, and Teresa of Avila, canonized in 1622; and Andrea Avellino, canonized in 1624) were assigned strong mystical traits in their iconography and drew strongly from the Franciscan tra-

dition. On the low canonization rate following the Council of Trent, perhaps as a result of a tightening of the criteria for determining the saintly status of an individual to be canonized, see Burke (1987, 49–50) and Fumaroli (1998, 263).

51. Or, in Endean's terms, "The fundamental principle is that [the Exercises] be applied to the dispositions of the person who wishes to receive them. . . . The stress is on the exercitant's distinctive experience, shaped as it is by a particular history" (2008, 53).

52. For an overview of the importance of codification of rhetorical strategy for early modern Jesuits, see, for example, Baffetti (1997, 79).

53. Again Baffetti: "It is thus not surprising to find that the third book [of Soarez's *De arte rhetorica,* a crucial Jesuit text first published in 1562 and circulating widely into the mid-1600s], the one on *elocutio,* is 'somewhat longer' than the other two, nor that he integrates within it the other two parts of rhetoric, *memoria* and *pronuntiatio,* which are usually autonomous in the writing of Latin rhetoricians. Along with *elocutio,* the latter two are not so much concerned with the argumentative efficacy of the proofs to be deployed; rather, they address the connotative efficacy of spoken language. . . . This underlines the prevalently oral application of Jesuit rhetoric, because once again the medium of transmission is the sense of hearing" (1997, 90–91).

54. As Endean (2008, 64) observes, during the generalate of Claudio Acquaviva (1580–1615), "the Society's distinctive spiritual resource, the Exercises, [became] a basis for daily life; Jesuits came to make a week's retreat on an annual basis, and normally to draw on the Exercises also for their daily prayer."

55. Treffers (1998, 77). As Treffers further observes, visual artworks and devotional tracts thus could function similarly as tools of "rapture."

56. As McGinness (1995, 99) observes, "The intended effect [of discourse on the virtues] was to create an ideal of holiness and a model of Christian life whose essential characteristic was an unconditional obedience to the hierarchical Church." This model of "right thinking" could be extended further: McGinness suggests that "though *recte sentire,* more properly conceived, moved along a continuum, in its fullest measure it admitted no dissent, questioning, or independent or insubordinate action. It manifested itself emphatically in the virtues of humility, obedience, justice, zeal for orthodoxy, intolerance of heresy, overflowing charity toward all within the Church, and a fierce animosity toward outsiders insofar as they violated the Church" (114). We will return to this issue in subsequent chapters.

57. As Richard Goldthwaite (1994, 98) has concisely remarked, "One of the chief reforms inspired by the spirit of the Council of Trent was to make the liturgy at once more accessible and more impressive in order to involve the worshipper more actively." In fact, the Catholic practice of First Confession and First Communion was introduced in the early seventeenth century and was highlighted by the Jesuits—as we have seen, spiritual instructors to the ruling classes—as a hallmark of conscious and active Christian participation, "a major event to be celebrated appropriately after adequate preparation" (Bireley 1999, 104). Note the stated importance of "adequate preparation" to this affirmation of spiritual connection, and the championing of these "elevating" rituals by the order most concerned with linking social and spiritual distinction.

2. AURAL COLLECTING

The chapter epigraph, in which Pietro Della Valle reminds Lelio Guidiccioni of his listening experiences, is from Della Valle's "Della musica dell'età nostra, che non è punto inferiore, anzi è migliore di quella dell'età passata; al sig. Lelio Guidiccioni [16 January 1640]," in *Le origini del melodramma: Testimonianze dei contemporanei*, ed. Angelo Solerti (Turin: Fratelli Bocca, 1903), 170. "E se V.S. tanto tempo fa si sentì andare una volta, come mi ha contato, quasi in eccesso di mente in sentir sonare in Parma il Correggio, ho anche inteso (se ne ricordi, per grazia) che un'altra volta in Roma, pochi anni or sono in casa di monsignor Raimondo, fu veduta liquefarsi, per dir così, di dolcezza, sentendo cantare alcuni di quei versi di Virgilio, che fra le opere del maggior fratello de' Mazzocchi si vedono con leggiadria messi in musica."

1. On the collection of scores, especially in the later seventeenth century, see Murata (1990; 1993), and more recently Ruffatti (2006; 2008), concerning the distribution of Italian cantatas in France and elsewhere in central Europe. On collections of instruments displayed by members of the Roman curia alongside other wonders, see Wazbinski (1994, esp. 136–38), Hammond (1994, 89–98, 299 n. 12), and Ehrlich (2002, 33); and on processes of "acquisition" of musical resources (objects as well as people), see Parisi (1996). Generally on the increasing and varied collecting practices of early modern Italian elites, see Findlen (1994; 1998).

2. "Magnificence was an outward sign of magnanimity, the greatness of spirit which is a central virtue in Aristotle's Ethics. . . . For families who had already arrived at the summit, conspicuous consumption was regarded as a duty, *L'obbligazione di viver con fasto*, as one leading Neapolitan lawyer, Francesco D'Andrea, described it [in the late seventeenth century]" (Burke 1987, 154).

3. On the rise in the consumption of artifacts generally in early modern Italy, see, for example, Goldthwaite (1987, 34). Specifically on Rome, and its combination of sacred and secular concerns, see Ago (2006); for instance, Ago characterizes early modern Rome as a place where "cultural production, in all its forms, and celebratory culture, also in all its aspects, whether secular or sacred, found active demand and a lively marketplace." (xx).

4. Tasso's critical dialogues (e.g., *La cavalletta*) were arguably the first texts to establish a tradition of discourse on the effects of literature from the reader's perspective. See Carapezza (1988, 3). On the prominence of Tasso and his theories in early seventeenth-century Rome, see Colantuono (1997, 174–75).

5. The notion of connoisseurship extended seamlessly from what we now define as "the arts" to many other aspects of Roman religious culture. For example, papal ceremonies required specific rituals, and only a few select individuals were versed in the exquisite details such rituals required; Peter Burke (1987, 176) cannily refers to these elites as "an important minority of connoisseurs of ritual."

6. See Fumaroli (1998, 275). As Fumaroli observes, the term *gustare* was much used in Catholic mystical writings before this point as a description of the deep understanding of the mysteries of the spirit; around this time it begins to come into common usage as a descriptive of physical experience, and through

the phenomenon of connoisseurship the secular meaning eventually eclipses the sacred one.

7. The historian Antonella Romano, for example, has argued (2004, 415) that early modern Rome "offered a kind of political, social, and cultural polycentrism that sustained the intellectual vitality of the Eternal City. . . . This complex society produced a new cultural and intellectual patrimony that was without equivalent in the early modern world."

8. For more on this issue, see Fabris (1999, 94–95).

9. On the systematic approach taken by Cardinal Guido Bentivoglio and his brother Enzo to build their connection to this "circuit," see Fabris (1999, 47ff., 84ff., 224, 228, and passim). For more on Bentivoglio and his perspective on the role of a cardinal in the early seventeenth century, see Bentivoglio (1648). See also Annibaldi's discussion of Cardinal Aldobrandini's participation in the "circuit" in Annibaldi (1987, 150ff.), and see the extensive documentation on musical activity in Cardinal Montalto's *famiglia* in Hill (1997).

10. "Il Card[ina]l del Monte hiermatt[in]a al suo Giardino vicino a Ripetta banchetto il card[in]al de Medici, e altri Cav[alie]ri fiorentini, con molto splendore quantità de cibi delicati, secondo la stagione, servitij di giacci, ornamenti di trionfi, et statue con grandiss[im]a esquisitezza; et oltre il trattenim[en]to de suoni, e canti delli primi virtuosi di Roma, gli diede gran gusto con mostrargli le distilatorie, ordegni di geometria, et altre curiosità delle quali Signoria Ill[ustrissi] ma grandamente si diletta" (Biblioteca Apostolica Vaticana, Urb. Lat. 1094, c. 307, quoted in Wazbinski 1994, 316 n. 85).

11. For a discussion of the expanding role of the secretary in early modern Rome, see Quondam (1981, 132ff.).

12. The combined term *virtuoso of taste* is one coined by Fumaroli (1994); however, the term *gusto* did have common currency in early modern Italy to describe the judging ability displayed by such individuals, and the term *virtuoso* was regularly associated with elite status and superior sensibility. Chapter 4 will examine this latter term and its context in more detail. In the discussion that follows, I am using the term rather than the more generic "connoisseur" because I want to emphasize what I consider to be a self-conscious attempt by such individuals to link these two seventeenth-century concepts as a marker of both status and social function.

13. For example, Giovanni Battista Agucchi, author of a noteworthy essay on painting (see Agucchi 1995), was *maggiordomo* to Cardinal Aldobrandini and later Gregory XV; Giulio Mancini, also the author of an important essay that we will consider at some length below, was a distinguished physician who treated many members of the church elite; and Lelio Guidiccioni, whose work we will examine at length in chapter 4, was a prelate who held a number of benefices, including a canonry in Santa Maria Maggiore in Rome. Stefano Pignatelli, a friend (possibly lover) of Scipione Borghese, was even raised by Paul V to the cardinalate; Ehrlich (2002, 32) suggests that his "role as Scipione's intellectual and artistic advisor may be likened to that played by Giovanni Battista Agucchi for Cardinal Pietro Aldobrandini." Pignatelli was also the dedicatee of an important collection of Roman *alfabeto* monody, Robletti's *Raccolta di varii concerti musicali* of 1621; see Gavito (2006, 178).

14. Janie Cole has examined processes of cultural brokerage enacted by Michelangelo Buonarroti the Younger. While Buonarroti was based in Florence, he had significant contact with the cardinal *famiglie* of the Barberini (more about this specific cohort below), and Cole's description of Buonarroti's role could apply generally to *virtuosi* of taste in early modern Rome: "A patron-broker-client relationship consisted of a three-party, indirect exchange in which a broker mediated between parties separated by physical, social, and political distances. His resources were usually the people he knew who could provide access to power and place, a strategic location, and ample time to devote to managing his social relations. A broker brought about communication for profit by manipulating people and information. . . . Here the role of a broker is carried out by a patrician, working primarily to secure and maintain his social position with his patron and in a wider courtly context, and whose activity may be suited to the broader ideology of a nobility without a profession growing up around courtly circles during the early seventeenth century" (2007, 748). On the flexibility and power of such patron-broker relationships, see also Weissman (1987, 36–37).

15. De Benedictis (1991, 114–15), paraphrasing Mancini.

16. Vincenzo Scamozzi, *L'idea della architettura universale* (Venice: Scamozzi, 1615), 3:305, quoted in Rebecchini (2002, 262–63).

17. "Studio di rari disegni di eccellenti pittori, pitture et compositioni d'intavolatura sopra il cembalo scritte a mano et non impresse dal famoso Girolamo Frescobaldi suo Padre" (Bellori 1664/2000, 26).

18. See, for example, De'Rossi (1645/1989), Cappelletti and Testa (1994, esp. 43), and Delbeke (2008).

19. Florence, Archivio di Stato, Fondo Mediceo del Principato, vol. 3622, c. 401v, transcribed in Camiz 1996, 286; my translation.

20. "Per poter collocare pitture, & scolture . . . statue, Pili, storie di basso rilievo, ritratti d'huomini illustri in arme, & in lettere, e simiglianti cose, che danno maniera di ragionare, e passar il tempo virtuosamente." Scamozzi, *L'idea della architettura universale*, quoted in Ehrlich 2002, 358 n. 111; my translation).

21. See, for example, Cuaz (1982, 174). Fumaroli (1998, 45–46) remarks on the crucial role played by Florentine and later Roman academies in building a discourse both about individual arts and about their synthesis. The unity of the arts on an idealized Parnassus/Arcadia-on earth was a crucial metaphor in the self-fashioning of Italian academies in the later sixteenth and seventeenth centuries; in this, of course, the Arcadians were following a tradition that was already well established by that point, though reaction to the poetry of Guarini can be seen as a crucial renewal of that tradition, one that sustained courtly (and especially Roman) aesthetics well into the eighteenth century. For an excellent discussion of the confluence of the Parnassus and Arcadia metaphors in academic life of this period, see Fumaroli (1998, 24–35). On the essential role played by the refined *conversazioni* in mid-seventeenth-century Roman cultural prestige, see also Brosius (2009).

22. On contemporary discussion by Cardinal Giulio Sacchetti (1587–1663), a prominent member of the curia, on the proper formation of a "perfect gentleman" within the church hierarchy, see Fosi (1997, 259).

23. "Ieri, pregato, condussi il S.r ambasciatore di Fiandra con tre o quattro altri SS.ri principalissimi fiamminghi a sentir sonar la Napolitana, e gli piacque in estremo e volsi sapere il nome e cognome di lei, e del marito, e lo notò sul libro; desiderava anco sentire la sig.ra Ippolita" (Vincenzo Landinelli to Enzo Bentivoglio, January 21, 1612, quoted in Fabris 1999, 240).

24. John Evelyn, *The Diary of John Evelyn,* ed. E.S. De Beer (Oxford: Oxford University Press, 1955), 2:364, quoted in Hammond (1994, 103).

25. As Laura Alemanno (1995, 100) observes, "The attitude [of the Accademia] reveals a more political than cultural outlook: it is evident that art is being used as a tool to make Roman political supremacy more attractive and advantageous." Still, the cultural and the political are here closely linked: the Accademia was designed to demonstrate how the members' political authority was a function of their shared cultural prestige as well as their religious status. Again Alemanno: "Popes Clement VII and Urban VIII participate in the meetings, surrounded by cardinals and high prelates: all this testifies to the fact that the Accademia is the space in which the curia makes its strategy manifest. The cultural politics of the Accademia degli Umoristi thus coincides precisely with that of the curia—indeed, in the public-private space of Palazzo Mancini, it can be pursued with more freedom and verve" (101).

26. For a more detailed discussion of the topics presented and discussed by the Umoristi, see Alemanno (1995, 103–5).

27. As Estelle Haan (1998, 105) observes, in Milton's epigrams in praise of Baroni—whom he may well have heard in the context of the Accademia degli Umoristi—"the emphasis is more on the effect of her song upon the listener than on the quality of her voice per se." Milton may have been connecting to a tradition of verses in praise of Baroni, many by members of the Umoristi, published in 1639; on this volume, and Cardinal Francesco Barberini's own copy, see Hammond (1994, 86) and chapter 4 of this book.

28. The phenomenon of "aural collecting" can thus be understood as operating smoothly within the consumption model that Richard Goldthwaite (1994, 203) has posited for seventeenth-century Roman elites—"At once urban in its emphasis on the architectural grandeur of the noble's residence and private in the exclusiveness of the life within: these were the values that informed the new consumption habits. The new material culture created by the Italian upper classes expressed their sense of what constituted noble status."

29. Fosi (2008, 35) observes, for example, that "national and regional ties were perhaps the strongest and the most important ones when it came to finding a place in the 'great sea' of the Roman court. Pietro da Cortona, just as he arrived in Rome in the 1620s, was picked out for his Tuscan dialect by Marcello Sacchetti, *depositario generale* and *tesoriere segreto* of Urban VIII. He went on to become the favourite painter of the Sacchetti family and of the Barberini pope, not to mention other Florentine families allied with them." Sacchetti was another *virtuoso* of taste—and the brother of a cardinal—with influence as an intermediary between artists and the heads of the cardinal *famiglie.*

30. For Del Monte's musical patronage, especially his role in the 1589 celebrations and his close collaboration with Emilio de'Cavalieri, see Wazbinski (1994, esp. 84ff.).

31. Quoted in Wazbinski (1994, 137–38; my translation). This would seem to be an early document of the type of "circuli" that is discussed above. Del Monte later acquired land in the outskirts of the city (the *vigna* in Via di Ripetta—see the reference to his entertaining there above, note 10—and in 1615 purchased the Palazzo Avogadro connected to the *vigna* and had his extensive collection of artworks and musical instruments transferred there. Del Monte was the dedicatee of several early seventeenth-century musical prints in the "nuove musiche" tradition, and from 1622 he became the protector of the Congregazione dei Musici, later to be known as the Accademia di Santa Cecilia. See Camiz and Zino (1983, 73).

32. Indeed, Carter (1991) points out the tendency in Medici circles to underplay the naming of musicians in official accounts of spectacles; it may well be that Del Monte was still working within a late sixteenth-century Medicean model of descriptive convention, while the collectors of the ensuing decades (whose writings we will examine shortly) developed new traditions of list making and categorizing to display their auditory *gusto*.

33. The connections between Del Monte, Montalto, and Giustiniani (and their link to the Medici court) are most thoroughly explored by art historians in connection with their collective patronage of Caravaggio; Claudio Strinati and Rossella Vodret (2000, 17) observe that the visual representation of "musical" subjects appears to be extremely powerful for this "handful of 'enlightened' noble intellectuals, who lived between Rome and Florence, [and] had in its hands the reins to guide the new course of cultural life and lay the groundwork for that which can be defined as an epochal renewal not only of art and music, but also in the new discoveries of science." Perhaps this formulation is a bit idealistic, but nonetheless the cultural liveliness of the Florentine nation in Rome, and its role in fostering professional artists and musicians, are significant. See also Onori (2000, 17).

34. In his travel diary, writing from Paris under the date June 29, 1606, Giustiniani says, "Si visitò poi monsignor Barberino, nunzio" (Bizoni 1995, 100).

35. A list of references on Barberini patronage of the visual arts would take up many pages, and I refer the reader to the bibliography at the end of this volume; the most thorough perspective on Barberini patronage of music is of course provided in Hammond (1994).

36. For example, Lorenza Mochi Onori attributes to Cassiano Dal Pozzo (1588–1657), one of the *virtuosi* of taste who was most prized by Maffeo/Urban and later by Francesco Barberini, the responsibility for "the elaboration of a new style of painting, which would be perfectly suited to the manifestation of the philosophical and political concepts of his patrons the Barberini" (Onori 2000, 18). Solinas (2000, 5) also emphasizes the role of Dal Pozzo in amplifying the practice, shared by the Medici and the Barberini, of harnessing connoisseurship for political/ dynastic purposes, and Fumaroli (1994, 56) specifically mentions Dal Pozzo and Giustiniani as important examples of the new model of *virtuoso* of taste.

37. Luigi Spezzaferro observes that the collections of professional *virtuosi*, "unlike those belonging to public individuals, . . . were of an ephemeral nature. In fact, it would almost seem that they were in many cases created specifically to not 'remain constant'" (1996, 243–44).

38. Quoted in Spezzaferro (1996, 242–43; my translation).

39. Fumaroli (1994, 54; my translation) has characterized this phenomenon as "the metamorphosis of literature on art, which shifts in 1620s and 1630s Rome from being the monopoly of artists to that of erudite spectators, enlightened judges of the Roman art scene."

40. For more on the fame and distribution of Mancini's *Considerazioni sulla pittura,* on which such later seventeenth-century critics as Baglioni and Bellori appear to have drawn extensively, see Olson (2005), Maccherini (1997), and especially Mancini (1956). Mancini regularly acquired artifacts as payment or "gifts" from his clients and provided them as gifts to his Barberini patrons and other luminaries of the cardinal circuit.

41. "Basta solo un buon giuditio ammaestrato con aver visto più pitture e da per sé e col giuditio di più intendenti . . . un huomo di buon giuditio naturale, con la peritia universale delle cose, con erudition del disegno possa giudicar della perfettione, del valore e del collocar' a loro luoghi le pitture" (Mancini 1956, 7).

42. Fumaroli has aptly described the connoisseur's combination of natural *gusto* and trained *giudizio:* "Knowledge of the history of painting, comparison of its various styles and its various schools, assiduous attendance at artists' ateliers and collections of drawings, sculpture, and paintings furnish the careful and methodical spectator with those delicate and precise antennae that are called *giudizio* in Italy and which the French have called *goût*" (1994, 54). Note, of course, that *gusto* is also a common early modern Roman term for the "antennae" that Fumaroli describes. On the importance of Mancini in the nascent definition of connoisseurship, see also De Benedictis (1991, 114–15). A similar suspicion of the artist is expressed a generation earlier by Gabriele Paleotti, who addresses his 1582 *discorso* on sacred and profane images primarily to patrons and "those who customarily embellish their churches and their homes with such ornaments" rather than to painters, who are (or should be) primarily "executors of [the patrons'] wills." See Paleotti (1961, 122). Indeed, Spezzaferro (2001, 22) has suggested that Mancini's essay is specifically directed to the aspiring *virtuoso* of taste—setting the parameters for the "professionality" of that role—rather than to the cardinals and noblemen who headed the Roman *famiglie.*

43. Mancini's four schools of living painters are (1) that of Caravaggio (Mancini lists a half-dozen artists in this school and describes it as most connected with expression of nature); (2) that of the Carracci family (described as having "per proprio l'intelligenza dell'arte con gratia et espression d'affetto"); (3) that of Cavalier Giuseppe (which is neither as natural as the Caravaggist nor as grave/solid as the Carraccist but which "ha in sè quella vaghezza che in un tratto rapisce l'occhio e diletta"); and (4) an "independent" group, apparently a catch-all category of sorts (Mancini 1956, 108–10); his extensive suggestions on the placement of art, both to reflect these categories and to serve other protoaesthetic and functional goals, follow on 112–14. Note the use of terminology that is simultaneously refined and connected to sacred considerations *(affetto, grazia, rapisce),* as well as nontechnical.

44. Giustiniani (1981, 43–44). Giustiniani's categories are a mixture of technique, subject matter, genre, and general artistic approach; the highest category comprises artists who can combine "di maniera" and "dalla natura," or idealized subject matter and depiction of nature. Indeed, Giustiniani was keen on

developing categories to display his *gusto* in a wide range of matters; in addition to the categories of visual art mentioned here and the parallel discussion of musical "categories" below, he lists ways of making sculpture seem old (73), various types of hunting (84), and varieties of fish to try on one's travels (108).

45. "Secondo le materie, il modo del colorito, il tempo nel quale sono state fatte e della schuola secondo la quale sono state condotte. . . . Si dovranno collocare prima le più antiche . . . e fra queste prima le tramontane, poi le lombarde, poi le toscane e romane, perchè in questo modo lo spettatore con più facilità potrà vedere e godere e, doppo haver visto e goduto, reservare nella memoria le pitture viste. Ma non vorrei già che fosse messa insieme la medissima schuola e maniera. . . . Ma vorrei che si tramezzassero con altre maniere e schuole del medessimo secolo, perchè in questo modo, per la varietà, deletteranno più e, con la comparation della varietà del modo di far, più si faranno sentir senza offesa di gusto, come sarebbe se fra queste si proponesse qualche pittura d'altro secolo" (Mancini 1956, 144–45).

46. Thus the collection of works of art in the 1620s-30s "tends to become a permanent exhibit of 'assembled taste.' . . . The art lover, whether princely or private, assembles the proofs and the sources of his taste" (Fumaroli 1994, 55). Fumaroli suggests that this phenomenon is tied to the Florentine-Roman cultural link at the turn of the *Seicento:* "This new, eclectic, and erudite concept of the gallery is set from the 1610s-1620s in Florence at Palazzo Pitti, under Cosimo II, followed by his son Prince Leopold, and in Rome, where cardinals Del Monte and Borghese lead the way" (55).

47. For a discussion of Giustiniani's collection in these terms, see Spezzaferro (2001, 12).

48. For example, Franco Piperno (2001, 134) describes Vagnoli's music making as "a performance art that placed musical consumers of the Pesaro court [of Guidubaldo] in the then-infrequent condition of mere [sic] listeners." Piperno observes that the more common model presented in the accounts of life at the court (taken from Ludovico Agostini's *Giornate soriane,* written retrospectively in the mid-1560s) reflects a collective practice similar to the court's literary discursive exchanges: for example, "Some music books were then brought, from which all sang many diverse madrigals by different authors" (135). As Piperno observes, on other days instruments were brought out and the amateurs played, or they sang Willaert motets, and this is fully in keeping with practices also described by Castiglione. For a discussion of the discourse around professional singers in Castiglione's *Cortegiano,* see Lorenzetti (2003, 79–80).

49. "Nel presente corso dell'età nostra, la musica non è molto in uso, in Roma non essendo essercitata da gentil huomini, nè si suole cantare a più voci al libro, come per gl'anni a dietro, non ostante che sia grandissime occasioni d'unire e di trattenere le conversationi. È ben la musica ridotta in un insolita e quasi nuova perfettione, venendo esercitata da gran numero de'buoni musici, che . . . porgono col canto loro artificioso e soave molto diletto a chi li sente. . . . Per i tempi passati era molto in uso il trattenersi con un conserto di Viole o di Flauti . . . [ma] l'esperienza ha fatto conoscere che tale trattenimento, con l'uniformità del suono e delle consonanze, veniva assai presto a noia, e più tosto incitava a dormire che a passare il tempo et il caldo pomeridiano" (Giustiniani 1628/1878, 30–31, 144–45).

50. Severo Bonini, who also moved in Tuscan circles at this time (though his specialization as a music theorist and his status outside the Roman court does not place him in the same category of connoisseur), likewise observed that "madrigals to be sung *a tavolino* without being concerted have been sent to oblivion" (1979, 100) [I madrigali da cantarsi a tavolino senza concertarsi si sono mandati in oblio].

51. "Oggi non se ne compongono tanti [madrigali] perchè si usa poco di cantare madrigali, nè ci è occasione in cui si abbiano da cantare; amando più le genti di sentir cantare a mente con gli strumenti in mano con franchezza, che di vedere quattro o cinque compagni che cantino ad un tavolino col libro in mano, che ha troppo del scolaresco e dello studio" (Della Valle 1903, 171).

52. "Sarà un valent'uomo quello che cantandosi una cosa non più udita da lui, ne possa capire la metà. Ma ciò forse non avvertiscono i Compositori, perche sapendo quello che si canta, pù facilmente ne comprendono le parole: il che non avviene à gl'uditori; che per ciò si partono il più delle volte mal sodisfatti di queste Musiche" (Doni 1635, 105).

53. On the changing role of singing in the definition of late sixteenth-century noble masculinity, see also Wistreich (2007, esp. 273).

54. "E questo è il frutto della moderna Musica concertata; fatta non per tutti, mà per puochi. Anzi che aggiungo, mentre la Concertata Musica non sarà accompagnata da Cantori, di Scienza pari, mai potrà haver garbo ... dove si gustarà dal perfetto Cantore soavità, e dolcezza, dal altro imperfetto, si perderà il gusto, scemandosi il valor della Musica, con puoca reputatione de buoni Musici" (Casali 1629, 185).

55. For the dynamics of the professional and semiprofessional musical establishment at the Collegio Germanico, see Culley (1970, esp. 133ff.).

56. See Camiz and Ziino (1983); Camiz (1988; 1989; 1991) (the last with specific reference to the spaces where music making took place in the Roman cardinal courts of the time); and for a concise summary, Strinati and Vodret (2000). On the version of the painting created for Cardinal Del Monte, see also Mahon (1990).

57. Camiz and Ziino (1983) and later Camiz (1989) speculate at some length about the significance of the specific madrigals depicted in the two Caravaggio paintings, pointing out that they do not fit any extant version of Arcadelt's *libro primo,* from which all four of the madrigals in the Giustiniani version of the image (currently in the Ermitage) are derived. The authors also observe that all four madrigals refer to sweetness and sensuality, though this is admittedly a very common theme in madrigal texts set by the Arcadelt generation. Building on speculations by Camiz (1991, 221ff.), I suspect that the works are iconic rather than specific and that their commonality lies in their general status as remembered sonic events of the kind that will be discussed in the context of "sonic galleries" below. A further meaning may reside in the depiction of the Arcadelt madrigals as "classics" to be remembered and revisited, much like the "older classics" (Michelangelo, Titian) that Giustiniani, Del Monte, and others collected alongside the works of living painters; this would further expand the analogy between the construction of an artistic and musical canon (dependent on the listener/spectator's understanding) on the part of the Roman connoisseur tradition.

58. See Bolzoni (1995, xxv). As Bolzoni further observes, "At the turn of the seventeenth century, the art of memory and collecting practices interact, come face to face, exchange models and ideas. . . . Closely connected to this process is a change in the way of perceiving human faculties: the mind begins to be portrayed as something situated in space, and sensory and intellectual processes are perceived and described in terms of motion. . . . Memory is thus also conceived in terms of space, as a collection of spaces within which images of memories are placed" (246–47).

59. On the conceptualization of memory as an "active" quality, see Bolzoni (1995, 177).

60. For an extended discussion of Augustine's theories of memory, see Furley (1999, 412ff.); on its connection with Aristotelian scholarly tradition, see Bloch (2007); and on the fundamental importance of memory to the resurgence of preaching in the post-Tridentine era, see McGinness (1980, 117).

61. For a discussion of the tradition of a variety of treatises that address memory and its bodily consequence, see Bolzoni (1998, 3ff.).

62. "Sempre che sentirò cantare l'aria d'un madrigale ch'abbia alcuna somiglianza con alcun altro, mi ricordo di quello e di chi lo cantava" (Porta 1996, 81). While *aria* could be translated in this context as "melody," the meaning of the term is more nuanced, as Tim Carter (1993) has ably argued, so I have left it in the original. On the complexity of the notion of "aria" in early modern Italian musical practice, see also most recently Cusick (2009, esp. xxv-xxvi, 113–53).

63. "Subbito che si arriva ad un luogo, sarà bene interrogare li padroni e garzoni dell'alloggiamento delle cose notabili del luogo, che son degne d'esser vedute, e particolarmente le fabbriche pubbliche e le private che eccedono la mediocrità, e così giardini, machine e fortezze ed edifizî d'acqua, pitture, statue, ed altro che parrà a proposito. E mentre si vedono simili cose degne, sarà bene che tutta la compagnia sia presente ed osservi e ciascuno dica quello che glien'occorre, perché così, oltre che e'meglio s'imprimono nella memoria, si ha più occasione di conferire e ricevere soddifazione nella reminiscenza, quando di poi si conferiranno" (Bizoni 1995, 176).

64. "Se nella compagnia vi sarà alcuno che scriva minutamente li progressi del viaggio con le sue circostanze e che faccia nota distinta, quasi come una relazione delle cose notabili che si vedono e che occorrono, sarà cosa che potrà arrecare molto gusto a tutti della compagnia, nel rivedere e conferire che potranno fare poi quando saranno tornati a casa e nell'occasioni poi servire anco in casi di non poca importanza" (Bizoni 1995, 184).

65. "Il vostro fine non sia la sola curiosità del veder cose nuove, ma il documento nell'apprender, dalla diversità dell'apprender altrui costume et governo, una regola più perfetta per il vostro Governo et per li vostri costumi et a tale effetto vi gioverà l'adoperar spesso la penna con far memoria di quanto vi occorra sentire et vedere, combinando anche le occorrenze moderne con le antiche, reflettendo in quelle Istorie, delle quali habbiate notitia et componendone un estratto che vi gioverà in ogni tempo non meno per il costume che per la cognitione degli Interessi Politici et delle cose naturali" (Fosi 1997, 260–61).

66. "Ed in ristretto concludo che, se non si osservano bene le cose degne che si vedono e non si procura di ritenerle bene nella memoria si potrà avanzare la

spesa e sfuggire gl'incomodi e patimenti del viaggio, che peraltro riuscirà super-fluo, con restarsene a godere la quiete della casa paterna" (Bizoni 1995, 177).

67. We shall return to the role of memory and collecting in shaping a "proper" identity within a defined hierarchy that values conformity to essential norms—both in social and religious terms—in the next chapter.

68. Bizoni's travel diary contains many musical episodes shared by Giustiniani's traveling *famiglia*. See Bizoni (1995, esp. 25–26, 33, 42, 47, 49, 50, 60, 76, 81, 102, 141).

69. It is perhaps significant that Pomarancio, a well-known artist who traveled with Giustiniani and Bizoni on this occasion, is described as sketching almost constantly as the party travels through their various experiences; it may well have been that visual "triggers" would have been as valued as verbal ones (or even musical ones?) in the collection and recollection of experiences. We will return in the next chapter to a specific episode involving both Giustiniani and Pomarancio and their comparative ability to evaluate an artistic work.

70. In Fabris (1999, 193; my translation).

71. Cesare Marotta, a composer who also worked as musical agent for the Bentivoglio, draws on a similar language of exclusivity—appealing to his *virtuoso*-of-taste patron through the reference to listening and the vague terms used by early modern nonmusician connoisseurs, including the transcendent buzzword *affetto* that we briefly considered in chapter 2—in describing a specific kind of song: "While it is a *romanesca*, nonetheless I call it *romanesca bastarda*, because it must be sung with emotional intensity in many places, and in others with a variety of effects, which cannot be written down but need to be heard live" (Marotta to Enzo Bentivoglio, March 3, 1614, quoted in Fabris 1999, 287; my translation).

72. Regarding earlier noble patrons' greater concern with the overall effect of a multimedia event, see Carter (1991).

73. Giustiniani's essay was translated into English by Carol McClintock (Bottrigari and Giustiniani 1962), though I have relied on the original Italian through the transcriptions and editions of the manuscript by Bongi (Giustiniani 1628/1878) and Banti (Giustiniani 1981). For the Della Valle essay I have relied on the transcription in Solerti's *Le origini del melodramma* (Della Valle 1903), which also contains a transcription of the Giustiniani essay. Excerpts from both the Giustiniani and Della Valle essays are translated in Strunk and Treitler (1998), respectively edited by Gary Tomlinson (352–57) and Margaret Murata (544–51); among the scholarly studies that make extensive reference to their essays are Holzer (1992), Carter (1993), and Hill (1997), but also see Wistreich (2007, esp. 201–2).

74. Wistreich (2007, 195–96) suggests that the twenty-two pitches may be a metaphorical reference to the twenty-two-pitch gamut—thus indicating that they could sing "all music"—rather than specifically indicating their range.

75. See most notably Holzer (1992), which provides the most careful discussion of Della Valle's reference to specific musical works as well as individual performers.

76. Della Valle (1903, 163–64) claims that formerly sopranos were all boys, who "while they did have a [good voice], as people who had no judgment be-

cause of their [young] age, sang without *gusto* and without *grazia,* as if they had memorized everything, and sometimes listening to them made me feel like I was being whipped mercilessly. Sopranos of today, being people of judgment, maturity, good sentiment, and exquisite skill in the art, sing their music with *grazia,* with *gusto,* and with true elegance; clothing themselves in the *affetti,* they are ravishing to hear." (Mentre pur l'avevano [la voce] come persone che per l'età non avevano giudizio, anche cantavano senza gusto e senza grazia, come cose appunto imparate a mente, che alle volte a sentirli mi davano certe strappate di corda insopportabili. I soprani di oggi, persone di giudizio, d'età, di sentimento e di perizia nell'arte esquisita cantano le loro cose con grazia, con gusto, con vero garbo; vestendosi degli affetti rapiscono a sentirli.) Once again, the ravishment of the hearer—presumably Della Valle himself, since he makes a point of telling us that he is drawing from personal experience—is the measure of judgment of the quality and relevance of the singers.

77. "I maestri dell'età nostra . . . premono negli affetti, nelle grazie, e nella viva espressione de'sensi di quello che si canta; che è quello che veramente rapisce e fa da dovero andare in estasi" (Della Valle 1903, 152–53).

78. Uberti (1630/1991). In his foreword (xx) to the facsimile edition, Giancarlo Rostirolla points out that Uberti—a jurist working in Rome—published a second volume from the same press the same year, on a legal topic, and dedicated that volume to Cardinal Francesco Barberini; while Uberti's connection to the Barberini *famiglia* is not entirely clear, it would seem that he was at least trying to gain favor with Francesco through that dedication. The *Contrasto musico* bears no dedication to a patron: in his foreword "Alli virtuosi lettori" (5), Uberti claims he has written his *discorso* "not because music needs praise, or the musician defense, but because I have been curious to hear some things during leisure hours, and so I have determined to have this printed to articulate my thought more fully" (Non perche la Musica habbia bisogno di lode, overo il Musico di difesa; ma per mia curiosità d'intendere certe cose in hore di ricreatione: hò risoluto farla stampare, per effettuare più copiosamente il mio pensiero). It would seem that Uberti is aiming his discussion at the interests and sensibilities of the upper strata of the cardinal *famiglie;* in modeling *virtuoso* conversation, he is perhaps attempting to display his suitability for same, in the hopes of gaining greater access to the "circuit."

79. Giorgio Adamo (2000, 69–70) has further argued that Giustiniani and Della Valle's descriptive passages about "popular" musics indicate a systematic (quasi-ethnographic) approach to comparative musical traditions assessed through listening.

80. "Non vi essendo altro che quest'osservanza fatta con lunghezza di tempo, non si dice altro che bisogna praticare, vedere e dimandare" (Mancini 1956, 330).

81. As Maravall (1986, 20) observes, the term *critic* (in both noun and adjective forms) came into use in the early seventeenth century.

82. "One of the means that proved effective in reaching this objective [of baroque culture to move its addressee]—which can very well be exemplified in art, but also in other areas—consisted in introducing or implying and, to a certain extent, making the spectators themselves participants in the work, which succeeded in making the spectators almost its accomplices. Such was the result

obtained by presenting a spectator with an open work that could come about in various ways. . . . Perhaps involvement comes about by turning the spectator into a coauthor, making use of the artifice by means of which the work changes along with the viewer's perspective. But obviously the individual confronted by the seventeenth century must be moved from within" (Maravall 1986, 75). Maravall returns to this point repeatedly; see also 220ff.

83. See Fumaroli (1998, 266–67) on Louis of Grenada, cited in chapter 1, note 21. Giving the example of a statue of Saint Biblena (by Bernini, ca. 1624) who is looking to heaven with one foot raised, Bert Treffers suggests that "she is ready to go. But the next step is up to the viewer. Only when he shares her intense faith and identifies with her completely will she truly come to life. As an image she lives in the beholder. It is in the heart that this transformation occurs" (Treffers 2001, 366). On the aesthetic of "completing incompleteness," see also Maravall (1986, 169).

84. Indeed, Colantuono remarks that "Guido [Reni]'s seventeenth-century interpreters operated within remarkably sophisticated interpretive parameters dictated by the conditions of their own seicentesque *concettismo,* in which the ingenious discovery of multiple and even contradictory meanings in the pictorial image was not only possible, but necessary" (Colantuono 1997, 11–12). Once again, the creative role of the recipient is emphasized and framed as potentially more sophisticated or dynamic than that of the creator of the artifact.

85. "Si rivolge con agio a contemplar una spatiosa pittura; oggetto, come noi sappiamo, doversi accuratamente vedere, e non come fanno i disapplicati, alla spensierità. Et ne caviamo che il gusto della pittura è da principe." Quoted in Bonfait (1994, 145).

86. "Dovrà aver l'occhio il pittore di sodisfare alle persone erudite in quella professione di che serà il soggetto suo, o sia di materie ecclesiastiche, o istorie profane, o cose naturali, o artificiali, o altre. . . . Altrimenti faranno errori, il che leva il credito a quell'opera e resta il pittore in concetto di non sapere se non copiare, e non essere abile da sé stesso a cose che siano ben fondate" (Paleotti 1961, 499).

87. See Annibaldi (1996, 64) and Piperno (2001, 10).

88. Nicoletta Guidobaldi (1990) traces the consequences of this transition in the conceptualization of music in a key visual-textual "resource manual" for early modern Italians, Ripa's *Iconologia.*

89. "Implied in the [semiotic] distinction [between "conventional" and "humanistic" patronage] is a further distinction between two ways of using music to represent the social status of a patron, which can be said to mirror Roman Jakobson's distinction between 'metaphoric' or 'metonymic' linguistic communication." Annibaldi argues that conventional patronage "achieves its ends by 'contiguity,' by proving to be a sort of musical accessory of the elite itself. In contrast, a piece generated by 'humanistic patronage' symbolizes the rank of its patron through a display of his artistic sensibility. It thus achieves its ends by 'similarity': by displaying compositional qualities that parallel the sophisticated tastes of the class in question" (Annibaldi 1998, 175–76). Annibaldi's focus is princely patronage, especially at the turn of the seventeenth century; but his observations work equally well for the *virtuosi* of taste from the following decades who are aspiring to a noble self-image connected to that of the idealized prince.

90. "Fu per un altro tipo di personaggio—per esempio i principi Barberini e Borghese degli anni Ottanta o Novanta del '600 che collezionare partiture di musica vocale si prospettò come un modo relativamente economico di dedicarsi passivamente alla musica, ovvero di continuare a esibire il proprio interesse per un'attività culturale divenuta troppo dispendiosa" (Murata 1993, 264–65). I would take issue with Murata's characterization of score collecting as "passive," though it certainly does indicate decreased financial and interpersonal sponsorship of (or even involvement with) musicians; we will return to this point in the final chapter.

91. See the exchange between Lydia Goehr and Reinhard Strohm summarized in Butt (2002, 62–64).

3. PROPER LISTENING

The chapter epigraph, from Grazioso Uberti's *Contrasto musico: Opera dilettevole*, ed. Giancarlo Rostirolla (1630; facs. ed., Lucca: Libreria Musicale Italiana, 1991), 130, reads in the original, "Così a mio giudicio potrebbe la persona spirituale, mentre le voci, e gli stromenti s'accordano, discorrere trà se stessa, come bene si accordino i suoi pensieri con li precetti della natura: e gl'affetti suoi con la legge di Dio, e mentre il Choro usa lo stile flebile, e poi lo varia nell'allegro, così potrebbe il divoto trà se stesso dolersi delle sue colpe, & al fine consolarsi nella misericordia del Signore."

1. Indeed, transcendent delight was seen as a result of the proper, intense enjoyment of the mysteries; see McGinness (1995, 106–9).

2. François de Dainville, *L'éducation des Jesuites: XVIe-XVIIIe siècles* (Paris: Éditions de Minuit, 1978), quoted in Baffetti (1997, 214). This is an example of how, as McGinness (1995, 6) observes, "[Rome's educators] sought to demonstrate the right way to approach intellectual, spiritual, and practical questions, offering a method or approach, a 'first principle and foundation,' a logic to sort through the maze of novel issues and spiritual claims."

3. On the Jesuit focus on pedagogy for the upper classes, see Grendler (1989, esp. 363–76, 389); on the notion of systematic teaching of knowledge procedures as "initiation," see Baffetti (1997, 27–43).

4. Toledo was professor of humanities at the Collegio Romano in the 1560s, and his teaching influenced the pedagogical approach of several generations at that institution, which was the central training ground for Italian curial elites; see Simmons (1999, 530).

5. As we saw in chapter 1, the *Exercises* was the model for a number of early seventeenth-century manuals—dealing with explicitly spiritual as well as broader moral issues—described by Dooley (1995, 15) as "what might for want of a better term be called self-education literature." For more on the increasingly important focus on "self-mastery" in court-related literature in the sixteenth and seventeenth centuries, see Haroche (1998).

6. Tarquinio Galluzzi, "De rhetorum ornamentis ab oratore divino non abhorrentibus," in Galluzzi, *Orationum tomus I* (Rome, 1611), quoted and paraphrased in McGinness (1995, 189).

7. The council's decrees of October 11, 1551, ch. 7, quoted in Wandel (2006, 222).

8. For a discussion of the complex arguments in the Council of Trent concerning the Eucharist, and the solutions proposed concerning the balance between action and reception of the sacrament, see Wandel (2006, esp. 212ff.).

9. Here we might recall Bourdieu's observation (1984, 60) that "explicit aesthetic choices are in fact often constituted in opposition to the choices of the groups closest in social space."

10. See Guazzo (1993) and Benzoni (1978, 145).

11. See, for example, Severo Bonini's argument about "men who are *virtuosi* and learned [but] who were lowly born in the countryside, who—while having a beautiful and noble surface of *virtù* and learning—nonetheless, having an element of wildness and roughness from their nature that is difficult to leave behind, occasionally show their origins through some bad behavior and through the coarseness of their demeanor" (1979, 67).

12. For an excellent overview of Barberini agency in sponsoring artistic/ cultural—and especially musical—projects, see Hammond (1994, 37–38).

13. As Cropper observes, "Unlike the uneducated crowd, which only enjoys or admires pictures, the intelligent judge can also understand the reasons behind them." Here Cropper (1984, 165–66) is paraphrasing Franciscus Junius, a copy of whose treatise on painting was in the Barberini library (currently at the Biblioteca Apostolica Vaticana, Stamp. Barb. O. VII (49)) and which, according to Cropper, was likely a structural guide for Giovanni Bellori's influential *Lives of the Painters* of 1672. For more on the role of Roman classicism as a guide to the sublime, see Briganti (1994, esp. 30ff.).

14. Compare Bourdieu (1984, 54): "[The] conditions of existence, which are the precondition for all learning of legitimate culture, whether implicit and diffuse, as domestic cultural training is, or explicit and specific, as in scholastic training, are characterized by the suspension and removal of economic necessity and by objective and subjective distance from practical urgencies, which is the basis of objective and subjective distance from groups subjected to those determinisms. . . . In other words, [the aesthetic disposition] presupposes the distance from the world . . . which is the basis of the bourgeois experience of the world." In the case of early modern Rome, the "distance from the world" is framed in very different terms (specifically as a religious construct), but the carryover of the rhetorical frame of "distance from practical urgencies" is an important instance of the permanence of rhetorical structures even with the decay of coherent rationales for such structures.

15. For an extensive discussion of gendered oppositions in discourse on the visual arts in early modern Italy, see Sohm (1995); Giustiniani, in his discourse on painting, states as the first necessary quality of a painting "that it be made . . . with good *disegno,* and with good and proportioned shape" (che sia fatto il lavoro con buon disegno, e con buoni e proporzionati contorni) and likewise praises the best statues as "very proportioned" (proporzionatissime) in his discourse on sculpture (1981, 44, 71).

16. For a discussion of Borromeo's iconographic project, see Menozzi (1997, esp. 36–37); and for resonance with his sponsorship of particular ideals of musical transcendence, see Kendrick (1996; 2002).

17. On the question of decorum in the controversy over Caravaggio, which came to a head with his *Death of the Virgin* (also discussed by Mancini, who seems to have both admired and suspected it), see Spezzaferro (2001, 2ff.) and, for more on the same topic, Poseq (1992). It is intriguing that some of Caravaggio's Roman patrons—foremost among them Cardinal Del Monte and Vincenzo Giustiniani, as we briefly discussed in chapter 3—were also those who arguably "flirted" most with the transcendent potential of unbalancing sound in the first decade of the century.

18. Mancini (1956, 141, 143). We must not forget that Mancini was a physician and probably would have viewed this as sound medical as well as moral advice.

19. The complexities of this issue, and its intersection with the problems of "policing" or otherwise monitoring (whether self-monitoring or otherwise) the potential discrepancy between the ideals of "proper fruition" and the realities of its practice, cannot be adequately addressed in this study and must await further research.

20. For example, Linda Austern (1998, 623) points out that reading pornographic material aloud was understood as "inescapably arousing" because the sense of hearing was so overpowering to the spirit. See also Austern (1993); while this latter essay centers on English Puritan writers, Austern points out that these authors clearly draw from Castiglione and sixteenth-century Italian moralists.

21. This effect was most powerful when the singer was female; see Cusick (1993a, 12ff. and esp. 17).

22. Cusick (1993a, esp. 19). Cusick ably argues the importance for the composer to project a competing ability to be "manly and in control" but does not address what I believe to have been an equally important need for the noble listener to respond in a similar fashion. See also Monson (1995, esp. 85ff.) for other examples of stated concerns about the threat posed by female musico-rhetorical power.

23. On the perceived dangers of female sonic "unruliness" both to the individual male listener and to the early modern Italian hierarchical social order, see Gordon (2004).

24. On courtesans and music making in early modern Rome, see Storey (2008, esp. 57ff., 108, 140).

25. Brosius (2009) is an outstanding study of these professional singer-courtesans, whose systematic labeling as *virtuose* may well have precipitated the anxiety about the nature of *virtù* that we will explore at some length in the next chapter.

26. See Monson (2002, 11) for this specific passage and passim for other discussions on reforms of Catholic musical practice before, during, and following Trent.

27. ASV, Misc. Arm. I–XVIII, 6492, cc. 78v–82n, 1604, orders from Mons. Antonio Seneca, under the heading *Delli divini officii*, quoted in Zannini (1993, 138).

28. An account by Cardinal Paleotti, reported by Monson in one of the first stages of his groundbreaking study of convent music in Bologna, puts the inherent lack of control in specifically musical terms: "But what was greatly scandalous

to the people was this: when they were singing to the book, after the sound of the organ had ceased, [the nuns] divided from each other so that one part of them followed this one with her novelties, and another followed the organist with the ordinary [singing], indicating discord among their minds and hearts ... so that those who were in the exterior church, hearing such 'un-concerted' [sconcerti] singing and such manifest discord among these nuns, became very scandalized by that occasion in which they began to create these 'un-concerts'" (Monson 1993, 153; my translation). Paleotti's account of audible disorder is especially damaging because those in the exterior church are "scandalized," so that the nuns' musical mayhem disrupts the lay devout community and the social order more broadly conceived. For a more thorough discussion of the imperative for women of the upper classes to maintain the quality of *continenza,* understood as the essence of proper womanhood, see Cusick (2009, 5–7).

29. Agostino Agazzari, *La musica ecclesiastica dove si contiene la vera diffinitione di musica come scienza* ... (Siena, 1638), quoted in Reardon (1994, 193); my translation. (Reardon provides a diplomatic transcription of the Agazzari without indicating page breaks from the original; the passage in question is about two-thirds through the original text.)

30. Bonini specifically refers to this as occurring "where God is found continuously incarnated as bread in the most sacred Host," perhaps a reference to musical activity at the *Quarantore;* both passages are in Bonini (1979, 43).

31. The passages are paraphrased from Augustine's *Confessions* 9.6, 10.33 in Bonini (1979, 105).

32. Misericordia Maggiore (MIA) Scritture 1606–19, segn. 540, fol. 31r, quoted in Padoan (1987, 377).

33. Guazzo (1993, 1:84). In his commentary (2:187–89), Amadeo Quondam expands on the crucial role of *prudenza* among the primary skills of both the prince and the courtier, emphasizing the perceived importance of a just balance between speaking and listening in conversation.

34. From an unpublished discourse by Lelio Guidiccioni on the preaching of Girolamo da Narni, quoted in Criscuolo (1998a, 434); for more on this specific *discorso* as well as Guidiccioni's broader interest in the power of Narni's manipulation of sound, see chapter 4.

35. The circumstances of this "competition" are documented in Antolini (1989, 352ff.).

36. Girolamo Tiraboschi (1824, 69) reports that "the ladies and princesses of Rome" (le gentildonne e principesse di Roma) were encouraged to view the Umoristi proceedings from a balcony in the hall, but the balcony placement seems to imply a separation from the activity of the academy.

37. "Oggi frequentati da'primi signori, e virtuosi di questa corte; prerogativa, che va del pari con qualsivoglia più famosa accademia che honori la nostra Italia." Domenico Benigni, ed., *L'idea della veglia* (Rome, 1640), quoted in Antolini (1989, 360). The wording may specifically allude to the Accademia degli Umoristi, which at the time was arguably considered the most prestigious gathering of *virtuosi* on the peninsula, as we saw in chapter 2. By creating a satellite *accademia* around her expressive strengths, Baroni may have been attempting to redefine herself as a *virtuosa* not in musical-practical terms but within the

parameters of the *virtuosi* of taste, trying to change her status in ways perhaps analogous to the efforts of Francesca Caccini in her later years, discussed in Cusick (1993b; 2009). On Baroni and her efforts to build expressive agency within the structurally misogynistic system of the Roman cardinal circuit, see Brosius (2009).

38. "Sacri cigni febei / Cui su'l Tebro distilla auree rugiade / NUBE, che dal Ciel cade / S'offra del vostro mar l'onda a costei." Benigni, "Non è pago il mio core," quoted in Antolini (1989, 356). Benigni is alluding to the device of the Umoristi, which was a cloud.

39. Haan (1998, 107–10). I have modified Haan's translations somewhat; my contributions are in brackets.

40. Diez (1986, 96). On the use of *Imprese* and other symbolic resources as a "common language" during the Barberini papacy, see also Hammond (1994, 124ff.).

41. Quoted and translated in Haan (1998, 106).

42. Gordon Campbell (1997, 64–65) specifically suggests that Milton's encomium was designed less as specific praise to Baroni than as a tribute to his Roman guests. This is especially likely because it is by no means certain that Baroni was schooled in the complicated literary tradition that would have made Milton's poem intelligible in all its nuanced classical allusion.

43. Indeed, several poems refer to Baroni as a "Sirena," creating a hint of seductive danger in her individual person, which can then be obviated by understanding her sound, separately from her as a physical individual, as transcendent and heavenly. See again Haan (1998, 107ff.).

44. As Furley (1999, 410–11) observes, "Augustine powerfully reiterates the Neoplatonist themes of conversion or return to oneself, of self-knowledge as the means to all knowledge, the fulfilment of a deep desire to possess wisdom, as deep as the desire to be happy. . . . The reproductive exercise of the imagination (often called phantasia by Augustine) depends on remembered images that are reactivated, but so does the creative activity of imagination . . . Creative imagination is a process of contracting and expanding the images of what we have perceived, or of combining or separating their data. In such cases concentration or will is operative."

45. See, for example, the exchange between Pope Urban VIII and Michelangelo Buonarroti the Younger about the "authorship" of the "text" underlying a performance by Francesca Caccini discussed in Cole (2007, 762–63).

46. Daniello Bartoli, *La ricreatione del savio* (Rome: de'Lazzeri, 1659), quoted in Lorenzetti (2003, 267–68).

47. For example, Murata (1990, 274) remarks that "the casual, household status [of Barberini-era manuscripts] is verified by the absence of composer attributions" and points out that well into the early 1650s manuscripts associated with the spread of the repertory to the court of Sweden and elsewhere in northern Europe "contain contemporary music by Luigi, Marazzoli, Pasqualini, and Carissimi—already in an anonymous state. Were the composers not known, or was naming them unimportant?" (275).

48. Note, furthermore, that the subject of the painting is not even mentioned: its relevance is provided by its authorship—or rather, by Giustiniani's

understanding of its authorship—and the network of associations that such authorship could provide for the learned *virtuoso*.

49. "De Statua, et eius Inspectore: Spectanti insinuat sese lapis; inscius ultro Spectator totum se lapidi insinuat. Inde trahunt homines, durum genus, unde rigescant; Inde unam e multis contrahit ille animam. Quid me spectantem mirum est lapidescere? Quid, quod Inspectus sese molliat ipse lapis?" "Brevius dictum: Vividus est hospes, rigidus lapis. Arte magistra, Hinc lapis, inde hospes, hic viget ille riget." Guidiccioni (1992, 174–75), translation by John and Frances Newman, though I have modified the second half of the translation of the second poem to make it follow the alternating rhythm of the original more closely, since I believe that alternation is crucial to the effect of the poem. The poems come from a group of works that accompany Guidiccioni's extended descriptive discourse on Bernini's newly constructed *Baldacchino* over Saint Peter's tomb in the Vatican basilica, which we will also consider in the following chapter.

50. Thus Fumaroli (1998, 13–14): "United by the revelation of truth, multiple in its ways and voices of persuasion, the church thus gives a wide margin of choice to the temperaments, characters, and tastes that divide and individualize Christian humanity on earth. . . . A Franciscan does not preach in the same style as a Dominican. An Oratorian can be distinguished from a Jesuit at first glance not only by his habit, but by his repertory of gestures, his culture, his way of speaking and preaching, his spiritual tastes (*goûts*)."

4. NOBLE AND MANLY UNDERSTANDING

The chapter epigraph, from Cesare D'Onofrio's "Note Berniniane 1: Un dialogo-recita di Gian Lorenzo Bernini e Lelio Guidiccioni," *Palatino* 10 (1966): 130, reads in the original as follows: "G[ian] L[orenzo]: Che hà dunque à fare un desideroso di gloria? L[elio]: Già s'è detto: presupporre di caminar per la vecchia strada, ma con virtù nuova, e con peregrinità. Chi non ha talento naturale, et nervo di studio, non si metta all'imprese. Ma chi è fornito dell'uno, e dell'altro, entri nel commun arringo, et vi faccia prove non usitate. . . . Per [la strada comune] bisogna andare, et mostrare con l'andamento, con l'opera, et con la maestria, quanto si sdegna, et si lascia à dietro la comunità."

1. For more on the importance of the masculine framing of *virtù*, and the concomitant complexities in positing the nature of a female "virtuosa" in early modern accounts, see Jacobs (1997, esp. ch. 7, 157ff.).

2. As McGinness (1995, 18) observes, "It was fitting that spiritual leaders above all be eloquent, for it was a virtue not merely appended to the list of their other virtues but a quality intrinsic to one's life as a prelate of the Church: eloquence epitomized a life well-rounded in Christian virtues." While McGinness is here using the term *virtue* in the plural and in the modern sense of "goodliness and piety," the trait of rhetorical eloquence corresponded most closely to the notion of *virtù* as articulated by Machiavelli, Castiglione, and other early modern authors concerned with noble masculinity.

3. This was, as Maria Antonietta Visceglia (1995, 37) suggests, "a phenomenon that expanded the competition and made the ascent through the curial ranks

more arduous for the members of the noble classes, changing the rules for selection and putting service in the forefront."

4. Della Valle (1903). Beyond an early mention by Oliver Strunk (1930, 491) as "the reactionary Lelio Guidiccioni, an Italian translator of Vergil," there are also useful (though passing) biographical references to Guidiccioni in Hammond (1994), but none mention the essay discussed below or any explicit involvement by Guidiccioni in musical matters. There is a translated excerpt from a letter from Guidiccioni to a contemporaneous prelate concerning the role of Palestrina's *Pope Marcellus Mass* in the deliberations on music at the Council of Trent, published in the commentary to Palestrina (1975) and subsequently anthologized in Weiss and Taruskin (1984, 141–42); I thank Cory Gavito for pointing me to this excerpt, which is very similar to a passage in the *discorso* to be discussed below (indicating that Guidiccioni most likely "recycled" and elaborated several of his ideas on music in various circumstances, as he did with several of his other writings). In her annotation to the translation of an excerpt from Della Valle's "Della musica ..." in Strunk and Treitler (1998), Margaret Murata mentions the Guidiccioni *discorso* in a single sentence, observing that it "argues that music teaches virtue" (545); this is the most detailed reference to the *discorso* of which I am aware in modern literature, and, as I will argue below, Murata's characterization may be somewhat deceptive.

5. The Barberini project may be understood as progressive in other ways; for example, Armando Petrucci (1982, 27) points to increasing literacy at all social levels in Rome under the Barberini papacy.

6. Where not otherwise specified, much of the basic biographical information is gleaned from the entry on Guidiccioni in the *Dizionario biografico degli Italiani* (Di Monte 1960). See also Bonfait (1994, 145) and Criscuolo (1998a, 373–75).

7. As the religious historian Jennifer Selwyn (2004, 17) observes, these authors "provided important models for the blending of the sacred and the profane. . . . Inspired by humanistic themes in their work, these theater artists shared with later missionary theater practitioners a preoccupation with developing and utilizing sophisticated techniques to promote a morally edifying message and to overwhelm spectators, leaving them 'exhausted and convinced.'"

8. For a broad overview of Guidiccioni's duties as "cultural facilitator" in the *famiglia* of Scipione Borghese, see Ehrlich (2002, esp. 32–33, 160–80).

9. For a discussion of Bernini's creations for the funeral—which were in stucco and were destroyed following the celebration—see D'Onofrio (1967, 288ff.). One of the statues, depicting "tranquillitas," is shown with a bowed string instrument (presumably a "viola"; see discussion of Guidiccioni's references to the instrument, below); it is unclear how influential Guidiccioni may have been in the selection of the iconographical choices for the event.

10. Concerning Guidiccioni and the Gentileschi, see Lapierre (2000, 180, 187, 189, 192, 205, 395). I use Lapierre's account with trepidation, since her book hovers between history and historical fiction; however, much of her archival work is acknowledged as accurate, and while I have not seen the documents to which she refers concerning the dowry, I believe this information is among the historically verifiable data on which she builds her sometimes fanciful story.

11. "Signas ac tabulas pictas, quibus ea villa referta est" (Di Monte 1960, 331).

12. Fumaroli (1978, 813–14) observes that Francesco Barberini (Antonio's elder brother) established an *accademia* in his palace at Monte Cavallo that included Guidiccioni as well as a number of younger *virtuosi* of taste such as Allacci, Naudé, and Cassiano del Pozzo; he characterizes the link between the Jesuit Collegio Romano, the Accademia degli Umoristi explored above, and Francesco's private *accademia* as "the Parnassus of official Roman *eloquentia*" (le Parnasse de l'*Eloquentia* officielle de Rome).

13. On the long-standing association of Guidiccioni with the Barberini, see Hammond (1994, 18) and more recently Cole (2007, 768–69), who mentions Guidiccioni as a regular presence in the "lively, predominantly Tuscan, intellectual circles that Urban VIII had created" in the 1620s, alongside a number of the individuals we have encountered in the previous chapters (for example, Mascardi) and prominent musicians such as Kapsberger and Mazzocchi, further quoting the Florentine poet Michelangelo Buonarroti's 1624 description of "Music always, and always poetry, / music and poetry morning and evening, / music every season and every day, /whether in autumn or in springtime" (Musiche sempre, e sempre poesie, / musiche e poesie mattina e sera, / musiche ogni stagione e ogni die, / vuoi l'autunno, o vuoi la primavera).

14. The *Ara maxima* was published the very year that Guidiccioni moved into the *famiglia* of Cardinal Antonio Barberini.

15. Both accounts—by Gian Vittorio Rossi, writing as Nicius Erythraeus (1645)—are provided in Briganti (1982, 130 n. 260); the quote by the same author on Baroni ("ita purum, ita elegans, ita argutum, ita venustum, prope ut dixerim, nihil me vidisse, in eo genere, elegantius neque politius") is from Lucchesini (1831, 48).

16. See Tetius (2005, esp. 385–87). Guidiccioni is featured in the *Aedes* in part through a poem he composed celebrating a Barberini musico-theatrical spectacle (which Murata [1981, 42] identifies as *Il palazzo incantato;* the poem is also transcribed and annotated in Murata [1981, 44), but also as the addressee of a long descriptive passage by the author of the book, Girolamo Tesi, who appears to have been closely connected to (perhaps mentored by) Guidiccioni through the Accademia degli Insensati of Perugia (Tetius 2005, 8–9).

17. For details on musical activities in the Borghese household in the second and third decades of the seventeenth century, featuring both instrumentalists and vocalists, see Lionnet (1993, esp. 524–27).

18. Unless otherwise specified, the biographical information on Mautini and his interactions with Guidiccioni in the following passage comes from Criscuolo (1998a, 372 ff.).

19. While Guidiccioni did not enter the *famiglia* of Antonio Barberini the Younger until the following year, it is entirely likely that he would have been present at such an important ceremonial acknowledgment of the order, since as we have seen the leader of his *famiglia*—Cardinal Scipione Borghese—was well placed within the Barberini sphere.

20. "Gela una lingua infocata . . . instrumento celeste, che rapiva gli animi, accendeva gli affetti, et, preparando alla gratia, apriva la gloria. . . . Si suol dire che l'habito del cappuccino parla e risuona; ma quanto è più sonoro in questo

suggetto, o vivo, o morto; di cui mi pare che, solo a toccarlo, debba mandar fuori il suono, come un instrumento organizato di metallo celeste" (Criscuolo 1998a, 452, 455).

21. Criscuolo (1998a, 385–431) provides a side by side comparison of the various drafts of Guidiccioni's "letter," indicating the careful shifts in rhetorical choices through the two decades of its gestation.

22. "Tiene un metallo di voce, in altri che in lui non udita, oltremodo sonoro et dolce, non tutto bronzo e non tutto argento, che rompe l'aria ben di lontano e sbaraglia le nemiche impressioni, ma in guisa che tonando molce e fulminando lusinga. . . . Parla con le reticenze, quanto con le parole. Ogni suo moto, ogni suo sguardo opera efficacemente. . . . Nell'action concitata è tremendo, nella composta et rimessa è gratioso. . . . Un suo girar d'occhio, un retirar di cappuccio, un raccogliersi e stendersi di persona, con tutta la quale (gravemente posta) dal piede alla testa, accompagna gli affetti del ragionamento, dispone gli animi altrui come piú gli piace. Se in ammonir si riscalda, esce da quel piccolo pulpito un fracasso et una tempesta come di machina militare. Se addolcisce e conforta, non è canto alcuno più grato all'orecchie dei detti suoi. In somma, alla presenza, alle parole, all'attione è venerando, sublime et penetrativo, et insieme è dolce, leggiadro et amabile." Quoted in Cargnoni (1998, 333).

23. "Et se V. S. Illustrissima fusse qui ad ascoltarlo, son certo che, dietro l'istessa regola, non gli resteria che desiderare. Ma dove manca la corporal presenza del primo, spesso il dicitor supplisce, parlandone espressamente con esquisita grandezza, che vuol dire con la debita dignità." Quoted in Cargnoni (1998, 336).

24. "Concedansi che le prediche del Mautino, fuor di sua bocca svaniscano, come succedeva ai versi di Virgilio; ma concedasi parimente che, quali sono in carta i versi di Virgilio, tali stiano in suo genere le prediche del Mautino." Quoted in Cargnoni (1998, 420).

25. Virgil's poetry had an especially important valence in the cultural sphere of the Barberini, since it was both specifically Roman and understood as coming from a pre-Christian author who had prefigured the arrival of Christ (see Shimp 2000, 139). Guidiccioni's role as a Virgilian exegete was thus a significant aspect of his contribution to the Barberini intellectual project.

26. "Memnonium quisquis simulacro, tactaque primo / Aera canit iubari, reddentia murmure certo / Eoos sonitus . . . / Protinus aetherias voces, atque intima aenis / Aligerum signis concusso murmura corde / Percipiet, radiis Solem indulgentibus auro / Perspicuum, inque sonos animantem fulva metalla. / Atque haec dicta bibet perculsi pecturis haustu; / Tanta viget virtus, tam vivax ardet imago." Guidiccioni, *Ara maxima Vaticana,* lines 1–3, 13–18, quoted and translated by John Kevin Newman and Frances Stickney Newman in Guidiccioni (1992, 120–21).

27. "Dulciloquis tales modulis, et voce quaterna / (Ceu totum a totidem compellent partibus Orbem) / Transmittunt Simulacra sonos; concordia quos dat / Impariles, mentique habiles. Spirantia cernis / Intuito primo, non aure loquentia sentis? / Nonne vides iubare Aligeros radiante coruscos? / At monita excipies penetrali pectore, mentem / Terrestres ni hebetent sensus, et terrea corda." Guidiccioni, *Ara maxima Vaticana,* lines 56–63, in Guidiccioni (1992, 122–23).

28. "In questi quaderni sono raccolte le fatiche meno scontie, le quali bisogna rivedersi, et meglio correggere, et ponere insieme, per non haverle buttate." Lelio Guidiccioni, "Della musica," I-Rvat Barb. Lat. 3879, fol. 1.

29. "Per mio ricordo. Quelle, che sono ridotte in netto, con una correttione potranno passare. Nell'altre s'ha da accender piu lume; et usar falce, et lima."

30. Note that 1632 was also the year of Mautini's death, and thus the date of the final redaction of Guidiccioni's "letter" on that subject; it may have been a year when Guidiccioni was pondering his "legacy." Della Valle's essay is dated January 16, 1640, in Gori's 1763 edition, which includes the essay in a miscellany of treatises on music by Giovan Battista Doni, another important intellectual in the Barberini circle (the edition was created in collaboration with Padre Giovanni Battista Martini, who provided an index); there is no known separate publication of the essay, and Gori may have found a manuscript copy among Doni's musical writings. While this might suggest that the Guidiccioni essay antedates Della Valle's "Della musica," there is no clear way in which either essay "answers" the other, so the chronology is unclear. Both appear to be written traces of a continuing *discourse-about* conversation between the two men—a conversation that would likely have been shared by Doni and other members of the Barberini *famiglia,* and probably more broadly among the Roman cardinal circuit.

31. We will return to Doni and the relationship of his approach to musical "neoclassicism" to the one articulated by Guidiccioni in the closing section of this chapter.

32. On this passage in Mascardi's *Pompe del Campidoglio* of 1623/24, see Hammond (1994, 59) and Fumaroli (1998, 137); the full *Pompe* are transcribed in Diez (1986).

33. The accompanied-singing event mentioned by Guidiccioni predates Caccini's *Nuove musiche* by at least two decades but is in keeping with Caccini's own contention that he had pioneered his monodic approach by the 1570s and also with recent scholars' observations about a "Roman" or at least South Italian "alla bastarda" tradition of accompanied singing within which Caccini may well have been trained; see most recently Wistreich (2007, esp. 185ff.). This tradition has not, however, generally been associated with the performance of sacred music; and this, along with Guidiccioni's identification of the individual as a repentant "Inglese," makes the image all the more intriguing. Is this Guidiccioni's anachronistic projection of early seventeenth-century practices onto an earlier generation, or does it reflect a tradition of sacred self-accompanied monody from the last quarter of the sixteenth century? And is the reference to the "double lyre" a classical abstraction or Guidiccioni's classicizing rendition of an instrument with double courses?

34. " [La] viola [tenore] trà gli istrumenti, che sopra ogni paragone intenerisce, et violenta" (39). By *viola* Guidiccioni probably means the six-string "da gamba" rather than the four-string "da braccio" instrument. It is interesting to speculate whether Guidiccioni was one of the dignitaries that Maugars impressed with his viol playing in Rome, according to the musician's "Lettre . . ." of 1639; Maugars's reference to Saint Francis and the musical angel and his report that the pope (presumably Urban VIII) told him, "We have heard that you have a singular *virtù,*

and would gladly hear you [play]" (Maugars 1993, 26) create interesting resonances between the French musician's terminology and Guidiccioni's own and
open up the question of possible interaction between those two individuals and
the Rome/Paris musical-discourse axis more broadly. See the brief discussion of
Maugars in chapter 1 and the general remarks about the transmission of the
model of musical connoisseurship to France in the Envoy.

35. Compare Guidiccioni's poem on viewing a statue discussed at the close of
chapter 3, and the argument in chapter 1 about viewer identification with Saint
Francis rather than the violin-playing angel.

36. For an excellent unpacking of the circumstances leading to this hard-to-
dispel myth, see Monson (2002). Guidiccioni's account here is similar to—though
subtly different from—a similar argument that he presented in a letter to Bishop
Jose Maria Suarez dated 1637, in which Palestrina is given more explicit agency;
for an excerpt of that letter and a brief discussion, see Palestrina (1975, 31), and
for a more extensive excerpt, see Baini (1828/1966, 1:190–91).

37. See, for example, ch. 2 ("Performing Baroque Travel: Pietro Della Valle's
Viaggi") of Hester (2008).

38. "il quale VS pure confessa, che già lo faceva stupire, e bene spesso com-
muovere" (Della Valle 1903, 158).

39. The reference to heavenly singers soothing Magdalen is intriguing and
requires further research on either literary or iconographic sources with which
Guidiccioni would have been familiar. As far as I have been able to determine,
there is no extensive iconographic tradition of musical consolation of the Magdalen analogous to that for Saint Francis as discussed in the Introduction; a
single example, but dating from the eighteenth century, is reproduced in Gentili
(2000, 207) and discussed briefly on 65–67 of that same volume. While the saint
was a favorite post-Tridentine resource for preachers concerned with the topic
of sin and redemption, her frequent iconographical depiction in a nude or semi-
nude state was also a topic of debate within the frameworks of propriety that
we have considered in earlier chapters (see Haskins 1994, 254–64). Urban VIII
was explicitly devoted to the Magdalen—after a number of requests, he finally
received a finger relic of the saint from Louis XIII in 1638 (Haskins 1994, 293–
94), providing yet another French-Barberini connection of which Guidiccioni
may have been aware.

Guidiccioni's use of the word *canzoni* is especially interesting to those of us
who are stymied by the scarcity of references to instrumental genres in early
modern commentary on music by nonmusicians: while the brief statement on
heavenly singers and the Magdalen is implicitly about vocal music, the much longer excursus on Saint Francis is very clearly about instrumental sounds (though
Guidiccioni maintains the ambiguity by referring to the angel preparing to restore Francis "con il tuo canto," and then providing an account of the sound of
the violin). Would Guidiccioni have been familiar with Frescobaldi's *Canzoni
da sonar*, first published in Rome in 1628, and scored from one to four melody
instruments and basso continuo? In any case, the ambiguity between vocal and
instrumental sounds here appears to argue for their expressive equivalency in
triggering divine transcendence.

40. See again Newman (1994).

41. Solerti (1905) provides an annotated transcription of several letters between Della Valle and Doni on their mutual endeavors to this end; what follows draws on Solerti's account as well as Ziino (1967). On Doni's notions of nature and artifice, see also Padoan (1992).

ENVOY

The first chapter epigraph, from Michel De Pure's *Idée des spectacles anciens et nouveaux,* facs. ed. (1668; repr., Geneva: Minkoff, 1972), 244–45, is worded as follows in the original: ".Cependant, qu'est-ce qui peut distinguer d'avantage l'honeste homme du trivial et du vulguaire, que cette curieuse education dans la connoissance des belles choses? Le sçavoir est un depart qui sepàre les hommes des hommes, les galants des grossiers, les habiles des sots, e ceux qui ont du merite de ceux qui n'ont point." The second chapter epigraph, from Marc Fumaroli's "Cicero Pontifex: La tradition rhétorique du collège romain et les principes inspirateurs du mécénat des Barberini," *Mélanges de l'École Française de Rome, Moyen Age, Temps Modernes* 90 (1978): 828, reads in the original: "À Rome, contrairement à ce qui se passera à Paris, il n'y a pas antithèse entre classicisme et baroque: une même mesure fait concerter l'ordre et l'inspiration, la transcendance du Beau et le génie individuel."

1. Holzer (1990, 23) suggests that even the last few years of Barberini rule saw a decay in the progressive elements of Roman culture and that the fall of the Barberini provided the final push toward the collapse of the cultural and political aspirations of the papacy—that "by the end of Alexander [VII]'s reign [in 1667], Rome was more repressive, more provincial, and politically weaker than it had been forty years earlier." On the quick cultural shift to conservatism among the curia following Urban's death, see also Lo Sardo (2004, 53).

2. Mazarin's ties with the broader cultural (and Tuscan-Francophile political) framework of early modern Rome that we have explored in the preceding chapters ran more deeply than just his close connection with the Barberini: for example, his sister married Michele Mancini, son of the founder of the Accademia degli Umoristi. After the death of the Pamphilij pope, he facilitated the rehabilitation of the Barberini nephews and their return to Rome. Antonio Barberini reciprocated by sponsoring celebrations at the church of the Roman "French nation," San Luigi dei Francesi, as well as later serving as intermediary for Bernini's service to Louis XIV in the design of statuary and other decorations for the palace at Versailles; see Wolfe (2008, esp. 116ff.).

3. Antonio's own relationship with the French court (as cardinal protector of France during the latter part of his uncle's papacy) and Mazarin himself was not ironclad: at the conclusion of the conclave that elected Pamphilij as Innocent X, Mazarin made a public show of "sacking" him from the cardinal protector position, ostensibly because of his willingness to vote for a candidate on whom Mazarin had placed a veto; see Poncet (2002, 167). On the other hand, given the fact that Antonio was then warmly welcomed in Paris, this may have been a way for Mazarin and the French court to express public distance from the newly disgraced Barberini (and may indeed have provided Antonio with a "cover" of sorts against postconclave suspicion of his Francophilia).

4. For more on these parallels, see Fragnito (1998, 108–9).

5. On the French Jesuits' use of music as a "spiritual training tool," whether in performance or in listening, see most recently Van Orden (2006, esp. 133ff.).

6. For more on Mersenne and French academic culture, see Yates (1988, 280ff.).

7. See, for example, Fumaroli (1978, 799ff.). On the "exporting" of French salon culture to the *conversazioni* of post-Barberini Rome, and especially the concerns that its empowering of women brought to the life of the curia, see also Brosius (2009, 114ff.).

8. See, for example, Jonathan Brown (1995, 185ff.), who also observes that Mazarin's mentor and predecessor as chief minister of France, Richelieu, was both influenced by Roman collecting practices and assisted by Mazarin in developing his collection, which was then amplified by his protegé. Patrick Michel (2001, 342–43) suggests that Mazarin was driven by "the desire to recreate in France a familiar atmosphere and a little bit of the grandeur of Rome. . . . He recreated in the *Palais Mazarin* the atmosphere of a Roman palace." See also Michel (1999), Guth (1999, esp. xiv ff.), and Dulong (1999, esp. 339ff.).

9. "Io vorrei in tal caso esser conduttore delli Bernini e Cortonesi e migliori musici perchè si ergessero statue, si facessero pitture e si formassero melodie per celebrare la gloria d'un tanto Re" (Biblioteca Apostolica Vaticana, Barb. lat. 8040, fol. 65), quoted in Laurain-Portemer (1981, 261 n. 2); I have here departed somewhat from the translation offered in J. Brown (1995, 229).

10. On Baroni and Melani, see Cowart (1980, 29), and more recently Freitas (2009) and Brosius (2009); on Rossi, see Hammond (1996) and especially Holzer (2001), who traces the close connections between Rossi and Antonio Barberini both in Rome and in exile. On the fortunes of Rossi and his music in midcentury France and beyond, see Ruffatti (2006; 2008).

11. Holzer (1990, 183) suggests that a number of musical manuscripts in the Bibliothèque nationale in Paris "are almost certainly products of midcentury Franco-Roman relations."

12. For Mersenne's comparison of preaching and music, the latter of which "has the same power to bring one to virtue and to despise vice as the voice of a good preacher," see Vendrix (2006, 44). On Mersenne's pro-Augustinian philosophical approach and its ties to his early Jesuit training, see Dear (1988), especially 81–85 and 107ff., which dwell on Mersenne's advocacy of Augustinian perspectives against Thomist arguments and his references to Augustine in his *Traité de l'harmonie universelle*.

13. "Par boutades, et par hazard, comme ils confessent eux-mesmes." *Harmonie universelle* 3:97, quoted in Vendrix (2006, 43).

14. For a specific comparison between Giustiniani's discursive strategies and those of the *honnêtes gens*—and a similar conclusion about the connection between the two approaches—see Ebert-Schifferer (1994, 104).

15. ["Le Tuaurbe et le Lut] sont des instruments de repos destinez aux plaisirs serieux & tranquiles, & dont la languissante harmonie est ennemie de toute action, & ne demande que des Auditeurs sedentaires" (De Pure 1668/1972, 273).

16. Lorenzetti (2003, 101–3) observes that the descriptions of music in French translations of Castiglione's *Cortigiano* change significantly in the seventeenth century, incorporating the emerging language of *goût* especially from the listener's

perspective: for example, the Abbé Duhamel, translating Castiglione in 1690, adds a significant "spin" to the original—sentiments not in the Castiglione, or signficantly modified, are in italics: "when a person *with a beautiful voice* can sing well on the viola; because, since *the harmony* is more simple, *one can evaluate* the sweetness better, *one listens* with more attention, one *judges* the *delicacy* of the composition with more pleasure, when the ears are occupied only with one voice, which on this instrument *gives tremendous force and grace to the words.*" (Quand une personne qui a la voix belle sçait l'accorder avec methode sur la viole; parce que l'harmonie étant plus simple, on en goûte mieux la douceur, on écoute avec plus d'attention, et on juge de la delicatesse de la composition avec plus de plaisir, quand les oreilles ne sont occupées que d'une seule voix, la quelle sur cet instrument donne une grace et une force merveilleuse aux paroles.) Castiglione's original, from bk. 2, ch. 13: "Bella musica . . . parmi il cantare bene a libro sicuramente e con bella maniera; ma ancor molto più il cantare alla viola perché tutta la dolcezza consiste quasi in un solo, e con molto maggior attenzion si nota ed intende il bel modo e l'aria non essendo occupate le oreccchie in più che in una sol voce, e meglio ancora vi si discerne ogni piccolo errore."

17. For example, Jonathan Brown (1995, 233) dwells on Roger De Piles's *L'idée du peintre parfait* and *Abrégé de la vie des peintres*, which he sees as one of the seminal texts in French writings on visual aesthetics; one of de Piles's key contributions, Brown suggests, is "the elevation of the amateur over the practitioner as the best judge of painting. However, this idea would not bear fruit until the eighteenth century, nor would thoroughly systematic treatises on the methods of attribution appear until that time." However, we have seen that Mancini—while not systematically laying out methodologies for attribution—was equally articulate about the greater judgment of the *virtuoso* over the practicing artist more than a half century earlier in Rome.

18. For an argument reinforcing this perspective with special reference to Poussin, see Ebert-Schifferer (1996, esp. 345).

19. For a discussion of this phenomenon, see Fumaroli (1978, 812ff.).

20. On this "rise of aesthetic rationalism," see Reiss (1997); a useful focus on music is on 188ff.

21. On the characteristics of early eighteenth-century French response to Roman sacred art, see Fumaroli (1998, 326–27).

22. Jean Lionnet (1991) observes that while young French noblemen traveled extensively to Rome especially after the midcentury to view visual artworks, there is less evidence of French musicians' presence in Rome in the third quarter of the century, though as Lionnet also points out there were not many prominent "foreign" musicians in Rome (from the rest of the Italian peninsula) at that time; this also reflects the relative decadence of Rome as a center of musical activity in that time frame compared to other Italian cities (Venice, Bologna, Naples).

23. Daniel Chua (1999, 68) suggests that French aesthetic discourses "attest to music's epistemological shift from the *quadrivium* to the *trivium*. . . . What the trivium demands . . . is not a cosmos but a forum in which music can be validated as a social sense rather than a global essence."

24. On Descartes's emphasis on the importance of trained memory in musical pleasure and understanding, see Vendrix (2006, 41).

25. See, for example, Dubost (1997, esp. 41ff. and 76ff.) for an extensive study of the rise in immigration and naturalization to French citizenship among wealthy and "socially dominant" individuals from the Italian peninsula in the first half of the 1600s, with a verifiable "spike" during the Mazarin regency. This increase was followed later in the century by an attempt by the French nobility to "close ranks" to distinguish true French blood from that of newly naturalized Italians, a gesture that corresponds chronologically to the various controversies between French and Italian music that characterize the later decades of the reign of Louis XIV.

APPENDIX

1. I have not translated *virtù* here and elsewhere because of the inadequacy of the term *virtue,* which a twenty-first-century reader of English is likely to associate with chastity or purity. See the discussion of this concept in chapter 4.

2. These categories that Guidiccioni postulates as "degrees" immediately below *virtù*—and most explicitly *gratia*—are also categories that Dalla Valle, in his essay dedicated to Guidiccioni, attributes to modern music. See Della Valle (1903).

3. This reference to Orpheus as soother of tigers is probably taken from the passage on Orpheus and Eurydice in Virgil's *Georgics* 4.510.

4. Probably from Psalm 18:5, and a common textual opening for items of the Common of the Apostles; a search on Latrobe University Library Online, Medieval Music Data Base, www.lib.latrobe.edu.au/MMDB/MusicDB/, yields several results on the phrase "In omnem terram exivit sonus eorum" in the antiphons for the hours of that common (sample search conducted December 20, 2010).

5. The citations are from Virgil's Eclogue 8, respectively lines 71 and 69.

6. This is the same statue that is featured in the opening rhetorical gesture of Guidiccioni's paean to Bernini's *Baldacchino*, discussed in chapter 4 above.

7. I have translated *adunanze virtuose* as "virtuous gatherings," but a more accurate (though more circuitous and awkward) translation might be "gatherings of men who have *virtù*"; again a subtle association of *virtù* in musical activity with elite individuals, following the cultural expectations of *virtuoso* conversation/discourse discussed in chapters 2 and 3. The citation is from Virgil's *Aeneid* 6.657; I am using J.B. Greenough's edition, *Bucolics, Aeneid, and Georgics of Vergil* (Boston: Ginn, 1900), available at www.perseus.tufts.edu/hopper/text?doc =Perseus:text:1999.02.0055:book=6:card=637. (Accessed March, 14, 2011)

8. The citation is from Cicero's "Dream of Scipio" (*De republica,* "Somnium Scipionis," 6.18), a description of the music of the spheres that was well known in Guidiccioni's day. Significantly, Guidiccioni focuses on the section of the passage that is most concretely about sound; the *Somnium Scipionis* continues with a more abstract discussion of proportions. A full text of the *Somnium* is online at www.ipa.net/~magreyn/somnium.htm. (Accessed March, 14, 2011)

Bibliography

Abbate, Carolyn. 2004. "Music: Drastic or Gnostic?" *Critical Inquiry* 30, no. 3 (Spring): 505–36.

Accademia della Crusca. 1612/1974. *Vocabolario degli Accademici della Crusca: Con tre indici delle voci, locuzioni, e prouerbi latini, e greci, posti per entro l'opera.* Facs. ed. Florence: Licosa Reprints.

Adamo, Giorgio. 2000. "Il nuovo interesse per la prassi esecutiva, il 'popolare,' e l'esotico nella cultura musicale tra Cinque e Seicento." In *Colori della musica: Dipinti, strumenti e concerti tra Cinquecento e Seicento,* ed. Annalisa Bini, Claudio Strinati, and Rossella Vodret, 65–73. Milan: Skira.

Ago, Renata. 2006. *Il gusto delle cose: Una storia degli oggetti nella Roma del Seicento.* Rome: Donzelli.

Agucchi, Giovanni Battista. 1995. "Treatise on Painting, ca. 1615" (excerpt). In *Italy in the Baroque: Selected Readings,* ed. Brendan Dooley, 426–36. New York: Garland.

Alemanno, Laura. 1995. "L'Accademia degli Umoristi." *Roma Moderna e Contemporanea* 3:97–120.

Annibaldi, Claudio. 1987. "Il mecenate 'politico': Sul patronato musicale del Cardinal Pietro Aldobrandini," pts. 1 and 2. *Studi Musicali* 16:33–94 and 17:101–76.

———. 1996. "Tipologia della committenza musicale nella Venezia seicentesca." In *Musica, scienza e idee nella serenissima durante il Seicento,* ed. Francesco Passadore and Franco Rossi, 63–77. Venice: Edizioni Fondazione Levi.

———. 1998. "Towards a Theory of Musical Patronage in the Renaissance and Baroque: The Perspective from Anthropology and Semiotics." *Recercare* 10:173–82.

Antolini, Bianca Maria. 1989. "Cantanti e letterati a Roma nella prima metà del Seicento: Alcune osservazioni." In *In Cantu et in Sermone: For Nino Pirrotta on*

His 80th Birthday, ed. Fabrizio Della Seta and Franco Piperno, 347–62. Italian Medieval and Renaissance Studies 2. Florence: L.S. Olschki.

Askew, Pamela. 1969. "The Angelic Consolation of St. Francis of Assisi in Post-Tridentine Italian Painting." *Journal of the Warburg and Courtauld Institutes* 32:280–306.

Augst, Bertrand. 1965. "Descartes's Compendium on Music." *Journal of the History of Ideas* 26, no. 1 (March): 119–32.

Austern, Linda Phyllis. 1993. "'Alluring the Auditorie to Effeminacie': Music and the Idea of the Feminine in Early Modern England." *Music and Letters* 74, no. 3 (August): 343–54.

———. 1998. "'For, Love's a Good Musician': Performance, Audition, and Erotic Disorders in Early Modern Europe." *Musical Quarterly* 82, no. 3/4 (Autumn–Winter): 614–53.

Baffetti, Giovanni. 1997. *Retorica e scienza: Cultura gesuitica e Seicento italiano.* Bologna: CLUEB.

Baini, Giuseppe. 1828/1966. *Memorie storico-critiche della vita e delle opere di Giovanni Pierluigi da Palestrina.* 2 vols. Facs. ed. Hildesheim: Georg Olms.

Battistini, Andrea. 1981. "I manuali di retorica dei Gesuiti." In *La ratio studiorum: Modelli culturali e pratiche educative dei Gesuiti in Italia tra Cinque e Seicento,* ed. Gian Paolo Brizzi, 77–120. Rome: Bulzoni.

Bellori, Giovanni Pietro. 1664/2000. *Nota delli musei, librerie, galerie et ornamenti di statue e pitture ne' palazzi, nelle case e ne' giardini di Roma.* http://biblio.signum.sns.it/cgi-bin/bellori//blrCGI?cmd=1&w=15&u=Cardinale+G.+Franzoni&pg=026.

Bentivoglio, Guido. 1648. *Memorie del cardinale Bentivoglio.* Venice: Baglioni.

Benzoni, Gino. 1978. *Gli affanni della cultura: Intellettuali e potere nell'Italia della Controriforma e barocca.* Milan: Feltrinelli.

Bini, Annalisa, Claudio Strinati, and Rossella Vodret, eds. 2000. *Colori della musica: Dipinti, strumenti e concerti tra Cinquecento e Seicento.* Milan: Skira.

Bireley, Robert. 1999. *The Refashioning of Catholicism, 1450–1700: A Reassessment of the Counter Reformation.* Washington, DC: Catholic University of America Press.

Bizoni, Bernardo. 1995. *Diario di viaggio di Vincenzo Giustiniani (1606).* Ed. Barbara Agosti. Porretta Terme: Quaderni del Battello Ebbro.

Black, Christopher. 1998. "'Exceeding every expression of words': Bernini's Rome and the Religious Background." In *Effigies and Ecstacies: Roman Baroque Sculpture and Design in the Age of Bernini,* ed. Aidan Weston-Lewis, 11–22. Edinburgh: National Gallery of Scotland.

Bloch, David. 2007. *Aristotle on Memory and Recollection: Text, Translation, Interpretation, and Reception in Western Scholasticism.* Philosophia Antiqua. Leiden: Brill.

Bolzoni, Lina. 1995. *La stanza della memoria: Modelli letterari e iconografici nell'età della stampa.* Turin: Einaudi.

———. 1998. "Il gioco degli occhi: L'arte della memoria fra antiche esperienze e moderne suggestioni." In *Memoria e memorie: Convegno internazionale di studi,* ed. Lina Bolzoni, 1–28. Florence: L.S. Olschki.

Bonfait, Olivier. 1994. *Roma 1630: Il trionfo del pennello.* Milan: Electa.

Bonini, Severo. 1979. *Severo Bonini's Discorsi e regole: A Bilingual Edition.* Trans. Mary Ann Bonino. Provo, UT: Brigham Young University Press.

Bonta, Stephen. 1969. "The Uses of the 'Sonata da Chiesa.'" *Journal of the American Musicological Society* 22, no. 1 (Spring): 54–84.

———. 1990. "The Use of Instruments in Sacred Music in Italy, 1560–1700." *Early Music* 18:519–35.

Boschloo, Anton. 1998. "Annibale Carracci: Rappresentazioni della Pietà." In *Docere, delectare, movere: Affetti, devozione e retorica nel linguaggio artistico del primo barocco romano,* ed. Sible de Blaauw, Pieter-Matthijs Gijsbers, Sebastian Schütze, and Bert Treffers, 41–60. Rome: De Luca.

Bottrigari, Ercole, and Vincenzo Giustiniani. 1962. *Il Desiderio; or, Concerning the Playing Together of Various Musical Instruments.* Ed. Carol MacClintock. Musicological Studies and Documents 9. [N.p.]: American Institute of Musicology.

Bourdieu, Pierre. 1984. *Distinction: A Social Critique of the Judgment of Taste.* Trans. Richard Nice. Cambridge, MA: Harvard University Press.

Bouwsma, William J. 2000. *The Waning of the Renaissance, 1550–1640.* New Haven: Yale University Press.

Briganti, Giuliano. 1982. *Pietro da Cortona, o, Della pittura barocca.* 2nd ed. Florence: Sansoni.

———. 1994. "Pietro da Cortona, o Della pittura barocca." In *Roma 1630: Il trionfo del pennello,* ed. Olivier Bonfait, 23–52. Milan: Electa.

Brosius, Amy. 2009. "*Il suon, lo sguardo, il canto: Virtuose* of the Roman *conversazioni* in the Mid-Seventeenth Century." PhD diss., New York University.

Brown, Beverly Louise. 2001. "Between the Sacred and Profane." In *The Genius of Rome: 1592–1623,* ed. Beverly Louise Brown, 276–303. London: Royal Academy of Arts.

Brown, Jonathan. 1995. *Kings and Connoisseurs: Collecting Art in Seventeenth-Century Europe.* A.W. Mellon Lectures in the Fine Arts. Princeton: Princeton University Press.

Burke, Peter. 1978. *Popular Culture in Early Modern Europe.* London: Temple Smith.

———. 1987. *The Historical Anthropology of Early Modern Italy: Essays on Perception and Communication.* Cambridge: Cambridge University Press.

Butt, John. 2002. *Playing with History: The Historical Approach to Musical Performance.* Musical Performance and Reception. Cambridge: Cambridge University Press.

Caccini, Giulio. 1614/1978. *Nuove musiche e nuova maniera di scriverle (1614).* Ed. H. Wiley Hitchcock. Recent Researches in the Music of the Baroque Era. Madison, WI: A-R Editions.

Camiz, Franca Trinchieri. 1988. "The Castrato Singer: From Informal to Formal Portraiture." *Artibus et Historiae* 9, no. 18:171–86.

———. 1989. "La 'musica' nei quadri di Caravaggio." *Quaderni di Palazzo Venezia* 6:198–221.

———. 1991. "Music and Painting in Cardinal del Monte's Household." *Metropolitan Museum Journal* 26:213–26.

———. 1996. "La bella cantatrice: I ritratti di Leonora Barone e Barbara Strozzi a confronto." In *Musica, scienza e idee nella serenissima durante il Seicento*, ed. Francesco Passadore and Franco Rossi, 285–94. Venice: Edizioni Fondazione Levi.

Camiz, Franca Trinchieri, and Agostino Ziino. 1983. "Caravaggio: Aspetti musicali e committenza." *Studi Musicali* 12:67–79.

Campbell, Gordon. 1997. *A Milton Chronology*. Author Chronologies. Houndmills: Macmillan Press.

Cappelletti, Francesca, and Laura Testa. 1994. *Il trattenimento di virtuosi: Le collezioni secentesche di quadri nei palazzi Mattei di Roma*. Rome: Àrgos.

Carapezza, Paolo Emilio. 1988. "Tasso e la seconda pratica." In *Tasso, la musica, i musicisti,* ed. Maria Antonella Balsano and Thomas Walker, 1–15. Florence: Olschki.

Cargnoni, Costanzo. 1998. "La predicazione apostolica di Girolamo da Narni." In *Girolamo Mautini da Narni e l'ordine dei frati minori Cappuccini fra '500 e '600,* ed. Vincenzo Criscuolo, 331–421. Bibliotheca seraphico-capuccina 56. Rome: Istituto Storico dei Cappuccini.

Carloni, Livia. 1996. "Le opere del Domenichino in Santa Maria della Vittoria a Roma: La Madonna della Rosa di Giulio Nolfi e la Cappella di San Francesco di Ippolito Merenda." In *Domenichino, 1581–1641,* ed. Richard E. Spear, 330–48. Milan: Electa.

Carter, Tim. 1991. "'Non occorre nominare tanti musici': Private Patronage and Public Ceremony in Late Sixteenth-Century Florence." *I Tatti Studies: Essays in the Renaissance* 4:89–104.

———. 1993. "'An Air New and Grateful to the Ear': The Concept of 'Aria' in Late Renaissance and Early Baroque Italy." *Music Analysis* 12, no. 2 (July): 127–45.

———. 2000. "Printing the 'New Music.'" In *Music and the Cultures of Print,* ed. Kate Van Orden, 3–37. New York: Garland.

Casali, Lodovico. 1629. *Generale invito alle grandezze, e maraviglie della musica*. Modena: Gadaldino.

Chauvin, Regina. 1970. "The *Sacrae modulationes* of Lorenzo Ratti." PhD diss., Tulane University.

Chua, Daniel. 1999. *Absolute Music and the Construction of Meaning*. Cambridge: Cambridge University Press.

Cima, Gian Paolo. 1610/1986. *Concerti ecclesiastici: A 1, 2, 3, 4, 5 e 8 voci*. Facs. ed. Archivum musicum / La cantata barocca 24. Florence: Studio per Ed. Scelte.

Colantuono, Anthony. 1997. *Guido Reni's "Abduction of Helen": The Politics and Rhetoric of Painting in Seventeenth-Century Europe*. Cambridge: Cambridge University Press.

Cole, Janie. 2007. "Cultural Clientelism and Brokerage Networks in Early Modern Florence and Rome: New Correspondence between the Barberini and Michelangelo Buonarroti the Younger." *Renaissance Quarterly* 60:729–88.

Couvreur, Manuel. 2006. "L'oreille épicurienne." In *Le plaisir musical en France au XVIIe siècle,* ed. Thierry Favier and Manuel Couvreur, 81–96. Sprimont, Belgium: Mardaga.

Cowart, Georgia. 1980. *Controversies over French and Italian Music, 1600–1750. The Origins of Modern Musical Criticism.* New Brunswick. Rutgers University Press.

Criscuolo, Vincenzo. 1998a. *Girolamo Mautini da Narni (1563–1632): Predicatore apostolico e vicario generale dei Cappuccini.* Rome: Istituto Storico dei Cappuccini.

———. 1998b. "Lineamenti bio-bibliografici di Girolamo Mautini da Narni (1563–1632)." In *Girolamo Mautini da Narni e l'ordine dei frati minori Cappuccini fra '500 e '600*, ed. Vincenzo Criscuolo, 233–329. Bibliotheca seraphico-capuccina 56. Rome: Istituto Storico dei Cappuccini.

Cropper, Elizabeth. 1984. *The Ideal of Painting: Pietro Testa's Düsseldorf Notebook.* Princeton: Princeton University Press.

Cuaz, Marco. 1982. *Intellettuali, potere, e circolazione delle idee nell'Italia moderna (1500–1700).* Turin: Loescher.

Culley, Thomas D. 1970. *Jesuits and Music: A Study of the Musicians Connected with the German College in Rome during the 17th Century and of Their Activities in Northern Europe.* Sources and Studies for the History of the Jesuits 2. Rome: Jesuit Historical Institute; St. Louis: St. Louis University.

Cusick, Suzanne G. 1993a. "Gendering Modern Music: Thoughts on the Monteverdi-Artusi Controversy." *Journal of the American Musicological Society* 46, no. 1 (Spring): 1–25.

———. 1993b. "'Thinking from Women's Lives': Francesca Caccini after 1627." *Musical Quarterly* 77, no. 3 (Autumn): 484–507.

———. 2000. "A Soprano Subjectivity: Vocality, Power, and the Compositional Voice of Francesca Caccini." In *Crossing Boundaries: Attending to Early Modern Women*, ed. Jane Donawerth and Adele Seeff, 80–128. Newark: University of Delaware Press.

———. 2009. *Francesca Caccini at the Medici Court: Music and the Circulation of Power.* Chicago: University of Chicago Press.

D'Onofrio, Cesare. 1966. "Note Berniniane 1: Un dialogo-recita di Gian Lorenzo Bernini e Lelio Guidiccioni." *Palatino* 10:127–34.

———. 1967. *Roma vista da Roma.* Rome: Liber.

Dear, Peter. 1988. *Mersenne and the Learning of the Schools.* Ithaca: Cornell University Press.

De Benedictis, Cristina. 1991. *Per la storia del collezionismo italiano.* Florence: Ponte alle Grazie.

De'Crescenzi Romani, Giovanni Pietro. 1693. *Il nobile romano, o' sia trattato di nobiltà libri due.* Bologna: Pisarri.

Delbeke, Maarten. 2008. "Individual and Institutional Identity: Galleries of Barberini Projects." In *Art and Identity in Early Modern Rome*, ed. Jill Burke and Michael Bury, 231–46. Aldershot: Ashgate.

Delcorno, Carlo. 1998. "La predicazione in Italia dopo il Concilio di Trento." In *Girolamo Mautini da Narni e l'ordine dei frati minori Cappuccini fra '500 e '600*, ed. Vincenzo Criscuolo, 119–48. Bibliotheca seraphico-capuccina 56. Rome: Istituto Storico dei Cappuccini.

Dell'Antonio, Andrew. 1997. *Syntax, Form and Genre in Sonatas and Canzonas, 1621–1635.* Quaderni di Musica/Realtà 38. Lucca: Libreria Musicale Italiana.

————. 2005. "'Particolar gusto e diletto alle orecchie': Listening in the Early *Seicento.*" In *Culture and Authority in the Baroque,* ed. Massimo Ciavolella and Patrick Coleman, 106–21. UCLA Clark Memorial Library Series. Toronto: University of Toronto Press.

Della Valle, Pietro. 1903. "Della musica dell'età nostra, che non è punto inferiore, anzi è migliore di quella dell'età passata; al sig. Lelio Guidiccioni [16 January 1640]." In *Le origini del melodramma: Testimonianze dei contemporanei,* ed. Angelo Solerti, 148–79. Turin: Fratelli Bocca.

De Pure, Michel. 1668/1972. *Idée des spectacles anciens et nouveaux.* Facs. ed. Geneva: Minkoff.

De'Rossi, Filippo. 1645/1989. *Ritratto di Roma moderna.* Ed. Maurizio Marini. Reprint, Rome: Logart Press.

Dietrich, Rita. 2005. "Palazzo Mancini: Per secoli cenacolo degli artisti d'oltralpe." *L'Osservatore Romano,* March 14.

Diez, Renato. 1986. *Il trionfo della parola: Studio sulle relazioni di feste nella Roma barocca, 1623–1667.* Biblioteca di storia della critica e delle poetiche 10. Rome: Bulzoni.

Di Monte, M. 1960. "Guidiccioni, Lelio." In *Dizionario biografico degli Italiani,* 61:330–32. Rome: Istituto della Enciclopedia Italiana.

Donà, Mariangela. 1967. "'Affetti musicali' nel Seicento." *Studi Secenteschi* 8:75–94.

Doni, Giovanni Battista. 1635. *Compendio del trattato de'generi e de'modi della musica.* Rome: Fei.

Dooley, Brendan, ed. 1995. *Italy in the Baroque: Selected Readings.* New York: Garland.

Dubost, Jean-François. 1997. *La France italienne: XVIe-XVIIe siècle.* Paris: Aubier.

Dulong, Claude. 1999. *Mazarin.* Paris: Perrin.

Ebert-Schifferer, Sybille. 1994. "Sandrart a Roma 1629–1635: Un cosmopolita tedesco nel Paese delle Meraviglie." In *Roma 1630: Il trionfo del pennello,* ed. Olivier Bonfait, 23–52. Milan: Electa.

————. 1996. "L'expression contrôlée des passions: Le rôle de Poussin dans l'élaboration d'un art civilisateur." In *Poussin et Rome: Actes du Colloque à L'Académie de France à Rome, 16–18 novembre 1994,* ed. Olivier Bonfait, Christoph Luitpold Frommel, Michel Hochmann, and Sebastian Schütze, 241–55. Paris: Réunion des musées nationaux.

Ehrlich, Tracy L. 2002. *Landscape and Identity in Early Modern Rome: Villa Culture at Frascati in the Borghese Era.* Monuments of Papal Rome. Cambridge: Cambridge University Press.

————. 2005. "Pastoral Landscape and Social Politics in Baroque Rome." In *Baroque Garden Cultures: Emulation, Sublimation, Subversion,* ed. Michel Conan, 131–82. Dumbarton Oaks Colloquium Series in the History of Landscape Architecture. Cambridge, MA: Harvard University Press.

Endean, Philip. 2008. "The Spiritual Exercises." In *The Cambridge Companion to the Jesuits,* ed. Thomas Worcester, 52–67. Cambridge Companions to Religion. Cambridge: Cambridge University Press.

Erythraeus, Janus Nicius. 1645. *Iani Nicii Erithraei Pinacotheca imaginum illustrium. Doctrinae vel ingenii laude, virorum, qui, auctore superstite, diem suum obierunt.* Colon. Agrippinæ: Apud Iodocum Kalcovium et socios.

Fabris, Dinko. 1999. *Mecenati e musici: Documenti sul patronato artistico dei Bentivoglio di Ferrara nell' epoca di Monteverdi.* Lucca: Libreria Musicale Italiana.

Fader, Don. 2000. "Musical Thought and Patronage of the Italian Style at the Court of Philippe II, Duc d'Orléans (1674–1723)." PhD diss., Stanford University.

———. 2003. "The Honnête Homme as Music Critic: Taste, Rhetoric, and Politesse in the 17th-Century French Reception of Italian Music." *Journal of Musicology* 20, no. 1 (Winter): 3–44.

Feld, Steven. 1996. "Waterfalls of Song: An Acoustemology of Place Resounding in Bosavi, Papua New Guinea." In *Senses of Place,* ed. Steven Feld and Keith H Basso, 91–135. Santa Fe, NM: School of American Research Press.

Ferrari Barassi, Elena. 1994. "Espressività, sensualismo e artificio nella musica strumentale protobarocca." In *Musicologia Humana: Studies in Honor of Warren and Ursula Kirkendale,* ed. Siegfried Gmeinwieser, David Hiley, and Jörg Riedlbauer, 327–43. Florence: Olschki.

Findlen, Paula. 1994. *Possessing Nature: Museums, Collecting, and Scientific Culture in Early Modern Italy.* Studies on the History of Society and Culture 20. Berkeley: University of California Press.

———. 1998. "Possessing the Past: The Material World of the Italian Renaissance." *American Historical Review* 103, no. 1 (February): 83–114.

Fioretti di S. Francesco. Ne'quali si contine la vita, & i miracoli, che egli fece per diverse parti del mondo. . . . 1576. Venetia: Franceschi et Nepoti.

Fosi, Irene. 1997. *All'ombra dei Barberini: Fedeltà e servizio nella Roma barocca.* Rome: Bulzoni.

———. 2008. "*Roma patria comune?* Foreigners in Early Modern Rome." In *Art and Identity in Early Modern Rome,* ed. Jill Burke and Michael Bury, 27–44. Aldershot: Ashgate.

Fragnito, Gigliola. 1998. "Buone maniere e professionalità nelle corti romane del Cinque e Seicento." In *Educare il corpo, educare la parola: Nella trattatistica del Rinascimento,* ed. Giorgio Patrizi and Amedeo Quondam, 77–90. Rome: Bulzoni.

Freitas, Roger. 2001. "Singing and Playing: The Italian Cantata and the Rage for Wit." *Music and Letters* 82, no. 4 (November): 509–42.

———. 2009. *Portrait of a Castrato: Politics, Patronage, and Music in the Life of Atto Melani.* Cambridge: Cambridge University Press.

Fumaroli, Marc. 1978. "Cicero Pontifex: La tradition rhétorique du Collège romain et les principes inspirateurs du mécénat des Barberini." *Mélanges de l'École Française de Rome, Moyen Age, Temps Modernes* 90:797–835.

———. 1994. "Rome 1630: Entrée en scène du spectateur." In *Roma 1630: Il trionfo del pennello,* ed. Olivier Bonfait, 53–82. Milan: Electa.

———. 1998. *L'école du silence: Le sentiment des images au xviie siècle.* Paris: Flammarion.

Furley, David. 1999. *Routledge History of Philosophy.* Vol. 2. *Aristotle to Augustine.* London: Routledge.

Galeries nationales du Grand Palais (France) and Palazzo Reale di Milano. 1988. *Seicento: Le siècle de Caravage dans les collections françaises: Galeries Nationales du Grand Palais, Paris, 11 octobre 1988–2 janvier 1989, Palazzo Reale, Milan, Mars-Avril 1989.* Paris: Ministère de la culture, de la communication, des grands travaux et du bicentenaire.

Gavito, Cory Michael. 2006. "The Alfabeto Song in Print, 1610-ca. 1665: Neapolitan Roots, Roman Codification, and 'Il Gusto Popolare.'" PhD diss., University of Texas at Austin.

Gentili, Augusto. 2000. "Le amorose musiche di Maddalena." In *Dipingere la musica: Strumenti in posa nell'arte del Cinque e Seicento,* ed. Sylvia Ferino Pagden and Luiz C. Marques, 273. Milan: Skira.

Giombi, Samuele. 1998. "Teorie sulla predicazione nei secoli xvi-xvii e l'ordine dei Cappuccini." In *Girolamo Mautini da Narni e l'ordine dei frati minori Cappuccini fra '500 e '600,* ed. Vincenzo Criscuolo, 149–84. Bibliotheca seraphico-capuccina 56. Rome: Istituto Storico dei Cappuccini.

Giustiniani, Vincenzo. Ca. 1628/1878. *Discorso sopra la musica de'suoi tempi . . .* Ed. Salvatore Bongi. Lucca: Giusti.

———. 1981. *Discorsi sulle arti e sui mestieri.* Ed. Anna Banti. Florence: Sansoni.

Goldthwaite, Richard. 1987. "The Economy of Renaissance Italy: The Preconditions for Luxury Consumption." *I Tatti Studies* 2:15–39.

———. 1994. *Wealth and the Demand for Art in Italy, 1300–1600.* Baltimore: Johns Hopkins University Press.

Gordon, Bonnie. 2004. *Monteverdi's Unruly Women: The Power of Song in Early Modern Italy.* Cambridge: Cambridge University Press.

Gravit, Francis W. 1935. "The Accademia degli Umoristi and Its French Relationships." *Michigan Academy of Science, Arts, and Letters* 20:505–22.

Grendler, Paul F. 1989. *Schooling in Renaissance Italy: Literacy and Learning, 1300–1600.* Baltimore: Johns Hopkins University Press.

Guazzo, Stefano. 1993. *La civil conversazione.* Ed. Amedeo Quondam. 2 vols. Ferrara: Franco Cosimo Panini.

Guidiccioni, Lelio. 1635 (?). *Discorso sopra la musica.* Cod. Barb. lat. 3879, fol. 28r—41v. Biblioteca Apostolica Vaticana.

———. 1992. *Latin Poems: Rome 1633 and 1639.* Ed. John Kevin Newman and Frances Stickney Newman. Hildesheim: Weidmann.

Guidobaldi, Nicoletta. 1990. "Images of Music in Cesare Ripa's *Iconologia.*" *Imago Musicae* 7:41–68.

Guth, Paul. 1999. *Mazarin.* Biographies historiques. Paris: Flammarion.

Haan, Estelle. 1998. *From Academia to Amicitia: Milton's Latin Writings and the Italian Academies.* Philadelphia: American Philosophical Society.

Habig, Marion Alphonse, ed. 1973. *St. Francis of Assisi: Writings and Early Biographies.* Chicago: Franciscan Herald Press.

Hammond, Frederick. 1994. *Music and Spectacle in Baroque Rome: Barberini Patronage under Urban VIII.* New Haven: Yale University Press.

———. 1996. "Poussin et les modes: Le point de vue d'un musicien." In *Poussin et Rome: Actes du Colloque à L'Académie de France à Rome, 16–18 novem-*

bre 1994, ed. Olivier Bonfait, Christoph Luitpold Frommel, Michel Hochmann, and Sebastian Schutze, 75–91. Paris: Reunion des musées nationaux.

Haroche, Claudine. 1998. "Il contegno nell'educazione del corpo." In *Educare il corpo, educare la parola: Nella trattatistica del Rinascimento*, ed. Giorgio Patrizi and Amedeo Quondam, 65–76. Rome: Bulzoni.

Haskins, Susan. 1994. *Mary Magdalen: Myth and Metaphor.* New York: Harcourt, Brace.

Hester, Nathalie. 2008. *Literature and Identity in Italian Baroque Travel Writing.* Aldershot: Ashgate.

Hill, John Walter. 1997. *Roman Monody, Cantata, and Opera from the Circles around Cardinal Montalto.* Oxford: Clarendon Press.

Holzer, Robert Rau. 1990. "Music and Poetry in Seventeenth-Century Rome: Settings of the Canzonetta and Cantata Texts of Francesco Balducci, Domenico Benigni, Francesco Melosio, and Antonio Abati." PhD diss., University of Pennsylvania.

———. 1992. "'Sono d'altro garbo . . . le canzonette che si cantano oggi': Pietro della Valle on Music and Modernity in the Seventeenth Century." *Studi Musicali* 21:253–306.

———. 1996. "Beyond the (Musical) Pleasure Principle: Sanctifying the Sensuous in Early Seicento Rome." Paper presented at the annual meeting of the American Musicological Society, Baltimore.

———. 2000. "Response to Noel O'Regan." *Journal of Seventeenth-Century Music* 6, no. 1. http://sscm-jscm.press.uiuc.edu/v6/no1/holzer.html.

———. 2001. "Rossi, Luigi." In *Grove Music Online.* Oxford Music Online, accessed March 20, 2009.

Jacobs, Fredrika Herman. 1997. *Defining the Renaissance Virtuosa: Women Artists and the Language of Art History and Criticism.* Cambridge: Cambridge University Press.

Johnson, James H. 1995. *Listening in Paris: A Cultural History.* Studies on the History of Society and Culture 21. Berkeley: University of California Press.

Kendrick, Robert L. 1996. *Celestial Sirens: Nuns and Their Music in Early Modern Milan.* Oxford: Oxford University Press.

———. 2002. *The Sounds of Milan, 1585–1650.* Oxford: Oxford University Press.

Kubitschek, Ernst. 1988. "Die Bezeichnung 'Affetto' in der frühbarocken Instrumentalmusik." In *Capella Antiqua München Festschrift*, 203–12. Tutzing: Schneider.

Lapierre, Alexandra. 2000. *Artemisia: The Story of a Battle for Greatness.* London: Chatto and Windus.

Laurain-Portemer, Madeleine. 1981. *Études Mazarines.* Paris: de Boccard.

Lionnet, Jean. 1991. "Une 'mode francaise' a Rome au XVIIe siecle." *Revue de Musicologie* 77, no. 2:279–90.

———. 1993. "The Borghese Family and Music during the First Half of the Seventeenth Century." Trans. Norma Deane and John Whenham. *Music and Letters* 74, no. 4 (November): 519–29.

Longatti, Mario, Alberto Colzani, Andrea Luppi, and Maurizio Padoan, eds. 1987. "La cappella musicale del duomo di Como." In *La musica sacra in Lombardia nella prima metà del Seicento*, 299–311. Como: AMIS.

Lorenzetti, Stefano. 1996. "La parte della musica nella costruzione del gentiluomo: Tendenze e programmi della pedagogia seicentesca tra Francia e Italia." *Studi Musicali* 25:17–40.

———. 2003. *Musica e identità nobiliare nell'Italia del Rinascimento: Educazione, mentalità, immaginario.* Florence: Olschki.

Lo Sardo, Eugenio. 2004. "Kircher's Rome." In *Athanasius Kircher: The Last Man Who Knew Everything,* ed. Paula Findlen, 51–62. New York: Routledge.

Lowe, Melanie Diane. 2007. *Pleasure and Meaning in the Classical Symphony.* Musical Meaning and Interpretation. Bloomington: Indiana University Press.

Loyola, Ignatius. 1914. *The Spiritual Exercises.* Trans. Mullan Elder, S.J. New York: P. J. Kennedy and Sons.

Lucchesini, Cesare. 1831. *Della storia letteraria del ducato lucchese, Libri sette.* Memorie e documenti per servire alla storia di Lucca. Lucca: Bertini.

Maccherini, Michele. 1997. "Caravaggio nel carteggio familiare di Giulio Mancini." *Prospettiva* 86:71–92.

Mahon, Sir Denis. 1990. "The Singing 'Lute-Player' by Caravaggio from the Barberini Collection, Painted for Cardinal Del Monte." *Burlington Magazine,* January, 5–23.

Mancini, Giulio. 1956. *Considerazioni sulla pittura (ca. 1621–1624).* Ed. Adriana Marucchi. Rome: Accademia Nazionale dei Lincei.

Maravall, José Antonio. 1986. *Culture of the Baroque: Analysis of a Historical Structure.* Trans. Terry Cochran. Minneapolis: University of Minnesota Press.

Marini, Biagio. 1617/1990. *Affetti musicali.* Ed. Franco Piperno. Monumenti musicali italiani. Milan: Suvini Zerboni.

Maugars, André. 1993. *Response faite à un curieux sur le sentiment de la musique d'Italie, escrite à Rome le premier octobre 1639.* Ed. H. Wiley Hitchcock. Geneva: Minkoff.

McGinness, Frederick J. 1980. "Preaching Ideals and Practice in Counter-Reformation Rome." *Sixteenth Century Journal* 11, no. 2 (Summer): 109–27.

———. 1995. *Right Thinking and Sacred Oratory in Counter-Reformation Rome.* Princeton: Princeton University Press.

Menozzi, Daniele. 1997. "La chiesa e le immagini." In *Mistero e immagine: L'Eucaristia nell'arte dal xvi al xviii secolo,* ed. Salvatore Baviera. Rome: Electa.

Meucci, Renato. 1996. "Domenichino 'musicologo' e le origini della sonata a tre." In *Domenichino, 1581–1641,* ed. Richard E. Spear, 311–17. Milan: Electa.

Michel, Patrick. 1999. *Mazarin, prince des collectionneurs: Les collections et l'ameublement du Cardinal Mazarin (1602–1661): Histoire et analyse.* Notes et documents des musées de France 34. Paris: Réunion des musées nationaux.

———. 2001. "Le cardinal Mazarin: Un collectioneur romain à Paris." In *Geografia del collezionismo: Italia e Francia tra xvi e il xviii secolo: Atti delle giornate di studio dedicate a Giuliano Briganti: Roma, 19–21 settembre 1996,* ed. Olivier Bonfait, 325–43. Collection de l'École française de Rome. Rome: École française de Rome.

Monson, Craig A. 1993. "La pratica della musica nei monasteri femminili bolognesi." In *La cappella musicale nell'Italia della Controriforma,* ed. Oscar Mischiati and Claudio Russo, 143–60. Florence: Olschki.

———. 1995. *Disembodied Voices: Music and Culture in an Early Modern Italian Convent.* Berkeley: University of California Press.

———. 2002. "The Council of Trent Revisited." *Journal of the American Musicological Society* 55, no. 1 (Spring): 1–37.

Montford, Kimberlyn Winona. 1999. "Music in the Convents of Counter-Reformation Rome." PhD diss., Rutgers University.

———. 2000. "*L'Anno santo* and Female Monastic Churches: The Politics, Business and Music of the Holy Year in Rome (1675)." *Journal of Seventeenth-Century Music* 6, no. 1. http://sscm-jscm.press.uiuc.edu/v6/no1/montford .html.

Morelli, Arnaldo. 1993. "Le cappelle musicali a Roma nel Seicento: Questioni di organizzazione e di prassi esecutiva." In *La cappella musicale nell'Italia della Controriforma,* ed. Oscar Mischiati and Claudio Russo, 175–203. Florence: Olschki.

Murata, Margaret. 1981. *Operas for the Papal Court, 1631–1668.* Ann Arbor: UMI Research Press.

———. 1990. "Roman Cantata Scores as Traces of Musical Culture and Signs of Its Place in Society." In *Atti del XIV congresso della Società Internazionale di Musicologia, Bologna, 1987: Trasmissione e recezione delle forme di cultura musicale,* ed. Angelo Pompilio, Donatella Restani, Lorenzo Bianconi, and F. Alberto Gallo, 272–84. Turin: EDT.

———. 1993. "La cantata romana fra mecenatismo e collezionismo." In *La musica e il mondo,* ed. Claudio Annibaldi, 253–68. Bologna: Il Mulino.

Newman, J.K. 1994. "Empire of the Sun: Lelio Guidiccioni and Pope Urban VIII." *International Journal of the Classical Tradition* 1, no. 1 (Summer 1994): 62–70.

Nussdorfer, Laurie. 1992. *Civic Politics in the Rome of Urban VIII.* Princeton: Princeton University Press.

O'Regan, Noel. 1999. "Music in the Liturgy of San Pietro in Vaticano during the Reign of Paul V (1605–1621): A Preliminary Survey of the Liturgical Diary (Part 1) of Andrea Amici." *Recercare* 11:119–50.

Olson, Todd P. 2005. "Caravaggio's Coroner: Forensic Medicine in Giulio Mancini's Art Criticism." *Oxford Art Journal* 28, no. 1 (March 1): 83–98.

Onori, Lorenza Mochi. 2000. "Il cavalier dal Pozzo ministro dei Barberini." In *I segreti di un collezionista: Le straordinarie raccolte di Cassiano dal Pozzo, 1588–1657,* ed. Francesco Solinas, 17–20. Rome: De Luca.

Ostrow, Steven F. 1996. *Art and Spirituality in Counter-Reformation Rome: The Sistine and Pauline Chapels in S. Maria Maggiore.* Monuments of Papal Rome. Cambridge: Cambridge University Press.

Padoan, Maurizio. 1987. "La musica liturgica tra funzionalità statutaria e prassi: Alcuni rilievi in area lombardo-padana." In *La musica sacra in Lombardia nella prima metà del Seicento,* ed. Maurizio Padoan, Alberto Colzani, and Andrea Luppi, 369–94. Como: AMIS.

———. 1992. "Nature and Artifice in G.B. Doni's Thought." *International Review of the Aesthetics and Sociology of Music* 23:5–26.

Paleotti, Gabriele. 1961. "Discorso intorno alle imagini sacre e profane" [1582]. In *Trattati d'arte del Cinquecento: Fra manierismo e Controriforma*, vol. 2, *Gilio—Paleotti—Aldrovandi*, ed. Paola Barocchi, 117–517. Bari: Laterza.

Palestrina, Giovanni Pierluigi da. 1975. *Pope Marcellus Mass: An Authoritative Score, Backgrounds and Sources, History and Analysis, Views and Comments.* Ed. Lewis Lockwood. Norton Critical Scores. New York: W.W. Norton.

Parisi, Susan. 1996. "Acquiring Musicians and Instruments in the Early Baroque: Observations from Mantua." *Journal of Musicology* 14, no. 2 (Spring): 117–50.

Pepper, D. Stephen. 1984. *Guido Reni.* Oxford: Phaidon.

Petrucci, Armando, ed. 1982. *Scrittura e popolo nella Roma barocca, 1585–1721.* Rome: Quasar.

Pigler, Andor. 1974. *Barockthemen, Eine Auswahl von Verzeichnissen zur Ikonographie des 17. und 18. Jahrhunderts.* 2nd enl. ed. Budapest: Akadémiai Kiadó.

Piperno, Franco. 2001. *L'immagine del duca: Musica e spettacolo alla corte di Guidubaldo II duca d'Urbino.* Florence: Olschki.

Poncet, Olivier. 2002. "The Cardinal-Protectors of the Crowns in the Roman Curia during the First Half of the Seventeenth Century: The Case of France." In *Court and Politics in Papal Rome, 1492–1700*, ed. Gianvittorio Signorotto and Maria Antonietta Visceglia, 158–76. Cambridge: Cambridge University Press.

Porta, Giambattista della. 1996. *Ars reminiscendi: Aggiunta L'arte del ricordare tradotta da Dorandino Falcone da Gioia.* Ed. Raffaele Sirri. Trans. Dorandino Falcone da Gioia. Naples: Edizioni Scientifiche Italiane.

Poseq, Avigdor. 1992. "Pathosformels, Decorum and the 'Art of Gestures' in Caravaggio's Death of the Virgin." *Konsthistorisk Tidsskrift* 51:28–44.

Quint, Arlene. 1986. *Cardinal Federico Borromeo as a Patron and a Critic of the Arts and His Musaeum of 1625.* Outstanding Dissertations in the Fine Arts. New York: Garland.

Quondam, Amedeo, ed. 1981. *Le "carte messaggiere": Retorica e modelli di comunicazione epistolare: Per un indici dei libri di lettere del Cinquecento.* Rome: Bulzoni.

Radinò, Simonetta Prosperi Valenti. 1982. "La diffusione dell'iconografia francescana attraverso l'incisione." In *L'immagine di San Francesco nella Controriforma*, ed. Simonetta Prosperi Valenti Radinò and Claudio Strinati, 159–88. Rome: Quasar.

Reardon, Colleen. 1994. *Agostino Agazzari and Music at Siena Cathedral, 1597–1641.* Oxford: Oxford University Press.

———. 2001. *Holy Concord within Sacred Walls: Nuns and Music in Siena, 1575–1700.* Oxford: Oxford University Press.

Rebecchini, Guido. 2002. *Private Collections in Mantua, 1500–1630.* Sussidi eruditi 56. Rome: Edizioni di Storia e Letteratura.

Reiss, Timothy. 1997. *Knowledge, Discovery, and the Imagination in Early Modern Europe: The Rise of Aesthetic Rationalism.* Cambridge: Cambridge University Press.

Riley, Matthew. 2004. *Musical Listening in the German Enlightenment: Attention, Wonder and Astonishment*. Aldershot: Ashgate.

Rizza, Cecilia. 1973. *Barocco francese e cultura italiana*. Cuneo: SASTE.

Roche, Jerome. 1966. "Music at S. Maria Maggiore, Bergamo, 1614–1643." *Music and Letters* 47:296–312.

Romano, Antonella. 2004. "Understanding Kircher in Context." In *Athanasius Kircher: The Last Man Who Knew Everything*, ed. Paula Findlen, 405–19. New York: Routledge.

Rosa, Mario. 2002. "The 'World's Theatre': The Court of Rome and Politics in the First Half of the Seventeenth Century." In *Court and Politics in Papal Rome, 1492–1700*, ed. Gianvittorio Signorotto and Maria Antonietta Visceglia, 78–98. Cambridge: Cambridge University Press.

Ruffatti, Alessio. 2006. "La réception des cantates de Luigi Rossi dans la France du Grand Siècle." *Revue de Musicologie* 92: 287–307.

———. 2008. "'Curiosi e bramosi l'oltramontani cercano con grande diligenza in tutti i luoghi': La cantata romana del Seicento in Europa." *Journal of Seventeenth-Century Music* 13, no. 1. http://sscm-jscm.press.uiuc.edu/v13/no1/ruffatti.html.

Selwyn, Jennifer D. 2004. *A Paradise Inhabited by Devils: The Jesuits' Civilizing Mission in Early Modern Naples*. Aldershot: Ashgate.

Shimp, Susan Parker. 2000. "The Art of Persuasion: Domenico Mazzocchi and the Counter-Reformation." PhD diss., Yale University.

Silbiger, Alexander. 2005. "The Solo Instrumentalist." In *The Cambridge History of Seventeenth-Century Music*, ed. Tim Carter and John Butt, 426–78. Cambridge: Cambridge University Press.

Simmons, Alison. 1999. "Jesuit Aristotelian Education: The *De anima* Commentaries." In *The Jesuits: Cultures, Sciences, and the Arts, 1540–1773*, ed. John W O'Malley, Gauvin Alexander Bailey, Steven J. Harris, and T. Frank Kennedy, 522–37. Toronto: University of Toronto Press.

Small, Christopher. 1998. *Musicking: The Meanings of Performing and Listening*. Hanover, NH: University Press of New England.

Smith, Bruce R. 1999. *The Acoustic World of Early Modern England*. Chicago: University of Chicago Press.

Sohm, Philip. 1995. "Gendered Style in Italian Art Criticism from Michelangelo to Malvasia." *Renaissance Quarterly* 48, no. 4 (Winter): 759–808.

Solerti, Angelo. 1905. "Lettere inedite sulla musica di Pietro della Valle a G.B. Doni ed una veglia drammatica-musicale del medesimo." *Rivista Musicale Italiana* 12:271–338.

Solinas, Francesco. 2000. "Cassiano dal Pozzo e le arti a Roma nella prima metà del Seicento." In *I segreti di un collezionista: Le straordinarie raccolte di Cassiano dal Pozzo, 1588–1657*, ed. Francesco Solinas, 1–11. Rome: De Luca.

Southorn, Janet. 1988. *Power and Display in the Seventeenth Century: The Arts and Their Patrons in Modena and Ferrara*. Cambridge: Cambridge University Press.

Spear, Richard E. 1982. *Domenichino*. New Haven: Yale University Press.

———, ed. 1996. *Domenichino, 1581–1641*. Milan: Electa.

―――. 1998. "L'espressione dell'affetto indefinito." In *Docere, delectare, movere: Affetti, devozione e retorica nel linguaggio artistico del primo barocco romano,* ed. Sible de Blaauw, Pieter-Matthijs Gijsbers, Sebastian Schütze, and Bert Treffers, 89–104. Rome: De Luca.

Spezzaferro, Luigi. 1996. "Le collezioni di 'alcuni gentilhuomini particolari' e il mercato: Appunti su Lelio Guidiccioni e Francesco Angeloni." In *Poussin et Rome: Actes du colloque à l'Académie de France à Rome, 16–18 novembre 1994,* ed. Olivier Bonfait, Christoph Luitpold Frommel, Michel Hochmann, and Sebastian Schütze, 241–55. Paris: Réunion des musées nationaux.

―――. 2001. "Problemi del collezionismo a Roma nel XVII secolo." In *Geografia del collezionismo: Italia e Francia tra xvi e il xviii secolo: Atti delle giornate di studio dedicate a Giuliano Briganti: Roma, 19–21 settembre 1996,* ed. Olivier Bonfait, 1–23. Collection de l'École française de Rome. Rome: École française de Rome.

Storey, Tessa. 2008. *Carnal Commerce in Counter-Reformation Rome.* Cambridge: Cambridge University Press.

Strinati, Claudio, and Rossella Vodret. 2000. "La nuova rappresentazione dei soggetti musicali tra Cinquecento e Seicento." In *Colori della musica: Dipinti, strumenti e concerti tra Cinquecento e Seicento,* ed. Annalisa Bini, Claudio Strinati, and Rossella Vodret, 17–29. Milan: Skira.

Strunk, W. Oliver. 1930. "Vergil in Music." *Musical Quarterly* 16, no. 4 (October): 482–497.

Strunk, W. Oliver, and Leo Treitler, eds. 1998. *Source Readings in Music History.* Rev. ed. New York: Norton.

Szendy, Peter. 2008. *Listen: A History of Our Ears.* New York: Fordham University Press.

Tagliavini, Luigi Ferdinando. 1998. "Gli 'affetti cantabili' nella musica di Girolamo Frescobaldi." In *Docere, delectare, movere: Affetti, devozione e retorica nel linguaggio artistico del primo barocco romano,* ed. Sible de Blaauw, Pieter-Matthijs Gijsbers, Sebastian Schütze, and Bert Treffers, 121–36. Rome: De Luca.

Tesauro, Emanuele. 1995. "Il cannocchiale Aristotelico" (excerpt). In *Italy in the Baroque: Selected Readings,* ed. Brendan Dooley, 460–86. New York: Garland.

Tetius, Hieronymus. 2005. *Aedes Barberinae ad Quirinalem descriptae.* Ed. Lucia Faedo and Thomas Frangenberg. Pisa: Edizioni della Normale.

Tiacci, Ennio. 1999. *Il predicatore apostolico Girolamo Mautini da Narni: Predicazione alla gerarchia nella chiesa post-Tridentina.* Perugia: S. Francesco.

Tiraboschi, Girolamo. 1824. *Storia della letteratura italiana.* Milan: Società Tipografica de'Classici Italiani.

Treffers, Bert. 1998. "Celerità come metafora della grazia e mezzo artistico: Lanfranco versus Van Baburen." In *Docere, delectare, movere: Affetti, devozione e retorica nel linguaggio artistico del primo barocco romano,* ed. Sible de Blaauw, Pieter-Matthijs Gijsbers, Sebastian Schütze, and Bert Treffers, 71–80. Rome: De Luca.

―――. 2001. "The Arts and Craft of Sainthood: New Orders, New Saints, New Altarpieces." In *The Genius of Rome: 1592–1623,* ed. Beverly Louise Brown, 340–71. London: Royal Academy of Arts.

Uberti, Grazioso. 1630/1991. *Contrasto musico: Opera dilettevole*. Ed. Giancarlo Rostirolla. Facs. ed. Lucca: Libreria Musicale Italiana.

Van Orden, Kate. 2006. "Le plaisir de pouvoir et le pouvoir du plaisir." In *Le plaisir musical en France au XVIIe siècle*, cd. Thierry Favier and Manuel Couvreur, 131–44. Sprimont, Belgium: Mardaga.

Vendrix, Philippe. 2006. "La place du plaisir dans la théorie musicale en France de la Rénaissance à l'aube de l'âge baroque." In *Le plaisir musical en France au XVIIe siècle,* ed. Thierry Favier and Manuel Couvreur, 29–48. Sprimont, Belgium: Mardaga.

Visceglia, Maria Antonietta. 1995. "Burocrazia, mobilità sociale e *patronage* alla corte di Roma tra Cinque e Seicento: Alcuni aspetti del recente dibattito storiografico e prospettive di ricerca." *Roma Moderna e Contemporanea* 3:11–55.

Wandel, Lee Palmer. 2006. *The Eucharist in the Reformation: Incarnation and Liturgy*. Cambridge: Cambridge University Press.

Wazbinski, Zygmunt. 1994. *Il cardinale Francesco Maria del Monte, 1549–1626*. Florence: Olschki.

Weber, William. 1997. "Did People Listen in the 18th Century?" *Early Music* 25, no. 4 (November): 678–91.

Wegman, Rob C. 1998. "Music as Heard: Listeners and Listening in Late-Medieval and Early Modern Europe (1300–1600): A Symposium at Princeton University, 27–28 September 1997." *Musical Quarterly* 82, no. 3/4 (Autumn—Winter): 432–33.

Weil, Mark S. 1974. "The Devotion of the Forty Hours and Roman Baroque Illusions." *Journal of the Warburg and Courtauld Institutes* 37:218–48.

Weiss, Piero, and Richard Taruskin, eds. 1984. *Music in the Western World: A History in Documents*. New York: Schirmer Books.

Weissman, Ronald. 1987. "Taking Patronage Seriously: Mediterranean Values and Renaissance Society." In *Patronage, Art, and Society in Renaissance Italy,* ed. F. W. Kent and Patricia Simons, 25–45. New York: Oxford University Press.

Weston-Lewis, Aidan, ed. 1998. *Effigies and Ecstacies: Roman Baroque Sculpture and Designing the Age of Bernini*. Edinburgh: National Gallery of Scotland.

Wistreich, Richard. 2007. *Warrior, Courtier, Singer: Giulio Cesare Brancaccio and the Performance of Identity in the Late Renaissance*. Aldershot: Ashgate.

Wolfe, Karin. 2008. "Protector and Protectorate: Cardinal Antonio Barberini's Art Diplomacy for the French Crown at the Papal Court." In *Art and Identity in Early Modern Rome*, ed. Jill Burke and Michael Bury, 113–33. Aldershot: Ashgate.

Yates, Frances Amelia. 1947/1988. *The French Academies of the Sixteenth Century*. London: Routledge.

Zacconi, Lodovico. 1592. *Prattica di musica . . . divisa in quattro libri*. Venetia: Polo.

Zannini, Gian Lodovico Masetti. 1993. "'Suavità di canto' e 'purità di cuore': Aspetti della musica nei monasteri femminili romani." In *La cappella musicale nell'Italia della Controriforma*, ed. Oscar Mischiati and Claudio Russo, 123–41. Florence: Olschki.

Ziane, Alexandra. 2007. "'Affetti amorosi spirituali': Caravaggio e la musica spirituale del suo tempo." In *Caravaggio e il suo ambiente: Ricerche e interpretazioni,* ed. Sybille Ebert-Schifferer, 161–79. Studi della Biblioteca Hertziana 3. Milan: Silvana.

Ziino, Agostino. 1967. "Contese letterarie tra Pietro Della Valle e Nicolò Farfaro sulla musica antica e moderna." *Nuova Rivista Musicale Italiana* 3:101–20.

Index

TEXT
Sabon

DISPLAY
10/13 Sabon

COMPOSITOR
Westchester Book Group, Inc.

INDEXER

PRINTER AND BINDER
Maple-Vail Book Manufacturing Group